Unemployment and Wage Determination in Europe

Previous titles in this series:

Unemployment and Wage Determination in Europe

Edited by
Bertil Holmlund
and
Karl-Gustaf Löfgren

Basil Blackwell

Copyright © Scandinavian Journal of Economics 1990

ISBN 0-631-17767-1

First published 1990

Basil Blackwell Ltd
108 Cowley Road, Oxford OX4 1JF, UK

Basil Blackwell Inc.
3 Cambridge Center,
Cambridge, MA 02142, USA

Library of Congress Cataloguing in Publication Data applied for

British Library Cataloguing in Publication Data
Unemployment and wage determination in Europe.
   1. European Community countries. Unemployment
   I. Holmlund, Bertil   II. Löfgren, Karl Gustav
   331.13794

Typeset by Unicus Graphics Ltd, Horsham
Printed in Great Britain by Page Bros, Norwich

Contents

Preface

This book presents the outcome of an international seminar on unemployment and inflation policies entitled "Unemployment and Inflation Tradeoffs in Europe", which took place at Saltsjöbaden/Stockholm on January 12–14, 1989.

The conference was hosted by the Swedish Economic Council. The Council was set up by the Swedish Government in 1987 to serve as a link between economic research and policymaking. Based at the National Institute of Economic Research, the Council forms a standing committee with the task of initiating the coordinating research and studies of particular importance for economic policy and transmitting them to public authorities.

It was with this purpose in mind that the Council decided to devote its first international conference to unemployment and inflation problems in Europe. Not only are the policy questions in this area important and acute; nowhere else are the answers given by economists so diverse and confusing to policymakers. The express aim of the conference was therefore to take a fresh look at the facts, summarize the experience of the countries in Western Europe and try to evaluate alternative policy proposals. It remains to be seen whether — out of our common experience — a new consensus as to the possibilities of stabilization policy will eventually emerge.

Bengt-Christer Ysander
Chairman of the Economic Council

Editors' Introduction

Bertil Holmlund
Uppsala University, Sweden

Karl-Gustaf Löfgren
University of Umeå, Sweden

Most European countries have experienced a huge increase in unemployment over the past 15 years. Economies where unemployment rates around 1 or 2 per cent were considered normal 20 years ago have registered double-digit unemployment during the 1980s. The rise in unemployment has, in general, been accompanied by some reduction in inflation, but the British experience reminds us that inflation is not easily killed, despite high unemployment.

The rise in European unemployment has inspired a great deal of new research on the causes of and cures for unemployment, analogous to the interest devoted to unemployment in the 1930s. The new research on unemployment has to a large extent focused on wage-setting behavior, as revealed by the rapid growth in theoretical and empirical studies of bargaining, insider–outsider models and efficiency wages. A common theme in this new work is the desire to provide satisfactory microeconomic foundations for price and wage rigidities and involuntary unemployment.

The papers collected in this volume bring together a number of contributions to current research on unemployment and wage determination. The papers fall into two broad categories. Four papers treat *empirical regularities*, drawing on multicountry econometric work (Drèze and Bean), recent microeconomic experience in the Nordic countries (Andersen) and microdata for Britain and the U.S. (Blanchflower and Oswald; and Hughes and McCormick). The second theme, *policy alternatives and equilibrium unemployment*, is represented by four papers (Lindbeck and Snower; Jackman and Layard; Malinvaud; and Phelps).

I. Empirical Regularities

The first paper in Part I, by *Jacques Drèze and Charles Bean*, reports some of the main results from the European Unemployment Program (EUP), an interesting attempt to understand the diversity of unemployment experiences by estimating a set of country models using the same broad specification. The framework adopted involves disequilibrium features in the short run, but prices and wages are allowed to respond to movements in capacity utilization and unemployment.

The EUP has found, for example, that productivity gains are rapidly fed into wage increases in Europe, whereas there appears to be no role for measured productivity in the U.S. wage equation. The wage increases induced by productivity growth lead to capital–labor substitution, thereby aggravating the European unemployment problem. The EUP also indicates that real wages are rather insensitive to the level of unemployment; an increase in the unemployment rate by one percentage point is associated with a fall in real wages by 1 to 2 per cent. Another interesting finding is that the Beveridge curve — the relationship between the unemployment rate and the vacancy rate — has shifted outwards in all countries, including the U.S. Demand pressure seems to have a negligible impact on prices, but leads to higher imports, thereby worsening the trade balance.

Drèze and Bean suggest that one key mechanism behind the high and persistent unemployment in Europe is the wage formation process, involving rapid incorporation of productivity gains into real wages and sluggish wage adjustment to unemployment.

Torben Andersen's paper is concerned with the various macroeconomic policy strategies pursued in the Nordic countries during the 1970s and the 1980s, focusing in particular on attempts to combine high employment with external balance. The Nordic countries have faced similar economic problems, but have chosen rather different policies. Denmark and Sweden are interesting polar cases. Sweden undertook two large devaluations in the early 1980s, while Denmark maintained a fixed exchange-rate policy. The aim in both cases was to improve competitiveness and facilitate expansion of production and employment in the private sector. Andersen describes the Swedish approach as a "once-and-for-all" policy, whereas the Danish strategy can be characterized as a "no more" policy. The Swedish strategy presumes that devaluations will not be used in the future, and the Danish approach aims at restoring credibility in the long run.

The "once-and-for-all" policy ensures an immediate change in the right direction, but may generate inflationary pressure and leads to credibility problems in the medium term. The "no more" strategy is problematic in the short run while credibility is building up, but offers promise of turning out successful in the long run. Both strategies have their pros and cons, and the choice between them is far from obvious. Andersen makes the interesting point that the Danish policy experiment may have been destroyed by its own success. Credibility was indeed established, but the resulting boom produced a current account deficit which in turn eroded credibility.

David Blanchflower and Andrew Oswald focus also on wage-setting mechanisms, but from a different econometric angle. They use cross-section microdata from the U.K. and the U.S. in order to estimate the "wage curve", i.e., the relationship between the (real) wage rate and the level of unemployment. The results for the two countries are largely similar. In both the U.K. and the U.S. there appears to be a nonlinear relationship between real pay and unemployment; the curve has a negative slope at low and moderate unemployment rates, but becomes flat (and possibly upward sloping) at high unemployment rates. A macroeconomic implication, noted by the authors, is that shocks to the economy may have substantial effects on employment if the wage-setting function is indeed flat at high levels of unemployment.

Microdata are also used in the paper by *Gordon Hughes and Barry McCormick*, but the focus differs from that of Blanchflower and Oswald. Unemployment data in Britain are based on workers receiving unemployment benefits. This criterion does not coincide with the search-based measures of unemployment used in other countries. Some nonemployed workers have no benefits but are engaged in active search, whereas other workers receive benefits but do not spend much time searching for a job.

The main issue raised by Hughes and McCormick is how expansion of labor demand will affect search efforts in the British labor market. The results indicate that the probability of searching does not respond to a tighter labor market, whereas the probability of employer-contact search is significantly increased as the labor market improves. Hughes and McCormick also report a number of other results, including the role of unemployment duration; they find that the probability of searching, as well as employer contact conditional on search, decline as the duration of unemployment increases.

II. Policy Alternatives and Equilibrium Unemployment

Part II focuses on policy alternatives and equilibrium unemployment. Over the past few years, *Assar Lindbeck and Dennis Snower* have developed the insider–outsider theory of employment and unemployment. The key aspect of their studies is to explain why underbidding does not seem to work in the labor market. Lindbeck and Snower emphasize turnover costs as the source of market power of incumbent workers; the replacement of insiders by outsiders is costly to firms, partly because insiders may refuse to cooperate with newly hired workers.

Their paper in this volume deals with policy implications of the theory. Lindbeck and Snower demonstrate the employment-enhancing effects of various supply-side policies, such as measures to reduce the insiders' market power, or policies which attempt to enfranchise the unemployed outsiders. Demand-side policies, such as aggregate spending in the product market, are also considered, but such measures have in general uncertain effects on employment when wages and prices are flexible.

The paper by *Richard Jackman and Richard Layard* is concerned with the effects of tax-based incomes policies (TIP). The issue in focus is how the equilibrium unemployment rate can be reduced by tax-subsidy schemes involving a tax on wage increases (or simply a tax on wages) offset by a subsidy to employment. The tax is used to finance a per-worker subsidy, and the subsidy is adjusted at the aggregate level so as to maintain a self-financed scheme.

TIP reduce equilibrium unemployment in an efficiency wage model as well as in a model with wage bargaining. Jackman and Layard also offer an interesting extension of their previous work on TIP by investigating the effects on workers' effort, assuming that effort is subject to bargaining between the union and the firm. It is shown that effort declines as the wage tax is increased, but plausible parameter values suggest that total output would still increase.

The paper by *Edmond Malinvaud* offers a discussion of the scope for more traditional price and incomes policies. Three objectives of such policies are considered: reducing inequalities, solving the inflation–unemployment dilemma, and restoring business profitability. Malinvaud discusses a possible tradeoff between employment and real wages that goes beyond the conventional neoclassical labor demand schedule. The relationship involves three routes: the choice of capital intensity, the choice of productive capacity, and the formation of aggregate demand. An increase in the real wage reduces employment through capital–labor substitution, and through a reduction in the growth of productive capacity. But higher wages may also increase aggregate demand for goods — and thereby the demand for labor — provided that the ensuing shift in income distribution decreases national saving. Malinvaud conjectures that the relationship between employment and real wages is positive in an interval with low wages and negative for high wages.

Edmund Phelps has made a series of lasting contributions to the theory of unemployment and inflation. In the final paper in this volume, he develops a model of a small open economy with imperfect competition in labor and product markets. The product market is modeled as a customer market following the seminal paper by Phelps and Winter (1970). The presence of informational frictions implies that a firm which deviates from the going price will only gradually lose its customers. The labor market model draws on the shirking version of the efficiency wage theory, and the worker's effort increases in the excess of the firm's wage over expected outside wages. The model delivers implications for the short run as well as the long run. A productivity decline, for example, leads to an increase in employment in the short run, although employment falls in the long run.

The implication of a long-run positive relationship between productivity and employment is not entirely plausible, however, since productivity has grown for centuries without marked trends in unemployment. Phelps's result, as noted by Michael Hoel in his comment, depends crucially on the specification of the effort function. A slight modification of this function yields a result that unemployment will be independent of productivity in the long run.

III. Concluding Remarks

The papers in this volume are good representatives of a current direction of research in macroeconomics that may be loosely referred to as "the new Keynesian approach". The approach is *Keynesian* in its focus on market imperfections, price and wage rigidities, and involuntary unemployment. The approach is *new* Keynesian in its attempt to provide solid microeconomic foundations for price and wage rigidities, rather than taking these rigidities as exogenously given.

There are two directions for future research that we would particularly like to emphasize. On the empirical side, we are convinced that the future lies in more systematic use of microdata. The macroeconomic interpretations of results from cross-section microdata are not unproblematic, of course, but properly designed microdata, including panel data on firms, seem to be crucial in order to resolve a number of the current controversies in macro and labor economics. It is discomforting, for example, that the rapidly growing literature on efficiency wages includes very few attempts to provide information about the nature of the effort function and the links between effort and unemployment.

On the theory side, there is a need to develop richer analyses of the welfare effects of interventions in the labor market. Jackman and Layard have taken several steps in this direction in their present paper as well as in their earlier work. The models developed so far, however, are often vulnerable to the criticism that they ignore the microeconomic costs of interventions; cf. Torsten Persson's comment on Malinvaud's paper. Microeconomic costs have to be analyzed within a framework of market imperfections, however. Noncompetitive wage setting is, after all, responsible for nonmarket-clearing outcomes in the labor market. The obvious distortions which arise from interference in competitive labor

markets do not necessarily carry over to economies with, say, efficiency
wage setting or wage bargaining.

Reference

Phelps, E. S. & Winter, S. G.: Optimal price policy under atomistic competition. In E. S.
Phelps *et al.*, *Microeconomic Foundations of Employment and Inflation Theory*, W. W.
Norton & Co. Inc., New York, 1970.

I. EMPIRICAL REGULARITIES

European Unemployment: Lessons from a Multicountry Econometric Study*

Jacques Drèze

CORE, Louvain-la-Neuve, Belgium

Charles Bean

London School of Economics, London, England

Abstract

The paper summarizes the principal empirical findings of the European Unemployment Program. It draws on 10 country studies which utilize the macroeconomic framework set out by Sneessens and Drèze (1986). The main conclusions are as follows: (i) a major problem in Europe is that productivity gains are quickly absorbed into wages and the effect of unemployment on wage settlements is generally weak; (ii) a wage-price-productivity spiral means the European economies are inflation-prone; (iii) demand pressures spill over into the balance of payments rather than leading to price increases; (iv) the major proximate determinant of employment in the 1980s is the level of effective demand.

I. Introduction

This paper summarizes some of the main empirical findings of the European Unemployment Program (EUP), a concerted effort by a group of researchers[1] from 10 countries (the U.S., the eight major EEC countries and Austria) to understand the forces behind the persistently high unemployment in Europe over the last decade. The Program itself was an outgrowth of the 1985 Chelwood Gate Conference on Unemployment, published as a special issue of *Economica* (1986). It is also somewhat

---

*This is an abridged version of the Introductory Chapter to the book *Europe's Employment Problem*, edited by Jacques H. Drèze and Charles Bean with Jean-Paul Lambert, Fatemeh Mehta and Henri Sneessens, to be published by MIT Press. Interested readers are referred to that book for further details. The authors thank Fatemeh Mehta for her very effective research assistance, and the Commission of the European Communities (DG II) for financial support under contract II/09602.

[1] See Drèze and Bean (1989) for a full list of personnel.

unusual in that authors agreed to work within a (broadly) common framework so that international similarities and differences could be identified more easily. This framework, derived from Sneessens and Drèze (1986), is described briefly in Section II. The empirical results are then discussed in Sections III (prices, wages and productivity) and IV (output, employment and demand). A concise summary and policy conclusions (to which hurried readers may turn) are then given in Section V.

II. Overview and Microeconomic Foundations

Employment

Our primary concern is (un)employment. At the heart of the model lies the recognition that for a filled job to exist three conditions must be satisfied. First, that there exists a worker in the right place and with the right skills for the job. Second, that there is the capital available to employ the worker. Third, that there is a demand for the worker's output.

The setting is one of imperfect competition where firms set output prices and choose input levels, given their observations or expectations regarding demand conditions and input prices. At any point in time, firms inherit a given capital stock as a result of past investment decisions. If *ex post* factor substitution possibilities are limited (in particular, take time), there is at that point an upper bound to employment dictated by the available number of job slots (capacity employment – LC) and an associated upper bound on the level of output (capacity output – YC) determined by the level of capital and the embodied technical coefficients.

However, employment may fall short of capacity employment because the firm cannot hire as many workers as it would like. In that case employment will be equal to the available workforce (labour supply – LS) and the output level will be determined accordingly (full employment output – YS).

Employment may also fall short of capacity employment and labour supply because at the prevailing output price there is insufficient demand forthcoming. In that case output will be determined by effective demand (demand-determined output – YD) and the employment level will be determined accordingly (demand-determined employment – LD).

These three employment concepts (and their output counterparts) correspond to the three prerequisites for the existence of a filled job outlined at the start of this section. In a given plant or shop i, actual employment L_i and output Y_i will correspond to the minimum of these three conceptual levels:

$$L_i = \min(LC_i, LD_i, LS_i) \tag{1}$$

$$Y_i = \min(YC_i, YD_i, YS_i). \tag{2}$$

Still relationships (1)–(2) are not the end of the story, because one needs to explain (i) the decisions of the firms about the level of capital, the embodied technical coefficients and the output price; (ii) the clearing of output markets; (iii) the aggregation of firm level variables into macro-economic variables; and (iv) the determination of input prices and "demand" for output. We take up these four items in sequence.

The Rest of the Model

(i) Firms treat factor prices as given when making their pricing and invest-ment decisions. Profit maximization dictates that prices are set as a mark-up over short-run marginal cost. The mark-up reflects either the elasticity of demand for output on imperfectly competitive markets, or the margin needed to cover fixed costs at normal rates of capacity utilization, or both. Short-run marginal cost depends on wages and the level of productivity embodied in the technology, at least when capacity and labour supply con-straints do not bite.

However, it is costly to continuously adjust prices, which consequently have to be posted in advance on the basis of demand expectations. If there is a chance that demand will be so high that capacity or labour supply constraints bite, then the firm may wish to increase its mark-up to choke off some or all of the excess demand. Alternatively, it may prefer to maintain a reputation for "fair" pricing, while running down inventories and possibly building up back orders. Which combination of these two policies prevails is an important empirical question; the specification of the price equations needs to be flexible enough to admit either answer.[2]

The embodied technical coefficients and the rate of capital accumula-tion will depend upon (expected) factor prices. Because the level of demand fluctuates over time, the expected level of utilization of new machines or facilities matters; having capital lying idle some of the time increases the effective cost of that capital and reduces the profitability of investment. Moreover, the investment rate will obviously depend on the gap between the desired stock of capital and existing capital. For these two reasons, investment should be positively related to the degree of capacity utilization.

(ii) Having set prices, on the basis of their demand expectations, firms which are not constrained by capacity or labour supply will always be willing to meet the level of demand forthcoming at the posted price, because that price necessarily exceeds marginal cost. There is no rationing of demand when supply bottlenecks do not operate. On the other hand, supply bottlenecks may lead to excess demand for output, which in-

---

[2] As explained in Section III, the combined evidence from the 10 countries supports the reputation argument.

dividual firms may not wish to choke off through price increases. In such
cases, the demand for the products of other firms producing close substitutes will increase accordingly. Some of these will be foreign firms, so the
level of imports may increase.[3] If some domestic suppliers choose to divert
output from the foreign to the domestic market, exports will fall, thereby
adding to the deterioration of the trade balance. The upshot is that
demand pressures will be associated with a combination of price increases
and trade spillovers. These demand pressures will also be accompanied by
undesirably high degrees of capacity utilization, spurring investment. The
model assumes that these mechanisms are sufficiently powerful that no
quantity rationing of domestic demand is ever observed (in aggregate
annual data).

(iii) The aggregation of the employment and output decisions of firms
into the corresponding macroeconomic variables recognizes the hetero-
geneity of the situations faced by individual firms. Because there are many
products, there will exist simultaneously cases where product demand
exceeds capacity output, and cases where it falls short of capacity.
Similarly, because there are many skills, there will simultaneously exist job
vacancies and unemployed workers. Aggregating equations (2), for
instance, yields

$$Y = \Sigma_i Y_i = \Sigma_i \min(YC_i, YD_i, YS_i) \leq \min(\Sigma_i YC_i, \Sigma_i YD_i, \Sigma_i YS_i)$$
$$= \min(YC, YD, YS). \tag{3}$$

With many firms, skills and products, the min conditions are smoothed
by aggregation. A simple functional relationship among the aggregate
variables — used in most of the papers — can be derived from plausible
(lognormality) assumptions about the distribution across firms of the
relative magnitudes of the three proximate determinants of output, viz.:

$$Y = [YC^{-\rho} + YD^{-\rho} + YS^{-\rho}]^{-1/\rho}. \tag{4}$$

The corresponding employment relationship is

$$L = [LC^{-\rho} + LD^{-\rho} + LS^{-\rho}]^{-1/\rho}. \tag{5}$$

(See Lambert (1988) for details.)

(iv) Turning to input prices and output demands, the model is fairly
standard. For simplicity, the papers generally do not model the financial
sector of the economy, instead treating interest rates as exogenous. To the
extent that (real) interest rates are determined in global rather than
national capital markets, this is a justifiable assumption.

---

[3] This is best understood as reflecting the activity of (wholesale) traders who chase supplies
wherever they can be found, either domestically or abroad, when not available from the
usual sources.

Wages however clearly do need to be endogenized. In general these will respond to tightness of the labour market, as well as to productivity growth. In addition, there are a number of variables, such as terms of trade movements, changes in taxes and changes in benefit levels that may affect wage settlements. Through the tightness of the labour market, unemployment affects wages; that is the only relationship where unemployment appears explicitly.

Aggregate demand is the sum of: consumption, mostly related to disposable income; investment, whose determinants were mentioned above; government expenditures (exogenous) and export demand minus import demand, both of which are related to the relevant measure of final expenditure (at the world level for exports, the domestic level for imports) and to international competitiveness (world prices relative to domestic prices). Through the trade equations, domestic prices and hence domestic costs (in particular wages) affect aggregate demand, output and employment.

Let us now turn to the details of the rest of the model.

Model Specification

Labour supply, LS, is exogenous. Capacity output, YC, is determined by the stock of capital, K, and the output/capital ratio, B, resulting from past, present and expected factor prices. Demand for labour at capacity output, LC, is similarly determined by K, or YC, and the output/labour ratio, A. Denoting wages by W, the appropriate user cost of capital by Q, and an appropriate lag structure by $\Theta(\Lambda)$, we write

$$B_t = B\left(t, \Theta(\Lambda)\frac{W}{Q}\right), A_t = A\left(t, \Theta(\Lambda)\frac{W}{Q}\right) \tag{6}$$

$$YC_t = B_t K_t, LC_t = \frac{B_t}{A_t} K_t = \frac{YC_t}{A_t}, \tag{7}$$

where t allows for technical progress. Note that YC and LC are latent variables and not directly observable. In principle, measured average productivities (Y/K and Y/L) are related to the technical productivities (B, A) by the identities defining the degree of utilization of the factors of production (DUC, DUL):

$$DUC = \frac{Y}{YC} = \frac{Y/K}{B}, DUL = \frac{Y/L}{A}. \tag{8}$$

Some data concerning DUC and DUL are available, but they do not correspond exactly to our needs. Thus business surveys yield estimates of

8   *J. Drèze and C. Bean*

DUC for the manufacturing sector; and there exist published series on "average hours actually worked", the ratio of which to "normal" or "conventional" hours provides an estimate of *DUL*. Because these data are subject to bias and measurement error, the estimated equations take the more general form:

$$\frac{Y}{K} = B\left(t, \Theta(\Lambda)\frac{W}{Q}\right) DUC^\alpha \tag{9}$$

$$\frac{Y}{L} = A\left(t, \Theta(\Lambda)\frac{W}{Q}\right) DUL^\beta \tag{10}$$

where the elasticities α and β (typically estimated well below unity, especially β) make allowance for the data inadequacies.

In line with the general principles outlined above, the models assume that domestic demand is never rationed. Aggregate demand *YD* is the sum of consumption *C*, investment *I*, government expenditure *G*, and export demand *XD* minus import demand *MD*. A stylized specification goes as follows

$$C = C(Y...) \tag{11}$$

$$\frac{I}{K} = \frac{I}{K}\left(\frac{\Delta YD}{YD}, \frac{YD}{YC}, ...\right) \tag{12}$$

$$XD = XD\left(WT, \frac{PW}{PX}, ...\right) \tag{13}$$

$$MD = MD\left(YD, \frac{PM}{P}, ...\right) \tag{14}$$

where *P* denotes the price (index) of value added; *WT* denotes World Imports with price index *PW*; and *PX*, *PM* denote export and import prices.

The excess of *YD* over *Y* is absorbed by inventories (not modelled) or spills over into the trade balance. Accordingly, realized imports and exports are allowed to deviate from the levels specified in (13)–(14) to an extent depending upon the degree of capacity utilization:

$$X = XD\left(WT, \frac{PW}{PX}, ...\right) DUC^{-\gamma} \tag{15}$$

$$M = MD\left(YD, \frac{PM}{P}, \dots\right) DUC^{\delta}. \tag{16}$$

As will be seen in Section IV, the empirical analysis yields significant parameter values for γ and especially for δ.

Wage and price adjustments are geared to each other, to productivity changes and to rates of excess supply; in terms of growth rates (denoted $\hat{W}, \hat{P}, \dots$):

$$\hat{W} = \hat{W}(\hat{P}, \hat{A}, UR, \dots) \tag{17}$$

$$\hat{P} = \hat{P}(\hat{W}, \hat{A}, DUC, \dots). \tag{18}$$

An additional definition is

$$K_t = (1 - d) K_{t-1} + I_{t-1} \tag{19}$$

where d is the scrapping rate.

Equations (4)–(5), (9)–(12) and (15)–(18) form a system of 10 equations in the 10 endogenous variables $B, A, C, I, X, M, Y, L, \hat{W}$ and $\hat{P}$.

In practice, all the equations except (4)–(5) are specified as loglinear. In principle, the simultaneous system is nonlinear in the parameters as well as in the variables. When formulated in terms of growth rates, however, the system is nearly linear, up to some parameters to be computed for each observation from the level values of the variables. That property is used repeatedly in Section III.

The common structure described above forms the basis of the 10 country papers. The exact specification of each equation was chosen by individual authors, and left to reflect national idiosyncracies. Although the resulting diversity of precise specifications sometimes restricts comparability of results, it turns out to be quite instructive. In particular, commonality of freely chosen specifications sometimes conveys a significant message, as we shall see.

III. Prices, Wages and Productivity

Prices

A first important empirical regularity of the empirical results is the lack of a significant influence of demand pressure on prices. Table 1 reproduces the point estimates of the elasticities of prices (the deflator of GDP) with respect to the degree of capacity utilization, used as a measure of demand relative to capacity output, and with respect to wages. Nine equations were estimated. In two countries (France, Netherlands), no significant influence of capacity utilization on prices could be measured. In three countries (Spain, U.K., U.S.), a significant but small negative elasticity was

Table 1. *Elasticities of prices* (GDP deflator) / (Upper rows = short run, lower rows = long run)

Variable	Austria	Belgium	Britain	Denmark	France	Germany	Italy	Netherlands	Spain	U.S.
Demand pressure (DUC)	0.225	(1) 0.188 0.003	(3) −0.054 −0.084	no price equation		0.155 0.277	0.720 0.970		−0.270 −0.443	−0.001 −0.005
Cost push (wages)	0.510 1	(2) 0.749 1	0.880 1	estimated	0.490	0.477 0.855	0.740 1	0.163 0.403	1 1	1.361 1

(1) The demand pressure variable is YD/YT, with YD estimated within the model.
(2) The cost variable is average production cost, estimated within the model.
(3) Numerical values not comparable to other countries.

estimated.[4] In three countries (Austria, Belgium, Germany) a significant but small positive elasticity was estimated. In Italy, the estimated elasticity is positive and quite high (0.72) — but it is partly offset by a negative elasticity with respect to the degree of utilization of labour (measured by the ratio of actual to normal working hours). The prevailing picture is thus one of negligible measured influence of demand pressure on prices. In that light, the reference to high rates of capacity utilization as a warning that demand stimulation would be inflationary is questionable.

The absence of a significant influence of demand pressure on prices is all the more instructive, because authors sought for such an influence, and tried alternative measures of demand pressure. One must hasten to add that the elasticity of prices with respect to wage costs is substantial everywhere[5] — ranging between 0.5 and 1 in the short run, and typically set equal to 1 (after suitable testing) in the long run. In that light, the more relevant question is whether demand stimulation is likely to generate upward pressure on wages, which would then promptly be transmitted to prices. We return to price-wage dynamics below.

Wages

The empirical results concerning wage equations are summarized in Table 2, which gives the elasticity of real product wages with respect to average labour productivity and the derivatives of the rate of growth of real wages with respect to the unemployment rate (measured in percentage points). In every single European country, measured productivity gains seem to be passed on quite rapidly into wages, with short-run elasticities ranging from 0.4 to 0.8 and with a long-run elasticity close to unity. Similarly, the dampening effect of unemployment on real wage growth is present everywhere, with sensible orders of magnitude, but the coefficients are not precisely estimated. In the U.S., measured productivity did not enter significantly, and was replaced by a time trend.

These wage equations, which are listed in Table 3, display two notable features. First, with the exception of France, they all embody an error correction mechanism which relates the level of real wages to the level of unemployment in the long run. This is in marked contrast to the orthodox "Phillips curve" relationship (of which the French equation is an example) which links the unemployment rate to the rate of change of real wages. This level specification originates in the classic paper of Sargan (1964).

---

[4] A negative influence could reflect increasing returns to scale or procyclical movements in perceived demand elasticities.

[5] Except in the Netherlands, where the dependent variable is the price deflator of output and where the equation is estimated for the period 1971-87; higher elasticities are obtained there when the dependent variable is consumer prices instead of output prices.

Table 2.   *Wages* (Upper rows = short run, lower rows = long run)

Variable	Austria	Belgium	Britain	Denmark	France	Germany	Italy	Netherlands	Spain	U.S.
Productivity (elasticity)	0.412	0.882	0.100		0.420	0.660	0.710	0.562	0.830	(2) 0.002
	1.060	0.821	(4) 1			1	1	0.839		0.017
Unemployment (semi-elasticity)	−0.025	(3) −0.004	(3) −0.011	−0.012	−0.003	−0.004	−0.014		−0.011	(3) −0.002
	−0.028	−0.007	−0.110	−0.055		−0.004	−0.020			−0.013
Vacancy rate			(1) 0.011					0.025		
			0.110					0.093		

(1) Vacancy rate is estimated from the percentage of firms reporting an excess demand for labour in business surveys.
(2) Productivity is proxied by a time trend; the coefficient 0.0017 may be compared with the estimated trend coefficient of 0.0023 in the labour productivity equation, suggesting an elasticity of real wages to labour productivity close to 0.8.
(3) Unemployment variable appears with a lag of one period.
(4) The explanatory variable is $(U_{\text{Effective}} - V)$. The nature of this variable means the numerical value of the semi-elasticity is not comparable with those for other countries.

Table 3.   *Survey of wage equations*

Austria

$$\Delta \ln\left[\frac{WH}{P}\right] = -0.4\left[\ln\left(\frac{WH\cdot L}{P\cdot Y}\right)_{-1} + 0.025 U_{-1} - 0.55\ln TAX2_{-1} + \text{const.}\right] - 0.65\Delta^2\ln P - 0.025\Delta U$$

$$+ 0.5\Delta\ln TAX2 - 1.2\Delta\ln TAX3 + \text{const.}$$

Belgium

$$\Delta \ln\left[\frac{WN}{PC}\right] = -0.5\left[\ln\left(\frac{WN\cdot L}{PC\cdot Y}\right)_{-1} + 0.01 U_{-1} + \text{const.}\right] + 0.88\Delta\ln\left(\frac{Y}{L}\right) + \text{const.}$$

Denmark

$$\Delta\ln\left[\frac{W}{PC}\right] = -0.21\left[\ln\left(\frac{W}{PC}\right)_{-1} + 0.055U_{-1} + 0.3HOURS_{-1} + \text{const.}\right] + 0.36\Delta\ln A - 0.76\Delta\ln\left(\frac{PC}{P}\right) + \text{const.}$$

France

$$\Delta\ln\left[\frac{W}{P}\right] = 0.4\Delta\ln\left(\frac{Y}{L}\right) - 0.6\Delta\ln\left(\frac{PC}{P}\right) - 0.08U + \text{dummies} + \text{const.}$$

Germany

$$\Delta\ln\left[\frac{W}{P}\right] = -0.17\left[\ln\left(\frac{W\cdot L}{P\cdot Y}\right)_{-1} + 0.004U_{-1} + \text{const.}\right] - 0.004\Delta U + 0.66\Delta\ln A + 0.18\Delta\ln\left(\frac{W}{WN}\right)$$
$$+ 0.04\Delta\ln\left(\frac{PM}{P}\right) + 0.27\Delta\ln\left(\frac{W}{P}\right)_{-1} + \text{dummies}$$

Italy

$$\Delta\ln\left[\frac{W}{P}\right] = -0.71\left[\ln\left(\frac{W\cdot L}{P\cdot Y}\right)_{-1} + 0.02U + 0.01\ln DUC - 0.9\ln TAX4 + \text{const.}\right] + 0.2\Delta\ln\left(\frac{PM}{P}\right)$$

Netherlands

$$\Delta\ln\left[\frac{W}{PC}\right] = -0.34\left[\ln\left(\frac{W}{PC}\right)_{-1} - 0.8\ln\left(\frac{Y}{L}\right)_{-1} - 0.1V_{-1} - TAX2_{-1} - 0.64TAX1_{-1} + \text{const.}\right]$$
$$+ 0.56\Delta\ln A + \Delta TAX2 + 0.4\Delta TAX1 + 0.025\Delta V + \text{const.}$$

Spain

$$\ln\left[\frac{W}{P(1+TAX3)}\right] = 0.16\ln\left(\frac{Y}{L}\right) - 0.01U - 0.27\Delta^2\ln P + 0.8[\text{mismatch} + \text{replacement ratio} + \text{import wedge}] + \text{dummies} + \text{const.}$$

U.K.

$$\Delta\ln\left[\frac{W}{P}\right] = -0.1\left[\ln\left(\frac{W}{P}\right)_{-1} - \ln\left(\frac{YC}{LC}\right)_{-1} + 0.11(U_{\text{Effective}} - V) + 0.65\ln(\text{replacement ratio})\right] - 0.1\Delta^2\ln P$$

U.S.

$$\Delta\ln\left[\frac{W}{P}\right] = -0.1\left[\ln\left(\frac{W}{P}\right)_{-1} - 0.02t + 0.013U_{-1} + 0.45\text{Wedge}_{-1} + \text{const.}\right] - 0.001\Delta U - 0.06\Delta DEMOG - 0.32\Delta^2\ln P + \text{const.}$$

*TAX*1: labour taxes paid by employees
*TAX*2: labour taxes paid by employers
*TAX*3: indirect taxes
*TAX*4: income taxes

WH: hourly wage cost
WN: take home wage
W: wage cost
PC: consumer prices

The second notable feature is that, with the exception of the Danish, French and American wage equations, the error correction mechanisms imply that in the long run, it is essentially the share of wages in GNP (rather than the real wage itself) that is related to the unemployment rate. This would seem to correspond to the notion that wage formation in Europe today is dominated by unions who are heavily concerned over distributional fairness, in contrast to the U.S.[6] As we shall see below, this has important implications for the susceptibility of the European economies to inflationary shocks.

There is also the issue of the responsiveness of wage demands to unemployment. There are two dimensions to this: the overall size of the effect; and the speed with which it operates. Measuring the overall size by the long-run semi-elasticities of the real wage to the unemployment rate (given in Table 2), we see that they range from 0.4 per cent in Germany to 2.8 per cent in Austria.[7] In all countries this sensitivity of real wages to unemployment is too low to ensure that unemployment is substantially self-correcting in the face of adverse shocks.

As far as the speed of the effect of unemployment on real wages goes, that too varies across countries. For instance in Austria and Germany lags in the response of wages to unemployment are very short — virtually all of the effect comes through in the first year — while for most of the other countries the effect of unemployment on real wages is quite drawn out. Some of these differences whether short or long run, will be attributable to differences in choice of specification and sampling error, but some also no doubt reflect real institutional differences.

There is another empirical regularity, in the EUP program, which bears relating at this point; namely the fact that the parameter ρ of equations (4)–(5) is trended, reflecting a growing "mismatch" of supplies and demands at the microeconomic level. That common feature may be interpreted as corroborating outward shifts in the so-called Beveridge, or U–V curve; see Drèze and Bean (1989, Section 4.3) for details.

Productivity

A natural benchmark is the identity relating the rates of growth of capacity output, *YC*, capacity employment, *LC*, and "full utilization" labour

---

[6] Hellwig and Neumann (1987) describe as follows the negotiating stand of West German trade unions: "As political organizations, they are very much concerned with the 'fairness' of the distribution of income. In principle, they want to raise or at least maintain the share of wages in GNP".

[7] The semi-elasticity for Denmark is even larger at 5.5 per cent but as noted in the Danish paper, this equation is less than satisfactory in a number of respects, despite its low standard error, suggesting that it should be treated as an anomalous outlier. Because of the nature of the pressure of demand variable used in the U.K. study, the figures for that country are not directly comparable to those for the other countries.

productivity, A (lower-case letters denote logarithms):

$$\dot{l}c = \dot{y}c - \dot{a}. \tag{20}$$

Figures 1a and 1b give plots of the time-series (1960–86) for the observed values of $\dot{l}$, $\dot{y}$ and the estimated values of $\dot{a}$ at normal rates of factor utilization. Except for equation residuals and variations in utilization rates, these three series satisfy equation (20).[8] Also plotted are the growth rates of labour supply, $\dot{l}s$; the vertical difference $\dot{l}s - \dot{l}$ measures the increase in unemployment, and can be cumulated over time to trace the unemployment rate.

The global picture for the seven European countries is one of stationary employment ($\dot{l} \approx 0$ on average), with a trend decrease in output growth offset by a trend decrease in productivity growth. By contrast, the U.S. series display no trend in output growth, but portray the so-called "employment miracle": employment growth is positive throughout — up to short lived recessions — and oscillates around the labour supply series. Labour productivity growth (at normal utilization rates) was positive in the sixties, but almost came to a halt in 1970.

From the productivity equations, one can obtain a decomposition of labour productivity gains into that part reflecting pure technical progress and that part reflecting choices of factor proportions induced by changes in relative prices. A common feature of most models is the measurement of the user cost of capital through a price index for investment goods. (Only in the U.K. and U.S. could an effect from interest rates be detected.) The productivity equations embody distributed lags on relative factor prices — both to model price expectations, and to reflect adjustment lags in technological choices. Mean lags of three years are typical.

The contribution of factor prices to labour productivity is negligible in the U.S. In Europe, where real wages as well as productivity grew faster than in the U.S., there is a distinct influence of relative factor prices on technical labour productivity. That influence hovered around 2 per cent to 2.5 per cent per year until the late seventies, then started declining towards levels of 0.5 per cent to 1 per cent around 1986.

Crude as these estimates may be, they have the merit of quantifying a phenomenon about which qualitative evidence seems undisputed, namely that substitution of capital for labour has been an important phenomenon in Europe over the past 30 years, including the period of high unemployment. Whereas productivity growth is the engine of progress under full employment, the substitution of capital for labour is wasteful when there is unemployment.

---

[8] Two countries (France and the Netherlands) are missing, due to data constraints at the time of writing.

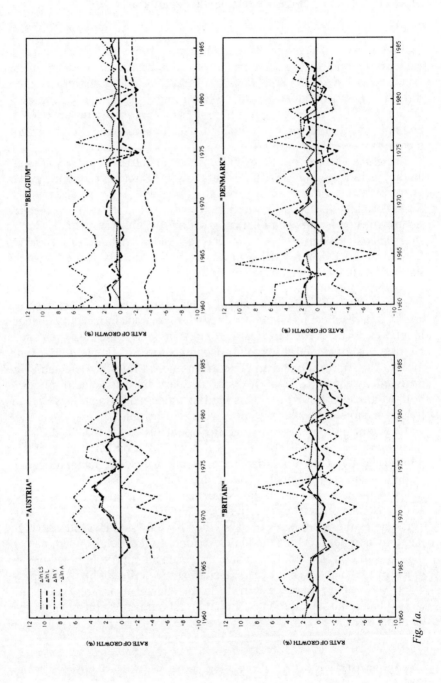

Fig. 1a.

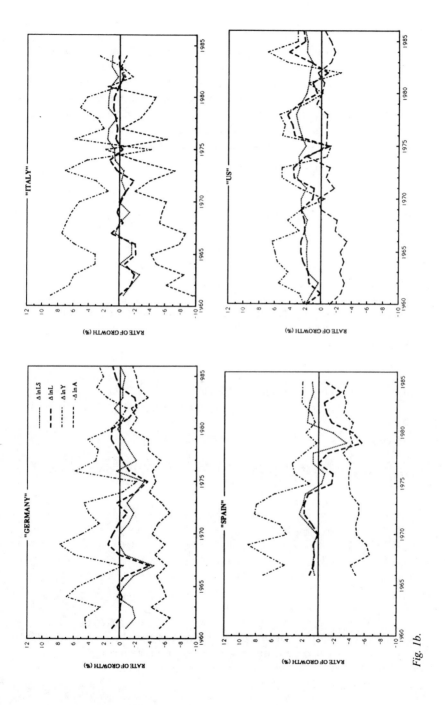

Fig. 1b.

The Wage-Price Spiral

The role of relative prices in guiding choices of factor proportions may be linked to the specification of the price and wage equations. To illustrate the phenomenon of induced substitution, we introduce a streamlined example, broadly consistent with the findings reported in this section. With a constant real interest rate, and with prices of investment goods moving closely with output prices, one may approximate relative factor prices by real product wages. Neglecting dynamics and cyclical fluctuations, a streamlined labour productivity equation then reads as follows:

$$a = y - l = \alpha_1 t + \alpha_2(w - p) + \text{constant}, \tag{21}$$

$$\dot{a} = \alpha_1 + \alpha_2(\dot{w} - \dot{p}), \tag{22}$$

where in the constant returns Cobb-Douglas case, α_2 is the capital elasticity of output.

If the error correction term in the wage equation may be written in terms of the labour share, a streamlined version of that equation is:

$$\dot{w} = \dot{p} + \dot{a} + z_1, \tag{23}$$

where z_1 denotes additional influences on wages, in particular unemployment. Under the assumption made about the cost of capital, prices are a mark-up on wage costs, up to additional factors z_2:

$$\dot{p} = \gamma(\dot{w} - \dot{a}) + z_2. \tag{24}$$

The solution to equations (22)–(24) is:

$$\dot{a} = \frac{\alpha_1 + \alpha_2 z_1}{1 - \alpha_2} \tag{25}$$

$$\dot{w} = \frac{\alpha_1}{1 - \alpha_2} + \frac{z_1}{1 - \alpha_2} \frac{1 - \gamma \alpha_2}{1 - \gamma} + \frac{z_2}{1 - \gamma} \tag{26}$$

$$\dot{p} = \frac{z_1 \gamma}{1 - \gamma} + \frac{z_2}{1 - \gamma} \tag{27}$$

$$\dot{w} - \dot{p} = \frac{\alpha_1 + z_1}{1 - \alpha_2}. \tag{28}$$

The rate of growth of labour productivity can thus be decomposed into an exogenous part corresponding to pure technological progress α_1 and an endogenous part induced by relative prices, $\alpha_2(\dot{w} - \dot{p}) = \alpha_2(\alpha_1 + z_1)/(1 - \alpha_2)$ or roughly, $(\alpha_1 + z_1)/2$.

In terms of equation (25), the downward pressure exerted by unemployment on wages (through z_1), will not reverse the capital/labour substitution $(\dot{a} < 0)$ unless it reduces real wages at a rate at least equal to α_1/α_2, or roughly $3\alpha_1$. Thus, with a typical value of α_1 like 0.02, and a rise in unemployment of one percentage point per year, the coefficient of U (or ΔU) in the wage equation should be as large as -0.06 in order for the downward pressure on wages to bring capital/labour substitution to a halt (after a mean lag of some three years...). In no single country do we find a coefficient that large. Clearly, the mechanism through which unemployment could be self-correcting is weak. We should not be surprised that unemployment has been persistent, in Europe.

We also note from equation (27), and from the elasticities in Table 2, that shocks affecting price (z_2) or wage (z_1) inflation are multiplied respectively by a factor of 3 or so $(1/1 - \gamma)$ and 2 or so $(\gamma/1 - \gamma)$ — revealing a high sensitivity to inflationary shocks. The sensitivity to wage shocks is less pronounced in the U.S. where measured productivity gains do not seem to be incorporated into wages.[9]

A more refined analysis should consider explicitly the "wedges" between consumption wages and product wages (including in particular labour taxes, which have increased everywhere), between the value added deflator and import prices (as influenced also by exchange rates), as well as between the prices of investment goods and those of consumer goods. In economies as exposed to inflationary spirals as suggested by equations (25)–(27), exogenous shocks affecting these wedges can have serious real consequences.

IV. Output, Employment and Demand

Trade Spillovers

Before reviewing the determination of output and employment in the EUP models, we wish to handle a simple question related to the comment made in Section III about the price equations. If prices do not react to demand pressure, how does one explain that quantity rationing of demand is hardly ever observed? In the EUP models, it is assumed that demand pressure spills over into foreign trade — either in the form of more imports, or in the form of less exports; see equations (15)–(16). To the extent that domestic producers may be reluctant to give up foreign markets, the penetration of which is a costly investment, the impact of capacity

---

[9] In the U.S. wage equation, $\dot{a}$ is replaced by a trend. Equation (27) then takes the form

$$\dot{p} = \frac{\gamma z_1 (1 - \alpha_2)}{1 - \gamma} + \frac{z_2}{1 - \gamma}.$$

utilization should be weaker for exports than for imports. These spillover terms in the import equations are all significant and quite sizeable, and, as expected, the quantitative order of magnitude is lower in the export equations. Adding together the import and export elasticities and looking at the median (over the nine countries) of the sums, we obtain for relative prices the values 1 in the short run, 1.5 in the long run; and for capacity utilization 1 in the short run and 2 in the long run (with no clear relationship to import shares).

Returning to the issue of demand pressure, and the lack of justification for the inflationary fears grounded in high rates of capacity utilization, it must now be recognized that domestic stimulation of demand in a country experiencing demand pressure is likely to generate import spillovers and hence a further deterioration of the trade balance. Since European governments are typically allergic to current account deficits, we find here an alternative explanation for the oft heard reference to capacity utilization as a ground for cautious fiscal policies.

Proximate Determinants of Growth

The models estimated under the EUP lead to a natural decomposition of the growth rate of output into three proximate components, corresponding respectively to the growth rates of output demand, of capacity output and of full employment output. The decomposition follows directly from the relationship defining output

$$Y = (YD^{-\rho} + YC^{-\rho} + YS^{-\rho})^{-1/\rho}, \tag{4}$$

$$\dot{y} = \eta_{Y \cdot YD} \dot{y} d + \eta_{Y \cdot YC} \dot{y} c + \eta_{Y \cdot YS} \dot{y} s \tag{29}$$

where $\eta_{Y \cdot YD}$ denotes the elasticity of Y with respect to $YD(=Y^{\rho}/YD^{\rho})$, and so on. These elasticities satisfy

$$\eta_{Y \cdot YD} + \eta_{Y \cdot YC} + \eta_{Y \cdot YS} \equiv 1. \tag{30}$$

This identity has theoretical foundations in the model of aggregation underlying (4). It leads to an interpretation of the three elasticities as the proportions π_D, π_C and π_S of micromarkets where domestic output is determined by demand, by capacity and by availability of labour, respectively; see Lambert (1988). In that notation, we may rewrite (29) as

$$\dot{y} = \pi_D \dot{y} d + \pi_C \dot{y} c + \pi_S \dot{y} s, \tag{31}$$

a linear relationship among growth rates.

Table 4 gives the values of (π_D, π_C, π_S) for various countries at selected dates. The main message is again the contrast between the European and U.S. patterns. In Europe the proportion of micromarkets where output is demand-determined grew markedly from 1975 and especially 1981

Table 4. Regime proportions

Year	Austria π_D	Austria π_C	Belgium π_D	Belgium π_C	Britain π_D	Britain π_C	Denmark π_D	Denmark π_C	Germany π_D	Germany π_C	Italy π_D	Italy π_C	Netherlands π_D	Netherlands π_C	Spain π_D	Spain π_C	U.S. π_D	U.S. π_C
1969	0.29	0.36	0.35	0.28	0.46	0.20	0.13	0.60	0.22	0.42	0.45	0.27	0.36	0.24	0.16	0.23	0.19	0.49
1974	0.24	0.11	0.33	0.34	0.37	0.15	0.34	0.45	0.33	0.34	0.21	0.31	0.66	0.15	0.13	0.63	0.20	0.54
1979	0.73	0.04	0.71	0.24	0.65	0.12	0.30	0.63	0.47	0.31	0.35	0.20	0.41	0.48	0.66	0.30	0.28	0.49
1984	0.74	0.06	0.71	0.28	0.78	0.13	0.38	0.44	0.74	0.20	0.60	0.20	0.65	0.34	0.78	0.22	0.53	0.30

onwards. In the U.S., there is less trend in the proportions: π_D moves pro-cyclically, and π_C countercyclically.

An alternative presentation of that message is offered by Figures 2a and 2b, which display the series $\pi_D \dot{y}d$, $\pi_C \dot{y}c$ and $\pi_S \dot{y}s$ — i.e., the decomposition of output growth into its three proximate determinants.

A remarkable feature of Figure 2 is the negligible contribution of capacity and labour supply growth to output growth in the eighties, for most European countries and particularly so for Austria, Belgium, Germany and the U.K. The proximate importance of demand for output growth since the second oil shock is thus clearly confirmed — in contrast again to the U.S. where capacity and labour supply availability retain significance.

Since demand for domestic output is the sum of consumption, investment, government expenditure and the trade balance, it is instructive to decompose in turn the rate of growth of *YD* into these four components:

$$\dot{y}d = S_C \dot{c} + S_I \dot{i} + S_G \dot{g} + (S_X \dot{x}d - S_M \dot{m}d), \tag{32}$$

where S_C is the ratio of consumption to *YD*, and similarly for the other shares. That decomposition is presented in Figures 3a–3b. In comparison to European countries, one may note for the U.S.: (i) the relatively limited amplitude of the foreign trade component in that relatively closed economy; (ii) the positive contribution of government expenditure ever since the mid-seventies and especially in the eighties; (iii) the sustained contribution of consumption, especially again in the eighties. In Europe, the amplitude of the foreign trade component is much more pronounced, especially in the smaller countries like Austria, Belgium and Denmark.

Another striking feature, shared by Europe and the U.S., is the amplitude of the contributions to GDP growth coming from investment. This is somewhat surprising, because investment amounts to less than 20 per cent of GDP; yet, it repeatedly contributes plus or minus four percentage points to GDP growth, because it is much more volatile than the other components. In particular, the sharp declines of aggregate demand in 1975 and 1981 (see Figure 2) are largely due to the collapse of investment in those years.

Output Dynamics

When looking at the evolution of demand components, one must remember first that most of them are endogenous, being simultaneously determined with output; and second that relative prices affect at least the trade component. A partial endogenization of demand growth is obtained from a stripped version of the demand block consisting of equations (11), (13) and (14). Treating provisionally investment and government expenditure as exogenous, one may rewrite these three equations in growth rates

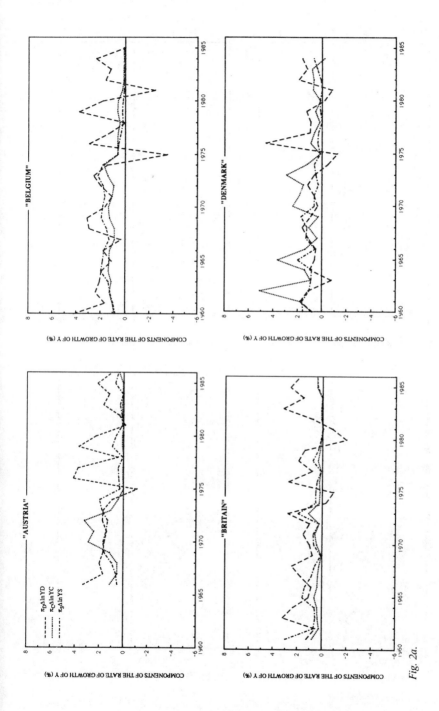

Fig. 2a.

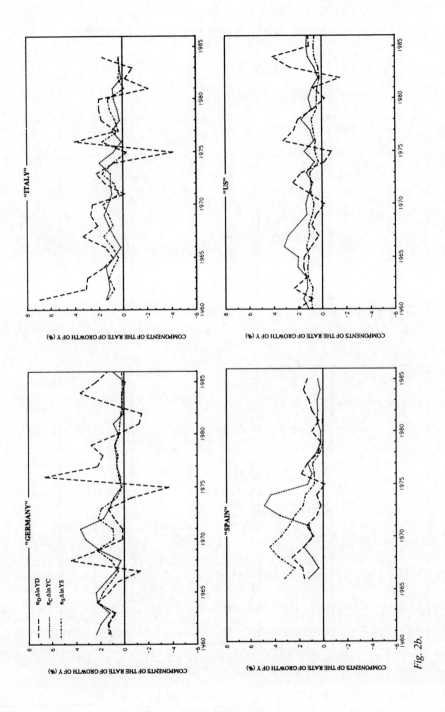

Fig. 2b.

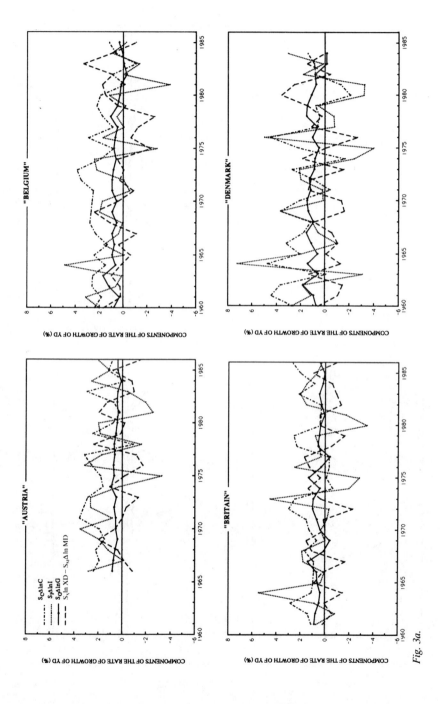

Fig. 3a.

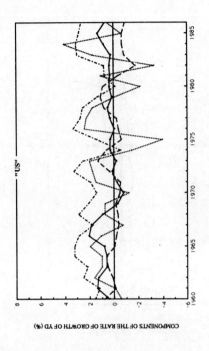

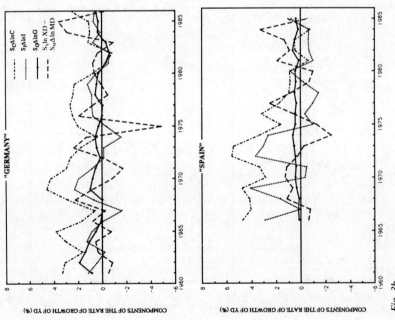

Fig. 3b.

form, then substitute them in (32) and (31), obtaining finally:

$$\dot{y} = \frac{\pi_D}{1 + S_M \eta_{M \cdot YD} - \pi_D S_C \eta_{CY}} \cdot \{ S_I \dot{i} + S_G \dot{g} + S_X \eta_{X \cdot WT} \dot{w}t$$

$$+ S_X \eta_{X \cdot (PW/PX)} (pw - px) - S_M \eta_{M \cdot (PM/P)} (pm - \dot{p}) \}$$

$$+ \frac{1 + S_M \eta_{M \cdot YD}}{1 + S_M \eta_{M \cdot YD} - \pi_D S_C \eta_{CY}} \{ \pi_c \dot{y}c + \pi_s \dot{y}s \}. \tag{33}$$

where $\dot{y}c = \dot{k} + \dot{b}$ and $\dot{y}s = \dot{i}s + \dot{a}$.

Although that expression may appear forbidding, its interpretation is in fact quite straightforward. A synthetic formulation would be:

$\dot{y} = \pi_D \times$ open economy multiplier

     $\times$ [contribution from growth rates of investment

       and exogenous demand components

     + contributions from price effects of trade component]

     + contributions from $\dot{y}c$ and $\dot{y}s$.

As is well known, the impact of demand shocks in such models is dampened by the factor π_D, because output adjusts only when it is demand-determined. For the same reason, the multiplier is reduced, because the propensity to consume (in the denominator) generates output only in the proportion π_D. Knowledge of the proportions (π_D, π_C, π_S) of Table 4 is thus important for policy evaluation.

Wages and Demand

We may now take up the difficult, but essential, question of the interplay of wages and demand. We should first of all note that the EUP models embody rather crude consumption functions (or no consumption function at all, in Austria, Denmark, Italy and the U.S.). Thus, the role of wages in sustaining consumer demand is not captured. According to some, little loss of information is involved, because they regard the hypothesis of a higher propensity to consume out of wage income than out of gross profits as unsubstantiated (presumably due to the chain from profits to asset prices to wealth to consumption). Even so, there would remain scope for unemployment to depress consumption through a "permanent income" effect. These issues will not be settled by the work under review. (Still, we note that the well-behaved German consumption function implies a fall in consumer demand of 0.25 per cent for a 1 per cent decrease in employment, at unchanged disposable income).

The direct channel through which wages influence final demand, e.g., in equation (33), comes from the price elasticities of foreign trade. It is important, in that connection, to draw a distinction between a wage shock in a single country and a wage shock affecting simultaneously several (most) European countries. In the former case, the wage shock being quickly transmitted to prices, and the sum of the price elasticities being of the order of one in the short run and higher in the long run, the impact on final demand is quite sizeable, and roughly proportional to the country's degree of openness, as measured by $S_M \simeq S_X$. In the latter case, the elasticity of prices to wage costs being of comparable magnitude in the different countries, and some 60 per cent of the trade being intra-European, the relative prices would be much less affected, and the influence on final demand would be significantly dampened, both for individual countries and for Europe as a whole (whose degree of openness is roughly comparable to that of the U.S.).

The difficult question concerns the interaction between wage formation and fiscal stance: Have European Governments adjusted their fiscal stance in response to wage shocks? (The adjustment could be contractionary, to fight inflation or to avoid current account disequilibria; but it could also be expansionary to prevent a rise in unemployment, resulting from the loss of competitiveness and from the induced capital-labour substitution.)

The econometric work within the EUP is not instructive in this respect, because government spending is exogenous in all models. But the papers contain a number of interesting anecdotes. These include such classics as the German fiscal contraction following the "locomotive experiment" of the late seventies. They also include the temporarily successful Austrian and Danish attempts to counter the first oil-shock through expansionary fiscal policies — and the reversal to budget consolidation as the public debt built up.

Beyond these individual anecdotes, there is a common experience. Temporary demand stimulation through fiscal policy exerts only temporary effects, in these models. That is, a temporary stimulus does not by itself raise the level of output permanently. It could in principle happen that growing public expenditures become self-financing as the growth rates of other components of final demand match that of government spending. But that would fail to happen if investment and exports lag behind. The fiscal deficit then results in a growing public debt and current account deficit, eventually inducing a reversal of policies. A wise use of the fiscal instrument rests on a comparative assessment of the state of the economy today, and tomorrow at the time of the policy reversal required to reimburse the debt. The chain of events which led European governments to tighten fiscal policy in the wake of the second oil shock was most unfortunate. That episode contains a lesson for the future.

The temporary nature of fiscal stimuli is confirmed by the simulations carried out with some of the EUP models.

A Synthesis

Bringing together the contents of Sections III and IV regarding the influence of wages on employment, we note that the models under review embody two explicit channels and one implicit channel through which that influence exerts itself. The two explicit channels are (i) the demand side, through the foreign trade elasticities — a channel of greater significance in case of single country wage movements than in case of parallel wage movements in several countries; (ii) the supply side, through capital-labour substitution — a channel that is equally significant in the single country case as in the multi-country case.[10] The implicit channel concerns fiscal policy reactions to wage shocks.

It is interesting to speculate briefly about the relative importance of the two explicit channels. From (25)–(27), and the figures in Table 2 and Section IV, one would guess that the two channels are of comparable importance in the case of single-country shocks — the exact answer being related to that country's degree of openness. In the case of European-wide shocks, the capital-labour substitution channel is probably the dominant one. As noted above, capital-labour substitution induced by the incorporation of productivity gains into wages are wasteful when the economy operates under inefficient unemployment.

One message from the work under review is that wage moderation has to fight the tide, in the supply channel as well as in the demand channel, if it is to pave the way for a reduction in unemployment. As noted in Section III, real wage adjustments will not increase the employment content of growth unless they amount to something like three times the rate of autonomous technological progress; the tide is thus quite strong along the supply channel. In the demand channel, the growth rates of capital, government demand and world trade define another tide. When these rates fall below the growth rate of labour productivity, the effects of wage adjustments on the trade balance again need to overcome that adverse tide before they result in employment growth. Lags in the reaction of wages to unemployment, then in the reactions of prices and factor proportions to wages, slow down the adjustment process. It is always difficult to fight the tide with insufficient boat speed...

---

[10] To this should be added all the general equilibrium interactions, like the investment accelerator, whereby the supply side reacts to demand conditions, and so on.

J. Drèze and C. Bean

V. Summary and Conclusions

Summary

The broad empirical regularities of the EUP may be summarized as follows:

(1) The measured influence of demand pressure on prices is negligible, but the elasticity of prices with respect to wage costs is substantial, ranging from minimal values of 0.5 in the short run to 1 in the long run.

(2) Real wages incorporate measured productivity gains quite rapidly in Europe, with short-run elasticities ranging from 0.4 to 0.8 and long-run elasticities close to 1. Measured productivity does not enter significantly in the U.S. wage equation.

(3) The level of unemployment typically enters the wage equations through an error correction term, relating the share of wages in value added to the level of unemployment. The estimated coefficients imply a reduction in the wage share, per percentage point of unemployment, ranging from 0.4 per cent in the high unemployment countries to 2.5 per cent in Austria — revealing the weak self-correcting mechanism for unemployment in the former group. That specification is consistent with the view that European labour unions are much concerned with the fairness of the distribution of income.

(4) The $U-V$ (Beveridge) curve has shifted outwards, in all countries (including the U.S.).

(5) The incorporation of measured productivity gains into real wages induces capital-labour substitution, which is wasteful in economies operating under inefficient unemployment. Employment growth in Europe was curtailed by factor substitution at an average rate of some 2 per cent per year until the late seventies, and 1 per cent per year more recently. If that substitution had stopped when it became wasteful, the rise of unemployment in Europe could have been avoided.

(6) Shocks on prices are multiplied by a factor of 2 to 4, and shocks on wages by a factor of 1 to 3, through the wage-price-productivity spiral. The European economies are thus inflation-prone.

(7) Demand pressures, which as suggested under point 1 are not choked off through price increases, spill over into imports, and to a lesser extent exports, thereby deteriorating the trade balance. That robust country-level finding remains to be analyzed in a multi-country setting.

(8) The main and nearly unique proximate determinant of output growth in the eighties in Europe has been effective demand. The

growth of demand is linked to the growth of its exogenous components, namely government expenditures and world trade. It is also linked to the relative growth rates of domestic and foreign prices, through the price elasticities of exports and imports. This last channel is much less significant for Europe as a whole than for individual countries.

(9) The degree of capacity utilization is a significant determinant of investment. (In line with the suggestion under point 1 that prices are geared to costs but not to demand pressures, the profitability of investment should depend largely upon utilization rates.)

(10) Besides affecting employment through their influence on the foreign trade component of demand, wages also affect employment through capital-labour substitution, as noted under point 5. For Europe as a whole, that second channel is probably more significant than the first.

(11) Temporary demand stimulation through fiscal policy exerts only temporary effects, in within-sample-period simulations of the EUP models. And the papers contain anecdotes about policy reversals induced by cumulated deficits.

Conclusions

The empirical findings suggest explaining the contrast between the U.S. "employment miracle" and the European persistent unemployment in terms of two proximate causes: (i) the wage formation process differs as between the two zones in particular regarding the incorporation of measured productivity gains into real wages; (ii) whereas the proportion of firms where output and employment are demand determined grew markedly in all European countries in the late seventies and mostly remained high, that proportion is not trended in the U.S. — presumably due to a combination of relative closedness, sustained consumption and lasting deficits.

The European wage-formation process makes non-declining employment dependent upon sustained output growth. In small open economies, this in turn requires parallel growth in exports — as determined by world demand and competitiveness. When some of these elements are missing, fiscal policy alone is not a very effective instrument.

These conclusions should be taken with a...pound of salt! After due pruning, it will probably remain inescapable that the elimination of European unemployment is a very difficult challenge. The work reviewed here suggests strongly that the mechanism through which unemployment could be self-correcting is weak and slow, in Europe. A gradual elimination will tautologically call for a prolonged period during which output grows faster than productivity — a situation not witnessed over the past 30 or 40 years. Because growth of real wages induces gains in measured productivity through capital-labour substitution, the goal will be easier to reach if medium-run expected wage growth is strictly contained. We do not know whether, and how, that condition could be met. Under that condition, the fear that faster output growth would rekindle inflation is probably misplaced — but a temporary deterioration in current accounts would need to be faced. And the expansion would require cooperation among several European countries, if national current account problems are to remain manageable. On the other hand, if demand stimulation through fiscal policy has only temporary effects, the accumulation of public deficits is unlikely to be tolerated.

We do not wish to eschew these dilemmas by resorting to fine tuning. Still the following remarks appear timely:

(a) Public deficits are more tolerable, from an intertemporal perspective, if they correspond to productive investments.

(b) Labour taxes have an obvious role to play in containing, or reversing, the growth of labour costs and medium-run expectations about them; one advantage of tax adjustments is that they are not apt to be perceived as transitory; granted that many among the currently unemployed are at best candidates for low-paid jobs, a reduction in labour taxes should be targeted towards the low end of the wage scale (for example by exempting minimum wages from social security contributions).

(c) In order to alleviate labour market tensions, it is important to increase the supply of those specific skills which are in excess demand; both training opportunities and wage differentials have a role to play. There is also scope for initiatives to make the wage differentials more acceptable, and to limit their unnecessary spreading to other skills. Still, it must be recognized that the required skills will not be supplied by the long-term unemployed; for these, special programs remain needed.

From a longer-run perspective, there is ground to be concerned about the vulnerability of Europe to inflation as well to output and employment fluctuations. The division into relatively open national economies compounds these problems, by creating complex interdependencies between countries. This also leads to a need for international cooperation in demand management, public investment, etc. The process of wage formation has almost certainly been destabilizing in the seventies, and the experience could be repeated. The goal of distributional equity needs to be implemented more efficiently. We need an operational way of separating out technical progress from measured productivity gains associated with capital deepening induced by wage increases. The incorporation into real wages of productivity gains following from capital deepening is entirely desirable when an economy is at full employment, but the resulting substitution of capital for labour becomes wasteful in the presence of unemployment.

References

Bean, C. R., Layard, P. R. G. & Nickell, S. J. (eds.): *The Rise in Unemployment.* Blackwell, Oxford, 1986.

Drèze, J. H. & Bean, C. R. (1989): Europe's employment problem: Introduction and synthesis. Forthcoming as Chap. I in J. H. Drèze & C. R. Bean (eds.), with J. P. Lambert, F. Mehta and H. Sneessens, *Europe's Employment Problem*, MIT Press, Cambridge, 1989.

Hellwig, H. & Neumann, M.: Germany under Kohl. *Economic Policy 5*, 103–45, 1987.

Lambert, J. P.: *Disequilibrium Macroeconomic Models: Theory and Estimation of Rationing Models Using Business Survey Data.* Cambridge University Press, Cambridge, 1988.

Layard, P. R. G. & Nickell, S. J.: The causes of British unemployment. *National Institute Economic Review 111*, 62–85, 1985.

Sargan, J. D.: Wages and prices in the UK: A study in econometric methodology. In P. Hart, G. Mills & J. Whitaker (eds.), *Econometric Analysis for Economic Planning*, Butterworths, London, 1964.

Sneessens, H. & Drèze, J. H.: A discussion of Belgian unemployment, combining traditional concepts and disequilibrium econometrics. *Economica 53*, 89–119, 1986.

Comment on J. Drèze and C. Bean, "European Unemployment: Lessons from a Multicountry Econometric Study"

Tohmas Karlsson

National Institute of Economic Research, Stockholm, Sweden

Karl-Gustaf Löfgren

University of Umeå, Sweden

Introduction

The approach used by the European Unemployment Program (EUP) is interesting for at least three reasons. First of all, it takes an explicit stance with respect to the causes of unemployment. Economic theory today is dominated by the neoclassical view that unemployment is a frictional phenomenon of a voluntary nature. If it becomes unnaturally high, because of demand or supply shocks, the self-regulating forces governed by price flexibilities will take the economy back to full employment or the natural rate of unemployment relatively quickly. The models of the EUP recognize price and wage rigidities. More precisely the markets for both goods and labor are modeled by a disequilibrium approach. Prices and wages are changing, but only gradually and not fast enough to create market clearing at each point in time. One of the aims of the EUP is to find out how quickly the economy approaches equilibrium.

Second, in an attempt to create a high degree of comparability and to be able to separate out real differences from differences of approach, the research teams have adopted a common framework which generated models for each country using approximately the same econometric specification.

Third, although the models, deal with nominal entities such as prices, they neglect money and financial markets. To the extent that real interest rates are determined globally rather than locally, this may be a justifiable assumption. On the other hand, it begs the question of the extent to which

---

*The authors acknowledge comments on an earlier version of this paper by Runar Brännlund, University of Umeå, Anders Vredin and Paul Söderlind, National Institute of Economic Research, Stockholm.

the rigidities created by the European Monetary System have contributed to European unemployment problems.

Drèze and Bean are able to present a huge amount of interesting econometric results, and it is an understatement to say that the project has been a success. We have few or no queries about the results. Sweden is not one of the countries included in the EUP, although has been subject to the same kinds of shocks (e.g., OPEC I and OPEC II), but considerably more successful in curbing the unemployment rate than most European countries. We are therefore curious about the extent to which the empirical regularities reported by Drèze and Bean are also valid for Sweden. Below we try to give a partial answer to this question.

The idea is that, given similar business conditions and similar poor self-correcting mechanisms, the fact that Sweden has been more successful in solving its unemployment problems than the average European country would cast some doubts on the appropriateness of the EUP approach as such. On the other hand, the existence of more flexible adjustment mechanisms in general in Sweden would add further credibility to the results reported in the Drèze and Bean paper.

In order to indicate that business conditions in Sweden and Europe have indeed been similar, we compare the EUP finding that the proportion of micromarkets where output is demand determined grew markedly from 1975 and especially from 1981 onwards, with a corresponding analysis for Sweden carried out by Karlsson (1988). This contains an estimate of the probability of Keynesian unemployment during the same period; see Figure 1.

Figure 1 indeed shows that the probability of Keynesian unemployment rises sharply between 1976–84 and is particularly high during the periods 1976–79, and 1981–83.

We concentrate on the following findings reported by Drèze and Bean:

(1) The measured influences of demand pressure on prices are negligible, but the elasticity of prices with respect to wage costs is substantial, ranging from minimal values of 0.5 in the short run and to 1 in the long run.

(2) Real wages incorporate measured productivity gains quite rapidly in Europe, with short-run elasticities ranging from 0.4 to 0.8, and long-run elasticities close to 1.

(3) The level of unemployment typically enters the wage equation through an error correction term, relating the share of wages in value added to the level of unemployment. The estimated coefficients imply a reduction in the wage share, per percentage point of unemployment, ranging from 0.4 per cent in the high unemployment countries to 2.5 per cent in Austria — revealing a weak self-

Probability for Keynesian Unemployment

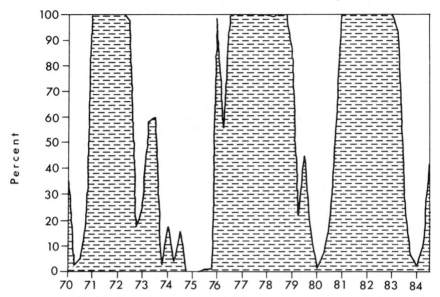

Fig. 1. The probability of Keynesian unemployment in Sweden.

correcting mechanism for unemployment in the former group. This specification is consistent with the view that European labor unions are greatly concerned with the fairness of the distribution of income.

(4) The U-V (Beveridge) curve has shifted outwards in all countries (including the U.S.).

To start with the last point, which means that the mismatch in European labor markets has increased, more vacancies are needed today to generate the same unemployment rate. We have drawn the Swedish U-V curve estimated on yearly data from the period 1963–88, as well as the data points as such in Figure 2. There is no way to distinguish any outward shift. An inward shift cannot be excluded since registration of vacant positions at employment offices has been mandatory since 1977, and data have not been appropriately corrected for this.

Turning to the real wage equation, we have chosen to work with semiannual data for the industry (SNI 2 + 4) and two different specifications of the error-correction mechanism. In one we entered the wage share as a function of the unemployment rate, and in the other the real product wage rate as a function of the unemployment rate, labour productivity and the tax on labor. The typical results are seen from equations (1) and (2) below.

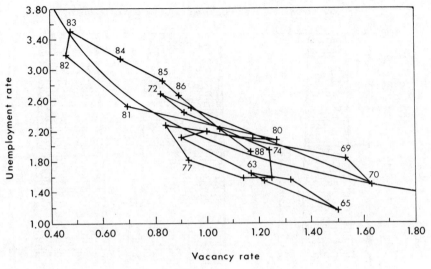

Fig. 2. The Swedish Beveridge curve[1] 1963–88.

The Long-Run or Equilibrium Relationship for Real Product Wages

Two alternative long-run or equilibrium relationships were postulated and estimated over the period 1971:1–1987:2. T-values, which are written below each estimated parameter, should not be taken too seriously, since the lack of dynamics in these long-run relationships induces a high degree of autocorrelation in the residuals.

(a) The wage share is assumed to be related to the level of unemployment in the long run.

$$\ln(WL/PQ)_t = -0.12 - 0.060\,U_t \qquad (1)$$
$$(-2.62) \quad (-2.63)$$

$$R^2 = 0.177 \qquad \sigma = 0.073 \qquad F(1,32) = 6.89\,[0.01]$$

(b) The level of the real product wage is assumed to be related to the level of productivity, the level of labor taxes paid by the employer and the level of unemployment.

---

[1] Both estimation and collection of the data set are due to Olle Westerlund, Department of Economics, University of Umeå. The estimated equation is

$$\ln u = 0.74 - 0.64 \ln v \qquad DW = 1.74$$
$$(12.77) \quad (-6.85) \qquad R^2 = 0.74$$

The residuals have been corrected for autocorrelation by the Cochrane-Orcutt method.

$$\ln(W/P)_t = 3.10 + 0.30\ln(Q/L)_t + 0.29\ln TAX_t - 0.0028 U_t \quad (2)$$
$$(7.55) \quad (3.38) \qquad (6.83) \qquad (-0.18)$$

$$R^2 = 0.912 \qquad \sigma = 0.0432 \qquad F(3,30) = 104.20\,[0.00]$$

We test for cointegration using the augmented Dickey-Fuller test (ADF), the Dickey-Fuller test (DF), and the cointegrating regression Durbin-Watson test (CRDW). In formulation (2) four variables are assumed to be related, which means that the cointegrating regression can be performed with any one of them as the dependent variable. In other words, the cointegrating vector is not necessarily unique. It is also not clear which regression should be chosen, but finite sample bias related to the overall goodness of fit of the regression suggests that the regression with the highest R^2 should be selected; see Stock (1984). We have followed this rule.

The lack of power of tests for cointegration when residuals are highly autoregressive, yet stationary, suggests that some caution is in order when interpreting the results. The results of these tests, with critical values taken from Hall (1986) in brackets, are:

	CRDW	ADF(4)	DF
eq. (1)	0.39 [0.367]	-0.41 [-3.13]	-1.23 [-3.37]
eq. (2)	0.82 [0.367]	-4.10 [-3.13]	-2.72 [-3.37]

On the basis of these findings we conclude that equation (2) is a cointegrating vector whereas equation (1) is not.

The magnitudes of the unemployment rate coefficients in equations (1) and (2) can be used as an indication of the strength of the self-corrective mechanism of unemployment. Compared with the corresponding coefficients in the Drèze and Bean paper, both are larger, but "the more reliable" one in the real product wage equation is not significantly different from zero.

The Short-Run Error-Correction Formulation for Real Product Wages

An important theorem by Engle and Granger (1987) states that a set of variables are cointegrated if and only if there exists an error correction representation of the dynamic model. In the second stage of the estimation we specify two different equations, one for each postulated equilibrium relationship. For both cases we initially estimate an overparameterized model with three lags on the dependent variable and each independent variable in addition to the error-correction term. After deleting insignificant lags we get the following parsimonious error-correction representation corresponding to the wage share formulation:

$$\Delta \ln(W/P)_t = 0.22 \Delta \ln(W/P)_{t-2} + 0.59 \Delta \ln(Q/L)_t$$
$$\quad (1.51) \qquad\qquad\qquad (3.41)$$

$$\qquad\qquad + 0.073 \Delta U_t - 0.069 \Delta U_{t-2} - 0.20 EC_{t-1} \qquad\qquad (3)$$
$$\qquad\qquad (2.76) \quad\;\; (-1.99) \qquad\;\; (-2.04)$$

$$R^2 = 0.58 \qquad\qquad \sigma = 0.0279 \qquad\qquad DW = 1.70$$

Note that the error-correction term is statistically significant even though we could not establish that equation (1) is a cointegrating vector. A further test of the error-correction specification would be to relax the restrictions on the coefficients on the level variables imposed by the cointegrating regressions in (1). Thus we use the same specification as in equation (3), but substitute the lagged values of the wage share and the level of unemployment for the error-correction term. The results are as follows:

$$\Delta \ln(W/P)_t = 0.013 + 0.20 \Delta \ln(W/P)_{t-2} + 0.70 \Delta \ln(Q/L)_t + 0.059 \Delta U_t$$
$$\quad (0.48) \quad (1.12) \qquad\qquad\qquad (3.39) \qquad\qquad (1.79)$$

$$\qquad\qquad - 0.10 \Delta U_{t-2} - 0.0065 U_{t-1} - 0.064 \ln WS_{t-1} \qquad\qquad (3b)$$
$$\qquad\qquad (-2.68) \qquad\; (-0.51) \qquad\; (-0.38)$$

$$R^2 = 0.52 \qquad\qquad \sigma = 0.0312 \qquad\qquad DW = 1.83$$

None of the level variables enter significantly, and the implied values for the error-correction term from the model in (3b), when normalized for a unit coefficient on the wage share, is:

$$\ln WS_t = 0.20 - 0.10 U_t. \qquad\qquad (1b)$$

Thus, the coefficient estimates are very different from the cointegrating regression in (1), which is not very surprising since we could not establish that (1) is a cointegrating vector. Let us now consider the second alternative (2) of the equilibrium relationship:

$$\Delta \ln(W/P)_t = 0.32 \Delta \ln(W/P)_{t-2} + 0.061 \Delta U_t - 0.085 \Delta U_{t-2}$$
$$\quad (2.39) \qquad\qquad\qquad (2.62) \quad\;\; (-3.05)$$

$$\qquad\qquad + 0.52 \Delta \ln(Q/L)_t - 0.40 EC_{t-1} \qquad\qquad (4)$$
$$\qquad\qquad (3.27) \qquad\qquad (-3.27)$$

$$R^2 = 0.66 \qquad\qquad \sigma = 0.0252 \qquad\qquad DW = 1.77$$

We note that the error-correction term is highly significant. Performing the same test as for equation (3), i.e., relaxing the coefficients for the level variables in the error correction term, gives the following results:

$$\Delta \ln(W/P)_t = 1.13 + 0.28\Delta \ln(W/P)_{t-2} + 0.059\Delta U_t - 0.070\Delta U_{t-2}$$
$$\qquad (1.94)\ (1.64) \qquad\qquad\qquad (2.03) \qquad (-1.63)$$

$$+ 0.51\Delta \ln(Q/L)_t - 0.40\ln(W/P)_{t-1} + 0.15\ln(Q/L)_{t-1}$$
$$\quad (2.63) \qquad\qquad (-3.04) \qquad\qquad\quad (1.36)$$

$$+ 0.10\ln TAX_{t-1} - 0.0086\,U_{t-1} \qquad\qquad\qquad (4b)$$
$$\quad (1.77) \qquad\quad (-0.51)$$

$$R^2 = 0.66 \qquad\qquad \sigma = 0.0272 \qquad\qquad DW = 1.75$$

The implied values for the corresponding error-correction term are:

$$\ln(W/P)_t = 2.81 + 0.37\ln(Q/L)_t + 0.25\ln TAX_t - 0.021\,U_t. \qquad (2b)$$

In this case the coefficients are quite close to the estimated ones in (2), except for the coefficient for u_t. This finding, of course, is in accordance with the result that (2) is indeed a cointegrating vector.

The results can be summarized as follows:

(1) The wage share formulation, i.e., a long-run relationship between the wage share and the unemployment rate (1) does not constitute a cointegrating vector, whereas the real product wage version (2) does. The coefficients in (3) and (4) are very similar. The rest of the comments below refer to the latter equation.

(2) The coefficients for changes in productivity and unemployment are significant and have the expected signs. The short-run elasticities with respect to changes in unemployment and productivity are -0.003 and 0.52, respectively.

(3) The results of various tests concerning the behavior of the residuals, parameter constancy, and forecasting performance are very satisfactory for the real product wage equation.

The Price Equation

For the price equation we tried different long-run or equilibrium relationships, e.g., relating the profit share to the degree of capacity utilization. As the error-correction terms turned out to be insignificant in the second stage of the estimation procedure, we do not present any results pertaining to these long-run equations. In our specification we relate changes in the value-added deflator to changes in unit labor costs, the difference between import prices and the value-added deflator and changes in the degree of capacity utilization. Our final version gives the following result:

$$\Delta \ln P_t = 0.03 + 0.22\Delta \ln ULC_t + 0.22\Delta \ln(PM/P)_{t-1}$$
$$\quad (6.28)\ (2.47) \qquad\qquad (2.27)$$

$$\quad + 0.23\Delta \ln(PM/P)_{t-2} + 0.42\Delta \ln CAP_{t-2} \tag{5}$$
$$\quad (2.57) \qquad\qquad (2.07)$$

$R^2 = 0.41 \qquad \sigma = 0.0178 \qquad DW = 0.904$

Sample period: 1973:1–1987:2.

The results for the price equation can be summarized as follows:

(1) The coefficients for changes in unit labor cost (ULC), the difference between import prices and the deflator of value added (PM/P), and changes in capacity (CAP) all have the expected signs and are significantly different from zero. The elasticity of price changes w.r.t. changes in capacity is equal to 0.42, whereas the corresponding elasticity w.r.t. unit cost is equal to 0.22. Thus, both cost and demand factors enter significantly in the determination of price changes. The elasticity of price changes w.r.t. the difference between import price and the deflator of value added is equal to 0.45.

(2) It has not been possible to include an error-correction term which has a significant influence. This should not be interpreted as a denial of the appropriateness of an error-correction specification, but rather suggests that we were not able to find a suitable equilibrium relationship with regard to prices.

(3) Using the same battery of tests as referred to above produced results that are not quite as good as those for the real wage equations.

Conclusions

If we compare our results for Sweden with the corresponding results from the European Unemployment Project, we find a few interesting differences. First, the measured impact effect of demand pressure on prices is considerable in comparison with the corresponding effect in the average country in the EUP. Unit labor cost and the "real" import price also have a nonnegligible short-run effect on the price level indicating that Sweden is a more open and more inflation-prone economy than the European average.

Second, real wages seem to incorporate measured productivity gains quickly, but to less an extent than the EUP countries. The long-run elasticity is less than one, and of about the same magnitude as the short-run elasticity.

Third, the level of unemployment enters the wage equation through error-correction terms relating the real product wage to the level of unemployment, labor productivity and the tax on labor. The estimated coefficient in the wage equation implies a reduction in the real product wage (wage share), per percentage point of unemployment, of 2.8 (6.0) per cent, which is higher than corresponding results in the EUP. The unemployment coefficient, however, is only significant in the less success-ful wage share equation. But why should real wages, productivity and unemployment have a common stochastic trend? One cautious interpreta-tion of our results in this respect, given the low short-run elasticity, is that unemployment in Sweden is subject to a fairly weak self-correcting mechanism.

Finally, the Swedish Beveridge curve has remained stable during the period 1963–88, revealing a better performance in this respect than both the U.S. labor market and the average European labor market. An ambitious labor market policy can, to some extent, explain this last finding, but hardly any of the other differences; see also Björklund 1989).

References

Björklund, A.: Why is Swedish unemployment so low? Paper presented at the IUI 50th Aniversary Symposium, Stockholm, Nov., 1989.

Dickey, D. A. & Fuller, W. A.: The likelihood ratio statistics for autoregressive time series with a unit root. *Econometrica 49*, 1057–72, 1981.

Engle, R. F. & Granger, C. W. J.: Co-integration and error correction: Representation, estimation and testing. *Econometrica 55*, 251–76, 1987.

Hall, S. G.: An application of the Granger & Engle two-step estimation procedure to United Kingdom Aggregate wage data. *Oxford Bulletin of Economics and Statistics 48*, 229–39, 1986.

Karlsson, T.: A macroeconomic disequilibrium model. An econometric study of the Swedish business sector 1970–84. *Lund Economic Studies No. 42*, Lund, 1988.

Stock, J. H.: Asymptotic properties of least squares estimators of cointegrating vectors. Manuscript, Harvard University, 1984.

Macroeconomic Strategies towards Internal and External Balance in the Nordic Countries

*Torben M. Andersen**

University of Aarhus, Denmark

Abstract

The aim of this paper is to clarify the policy strategies pursued in the Nordic countries in the 1970s and 1980s to attain internal and external balance. A distinction is made between (i) a bridging strategy, (ii) a sheltering or adaptive strategy, and (iii) a production strategy of export-led growth. These strategies are characterized and related to the experience of the Nordic countries.

I. Introduction

A primary concern for economic policy in small and open economies is how to strike an acceptable balance between internal (unemployment) and external (trade balance) objectives. The experiences of the Nordic countries (Denmark, Finland, Norway and Sweden)[1] exhibit striking differences in their performance with respect to these objectives; cf. Table 1.

During the period up until the first oil crisis, all of these countries fared reasonably well. Unemployment was low, as were current-account deficits, and there was an apparent tradeoff between low unemployment, high inflation and current-account problems or higher unemployment, moderate inflation and reduced current-account deficits. The oil-price crisis marked the beginning of a period of difficulties in reconciling internal balance with external balance, and a significant deterioration in the tradeoff between unemployment and the current account was experienced

---

*Comments by participants at the conference, the discussants Lars Calmfors and Peter Englund, an anonymous referee, Jan Rose Sørensen, Bo Sandemann Rasmussen and Nils Gottfries, are gratefully acknowledged. Tue Gørgens provided excellent research assistance.

[1] This paper is not an exhaustive discussion of the Nordic countries since it leaves out Iceland, the Faroe Islands and Greenland.

46   *T. M. Andersen*

in the mid-1970s. The four countries faced quite different problems, however. Denmark found itself in a situation with high unemployment and a persistent current-account problem, accentuated by the burden of debt servicing due to a continuous deficit. In the mid 1970s Finland swapped a huge current-account deficit for an increase in unemployment, and while the current-account deficit has been relatively moderate since then, it was difficult to return to previous levels of unemployment. The revenue from oil and gas extraction allowed Norway to maintain a low level of unemployment without much immediate concern for the current account, although the double balance problem has recently become more apparent. Sweden has been able to ensure a relatively low level of unemployment while avoiding substantial current-account problems, although external balance difficulties developed during the 1970s.

These different experiences are brought out clearly by the performance index in Table 2, defined simply as the sum of the unemployment rate and

Table 1. *Main economic indicators — Nordic countries*

	1963–67	1968–72	1973–77	1978–82	1983–87
Denmark					
Growth in GDP	4.1	4.1	2.0	1.3	2.7
Inflation	5.4	5.3	10.5	8.8	5.2
Unemployment	1.4	1.0	4.6	8.4	7.6
Current-account deficit in % of GDP	− 1.7	− 2.2	− 3.1	− 3.7	− 3.7
Finland					
Growth in GDP	3.7	5.8	2.3	4.0	3.2
Inflation	6.0	5.4	14.6	9.7	5.8
Unemployment	1.7	2.6	3.2	5.6	5.2
Current-account deficit in % of GDP	− 1.8	− 1.1	− 3.7	− 0.7	− 1.3
Norway					
Growth in DGP	4.8	3.7	4.8	3.0	4.2
Inflation	3.5	6.1	9.4	9.7	7.3
Unemployment	0.9	1.1	1.7	2.0	2.7
Current-account deficit in % of GDP	− 2.3	− 0.9	− 8.2	− 0.1	0.6[1]
Sweden					
Growth in GDP	4.3	3.7	1.8	1.6	2.4
Inflation	3.8	4.0	10.0	10.7	5.9
Unemployment	1.6	2.2	1.9	2.4	2.8
Current-account deficit in % of GDP	− 0.2	0.1	− 0.7	− 2.4	− 0.3

Definition and Sources: GDP: Gross domestic production in fixed prices (OECD, National Accounts); Inflation: Consumer price increases (OECD, Main Economic Indicators); Current account deficit (OECD, National Accounts); Unemployment rate: unemployed in percentage of labor force (OECD, Labor Force Statistics).

Table 2. *Performance index: Rate of unemployment plus current-account deficit in percent of GDP*

	I	II	III
	average: 1963–72	average: 1973–87	change: II–I
Denmark	3.2	10.6	7.4
Finland	3.6	6.5	2.9
Norway	2.6	5.6	3.0
Sweden	2.0	3.6	1.6

the current-account deficit in percentage of GDP. Despite these different records, it is nonetheless the general case that policies were designed with concern for both internal and external objectives. Hence, we are left with the puzzle of why the experience of these countries is so dissimilar.

Recently, efforts have been devoted to investigating whether different institutional settings can explain different economic performances; see Calmfors and Driffill (1988). Rankings of countries according to their degree of centralization usually assign the four Nordic countries to the group of highly centralized countries. Hence, the institutional hypothesis does not fully explain the different economic performance of the Nordic countries. On the other hand, similar institutions allow an "almost" controlled experiment on the importance of other factors which can explain different economic performance, i.e., different economic structures and policy strategies. The aim of this paper is to address these issues in a case study of macroeconomic strategies in the Nordic countries. The overall strategies pursued are described in Section II. Some theoretical aspects relating to these strategies are briefly reviewed in Section III, after which the details of the three main strategies are discussed in Sections IV–VI. Some lessons from the experiences of the Nordic countries are summarized in Section VII.

II. Policy Strategies in the Nordic Countries

The purpose of this study is to clarify the policy strategies pursued in the Nordic countries[2] in the 1970s and 1980s to attain internal and external balance. At the risk of oversimplification, it is possible to distinguish between (i) a bridging strategy, (ii) a sheltering or adaptive strategy and (iii) a production or aggressive strategy. By a bridging strategy is understood policies pursued in the mid-1970s to mitigate the effects of the international recession associated with the oil crisis, which was perceived as

---

[2] Comparative studies of the Nordic countries can also be found in Calmfors (1984) and Söderström (1985).

temporary. The sheltering or adaptive strategy was aimed at adjusting the domestic economy to the changed economic environment by making it less dependent on international economic developments. The intention was to expand domestic production to avoid current-account problems while maintaining employment. This was to be accomplished by a demand management policy that reduces private demand and expands public demand. This demand switch was intended to reduce excess demand for tradeables while expanding activities in the nontradeable sector such that the trade deficit would be transferred into more employment. The final strategy conceived that the double balance problem could be solved by expanding the private sector in general, and the tradeables sector in particular. Increased production of tradeables would create employment while at the same time reducing the trade deficit. It aimed at enhancing supply incentives in the tradeable sector, possibly in part by transferring supply capacity from the nontradeables sector. This adjustment process was assumed to be speeded up by a reduction in aggregate demand, especially for nontradeables. This aggressive strategy of export-led growth, denoted the production strategy, addressed the double balance problem directly.

All four countries pursued some form of bridging policy to moderate the effects of a perceived temporary international recession in the early 1970s. A sheltering strategy came to dominate economic policy from the late 1970s until the early 1980s, when it was replaced by the production strategy in Denmark and Sweden. Norway also followed a form of sheltering strategy with respect to nonresource sectors in the sense of maintaining a high level of activity financed by oil and gas revenues. However, this implied that the main concern for economic policy in the 1970s was the problem of internal balance. During the 1980s it became apparent that such a policy was not viable in the long run and a shift towards a production strategy was contemplated. Finland, on the other hand, placed more emphasis on a production strategy in the 1970s and early 1980s, but since then demand management policies have become consistent with the sheltering strategy. Finland has thus pursued the two strategies in reverse order to that of Denmark, Norway and Sweden. This, however, should be related to the late industrialization in Finland, and the implied delay in the expansion of service sectors including the public sector.

It is obviously an oversimplification to categorize the policies pursued in four different countries over two decades into a few broadly defined strategies. This is nonetheless taken to be useful in clarifying the policy views that underlie specific policy initiatives in the Nordic countries. Needless to say, specific policies pursued in a given country might contain aspects which concur with more than one strategy, but the classification pertains to the dominating strategy in a particular period.

Institutions and wage-formation processes in particular are not considered in great detail since this has recently been done elsewhere; see Calmfors (1990). Comparative studies usually point out the highly centralized wage-formation process in the Nordic countries, cf. Calmfors and Driffill (1988) and Jackman (1990), which at face value leaves little room for explaining different economic performances.

III. Theoretical Aspects

Next we review theories of stabilization policy towards internal and external balance[3] in a small and open economy with a fixed exchange rate and centralized wage setting. It is useful to consider the problem of internal and external balance by distinguishing between a tradeable and a nontradeable sector. The goods produced by the tradeable sector have perfect substitutes which are internationally produced, and prices are determined by world-market prices measured in domestic currency. There are no internationally produced goods which are perfect substitutes for nontradeables, and their price is determined by a market-clearing condition.

Let us begin in a situation with a fixed nominal wage. Figure 1 shows an economy with both internal and external balance problems. Given supply and demand for nontradeables, this market clears at a price p_N^* and a level of output y_N^*. At the given international price for tradeables $(\bar{p})$ measured in domestic currency $(p = \bar{p}E$ where E is the exchange rate,

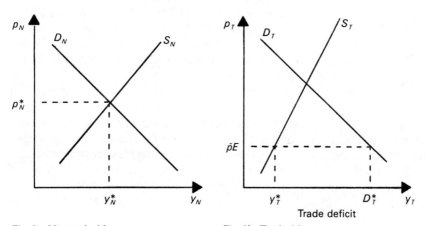

Fig. 1a. Nontradeables.　　　　　*Fig. 1b.* Tradeables.

---

[3] The aim of external balance is taken for granted, thereby ignoring the interesting question of whether this is a reasonable concern in open economies which are well integrated in international financial markets.

assumed fixed), there is excess demand for tradeables and thus a trade deficit. An internal balance problem exists if the level of activity in the two sectors (y_N^* and y_T^*) implies too low a level of employment.

Demand Management Policies[4]

The sheltering strategy hypothesizes that internal and external balance can be attained by a suitable fiscal policy that switches demand from the tradeable to the nontradeable sector. The argument goes roughly as follows: substitution of tradeables demand for nontradeables demand[5] will improve the trade balance and reduce unemployment since the reduction in tradeables demand has no consequences for employment, while the increased demand for nontradeables raises employment; cf. Figure 1.[6]

But it is an open question whether wages remain invariant to such a policy. Higher prices of nontradeables imply higher employment but lower purchasing power of wages. In the context of centralized wage bargaining which characterizes the Nordic countries, it is plausible to expect wages to increase, but by less than the rise in nontradeables prices such that the adjustment is split between higher employment and lower real-consumption wages.

Such a response of wages to output prices gives rise to an interesting sectoral interdependence since an increase in profitability in one sector, induced by higher output prices, spills over into the other sector in the form of higher wages, and thus reduced profitability. Higher prices of nontradeables increase the supply of nontradeables since wage increases do not eliminate the increase in profitability, whereas the supply of tradeables falls since wages rise at unchanged output prices. This supply response is illustrated in Figure 2, where the price of tradeables is not influenced by domestic economic conditions. The demand curves are similar to those in Figure 1.

Consider now the effects of an increase in government demand for nontradeables. The increased government demand for nontradeables does not produce a proportional rise in the level of activity in this sector since private demand is crowded out via price increases caused by rising wages, thereby inducing demanders to substitute nontradeables for tradeables.

There is, however, also an indirect crowding-out effect on the supply of tradeables arising from the wage increases induced by higher prices of nontradeables. Consequently, the level of activity in the tradeable sector

---

[4] This subsection is based on Andersen (1989) which also includes detailed references to the literature on stabilization policies in the presence of centralized wage bargaining.

[5] This is usually stated in terms of substitution from demand with a high marginal import content towards demand with a low marginal import content.

[6] See e.g. Söderström and Viotti (1979).

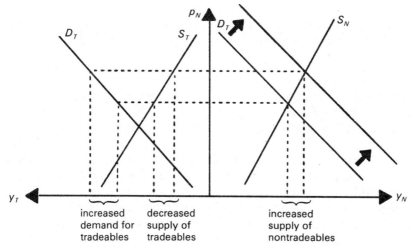

Fig. 2. Effects of increased government demand for nontradeables.

decreases; cf. Figure 2. The expansion of the nontradeables sector is achieved at the cost of a reduction in the tradeable sector! The negative effects of increased private demand for tradeables on the trade balance is thus reinforced by a fall in the supply of tradeables. This crowding-out effect is due to the wage-formation process and not the traditional crowding out induced by higher interest rates. Actually, this type of crowding out is ruled out in the present setting by the implied small open economy assumption with respect to financial markets. Hence, the analysis modifies the Mundell-Fleming result that fiscal policy is an effective means of affecting activity under a fixed exchange-rate system.

It is uncertain whether an expansion of government demand for nontradeables actually increases employment, since the increase in employment in the nontradeable sector is counteracted by a decrease in employment in the tradeable sector. The increased demand for nontradeables unambiguously raises the wage but has an ambiguous effect on employment. Obviously, the higher the share of employment in the tradeables sector, the more likely it is that increased demand for nontradeables lowers total employment and vice versa. These findings indicate that there is no well-defined tradeoff between either employment and wages or employment and trade deficits which can be exploited by demand-management policies and it is uncertain whether the sheltering strategy improves on the double balance problem.

If the government is perceived to follow a policy which counteracts any tendency for unemployment to rise by e.g. increased public employment, wage crowding out takes an even stronger form. Such a policy effectively reduces the perceived sensitivity of employment to wages, and wages are bound to increase. By the end of the day, such a policy may create wage increases without reducing unemployment; see Calmfors (1982).

Supply Policies

Policy initiatives may also be directed towards supply incentives more directly, and by means of a diagram such as Figure 2 it is easy to see that increased supply incentives in both sectors — created by, say, lower payroll taxes — have a great potential effect on both the internal and external balance. This tends to increase output and lower prices for nontradeables. In the tradeable sector activity is increased, demand is reduced and, consequently, the trade balance improves through three channels: (i) the effect of increased supply of tradeables at prevailing output prices, (ii) the increase in the supply of tradeables is reinforced by lower wages (crowding in!) as a result of the fall in prices of nontradeables and (iii) the shift in demand from tradeables to nontradeables due to falling prices of nontradeables.

A subsidy to capital is another supply-oriented policy option.[7] Such subsidies will also improve employment to the extent that labor and capital are cooperating factors of production, but this will in turn induce wage increases. Hence, even though such subsidies increase the use of both labor and capital, they tend to favor the latter as the capital-labor ratio increases. The net effect is an expansion of the supply capacity in the economy which favors capital relatively more than labor, but the policy may still improve upon the internal–external balance problem.

Sluggishness in the adjustment of capital stock is also critical for the effects of demand-management policies. After a prolonged recession, firms have adopted their capital stock to a low level of activity, and a sudden increase in demand is likely to make the available production capacity insufficient. Consequently, in the short run, activity is affected only moderately by an expansionary demand-management policy and the trade balance is likely to be the buffer.

Competitiveness

Any discussion of stabilization policies in open economies has to consider the effects of devaluation. Fiscal-policy changes affect relative prices between nontradeables and tradeables, and in this way influence the competitiveness or terms of trade like commercial policies with con-

---

[7] Such subsidies can be motivated by capital being employed inefficiently if firms perceive that wages depend positively on the capital stock; see e.g. Anderson and Devereux (1988).

sequences for the allocation of resources between sectors. This finding is important in regard to policies intended to change the real-exchange rate, e.g. a discrete devaluation in a managed exchange rate system.

A devaluation leaves all relative prices and hence quantities unchanged, while all domestic prices and wages adjust proportionally if all decisions depend only on relative prices, and wages and prices are fully flexible. In the short run,[8] however, there are good reasons why nominal wages and prices may not adjust proportionally to changes in the exchange rate. A reduction in the relative price of nontradeables to tradeables in order to improve upon internal–external balance problems may thus in the short run be accomplished by a devaluation. Left on its own, a devaluation does not contribute to a permanent change in relative prices since this requires some real changes. But exchange-rate changes are not useless if they are consistent with underlying real changes in the economy. Such consistency requires, for instance, a fiscal policy change to validate the change in relative prices induced by the exchange-rate change.

Why is a devaluation required when it is the fiscal policy change which eventually causes the desired change in relative prices? The answer depends on how the labor market works in the short run. If wages adjust sluggishly, there is a case for undertaking a devaluation along with a fiscal policy change since adjustment to the fiscal policy change takes time. A devaluation has the potential of changing relative prices in the short run and thus speeding up the changes which are needed given the fiscal policy changes. If the labor and product markets, on the other hand, adjust fairly quickly, there is no need to let a fiscal policy change be accompanied by a devaluation, since in this case it only fuels inflation. These considerations make it clear that the exchange-rate policy cannot be judged in isolation; it is part of a stabilization program. Whatever can be accomplished by exchange rate management depends on the entire stabilization program.

Devaluations without accompanying real changes may induce widespread devaluation expectations which in themselves contribute to a deterioration of internal–external balance problems; see Horn and Persson (1988) and Andersen and Risager (1988b). Against this background there are some gains to be reaped if a fixed exchange rate policy can be made credible. This would eliminate the devaluation premium from nominal wages and, moreover, possibly contribute to a reduction in real wages by reducing price risks; see Sørensen and Andersen (1988).

Incomes policies are often taken to be a necessary backup policy for a devaluation. Models of wage bargaining imply that incomes policies

---

[8] The effects of a reduction in real wealth and the induced wealth dynamics are disregarded here; for an analysis see e.g. Marston (1985). Likewise, we disregard contractionary supply effects induced by higher costs of imported raw materials and the like.

cannot have lasting effects if they are inconsistent with incentives in the labor market. Therefore, they do not provide sufficient backup, and real changes in the form of e.g. changes in fiscal policy are required. But incomes policies may serve a useful role in the short term by signalling that relative price changes are needed, although this is, obviously, effective only if it is consistent with underlying real changes in the economy.

Temporary shocks may have persistent effects in the presence of e.g. insider–outsider or hysteresis mechanisms; see Lindbeck and Snower (1989). To the extent that devaluation has short-term real effects, it might therefore have a permanent real effect by moving the economy from one equilibrium to another. Although such phenomena cannot be ruled out it is doubtful whether sufficient information is available for policymakers to exploit such mechanisms effectively.

To summarize, reliance on demand-management policies may make it difficult to reconcile internal and external objectives in the medium run, whereas supply-oriented policies have a greater potential, although they may affect external objectives more than internal objectives if too much capital-labor substitution is induced. It has been argued that devaluations are most effective if adjustment mechanisms are sluggish and provided that they are consistent with real changes induced by policy or shocks. These conclusions turn out to be important when interpretating the policy experience of the Nordic countries.

IV. Bridging Strategies

Bridging strategies relate to a specific problem and period in time, and they provide information needed to understand subsequent problems for economic policy. As revealed by Table 3, there are important differences in the background against which these policies were pursued as well as in the use of instruments.

All of the countries except Denmark had an expansionary policy stance when the international recession set in. Consequently, bridging policies were not contemplated in Denmark until a substantial increase in unemployment was experienced, whereas such policies were a continuation of policy initiatives already taken in the other countries. As a result, only Denmark experienced a substantial rise in unemployment; Norway and Sweden managed to avoid it altogether, whereas unemployment did not rise in Finland until the late 1970s as a result of restrictive policies intended to eliminate the record current-account deficit in 1975. Likewise, a record current-account deficit in 1976 put an end to the bridging strategy in Denmark. It is noteworthy that, in contrast to most other countries, the Nordic countries — except Denmark — experienced growth in 1974–75.

Table 3. *Bridging policies and their background*

	Policy stance prior to oil crisis	Bridging policies
Denmark	Tight demand management policy following the boom period 1971–73	Expansionary demand management policy to boost domestic demand in late 1975
Finland	Recession in the early 1970s induced an expansionary demand management policy	Expansionary demand management policy in 1974
Norway	Expansionary demand management and a boom period	Expansionary demand management policy and selective policies
Sweden	Selective policies to increase employment as a response to the recession 1971–72	Selective policies supplemented by tax cuts in 1974

The varying importance of the oil crisis for the four countries should also be pointed out. Among them, Denmark was most heavily dependent on energy imports as it had no domestic supply at that time. Finland was less severely affected due to the dominance of raw materials in its exports and the fact that the substantial amount of energy imports originating from the Soviet Union was matched by increases in exports as a result of bilateral trade agreements. Reliance on oil as a source of energy was relatively small in Norway and, more importantly, expected revenue from oil and gas provided a basis for optimistic prospects for future economic growth. Essentially this implied that policies were planned without much concern for their effects on the public debt and the current account. Hence, the bridging policy in Norway was dependent on expected revenue from oil and gas rather than a possible international upswing. With some domestic production of energy and substantial exports of raw materials, Sweden was affected only moderately by the oil crisis.

It is worth noting that unemployment figures might give a misleading impression of the problems in ensuring internal balance if the growth rates of labor supply differ significantly among the four countries. Of course, growth of labor supply depends on a number of economic variables including unemployment, unemployment insurance, tax treatment of spouses, etc. Nonetheless, Table 4 reveals that the Nordic economies have faced rather different development in the need for jobs. These differences should be kept in mind when evaluating the relative success of these countries in reconciling internal and external objectives. This must be the case, regardless of how the evolution of labor supply is interpreted. If the differences are due to exogenous reasons, they show that the four countries have fundamentally different employment problems, whereas if the differences are attributed to endogenous causes, it would be tempting

Table 4. *Growth in labor supply and employment* (number of persons) *from 1960 to 1986*

	Labor supply	Employment
Denmark	34.5%	29.6%
Finland	20.6%	15.9%
Norway	46.1%	44.9%
Sweden	19.8%	18.6%

Source: OECD, Labor Force Statistics.

to conclude that unemployment figures give a distorted impression of the slack in the labor market.

V. Sheltering Strategies

Sheltering strategies aim at adapting the economy to a changed economic situation. In relation to the current-account problem, this essentially means (i) switching demand from tradeables to nontradeables which, in turn, should also improve employment, and (ii) selective subsidies to maintain activity in industries which face difficulties, combined with employment programs to preserve the working capabilities of the workforce.

Demand Policies

In one way or another all four countries attempted to shift demand from tradeables to nontradeables by means of both fiscal and monetary policy instruments.

Fiscal policy initiatives directed towards the double balance problem implied increases in public consumption and employment, whereas private demand was curtailed by tax increases. These policy initiatives were not necessarily effected simultaneously, as policy changes often had a stop-go character. In periods where unemployment was a chief concern, public consumption and employment were increased, the induced expansion tended to worsen the current account and authorities eventually resorted to tax increases to reduce private demand. Such increases were believed to help control the current account without jeopardizing the employment gain following from the initial fiscal expansion. The asymmetric use of instruments for expansion and contraction reflects the objectives of a selective demand-management policy. The need to balance the public budget was given less consideration in the short run.

Some signs of a fiscal cycle became visible in the sense that the public sector grew without significant improvement in the double balance problem. The reason might be that fiscal expansion in the medium run crowds out private activity, as argued in Section III. With little effect on employment in the medium term and a deterioration of the external balance, tax increases were implemented. By reducing demand, these increases also released a contractionary effect, thus giving rise to the need for another fiscal expansion. The end result was a deterioration of the current account without much effect on the unemployment problem. Denmark is a good example of fiscal policy attempts to switch demand between the tradeable and the nontradeable sector (see Figures 3 and 4),

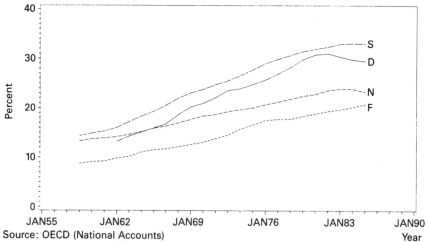

Source: OECD (National Accounts)

Fig. 3. Share of public employment in total employment.

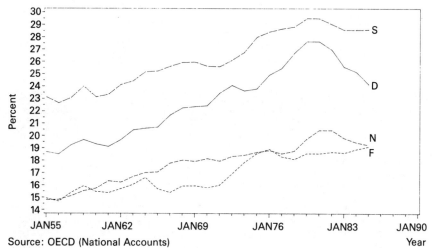

Source: OECD (National Accounts)

Fig. 4. Public consumption share in GDP.

58   T. M. Andersen

which in turn implied an increase in public consumption and taxes. The implications of an expansionary demand-management policy are also seen clearly in the case of Norway where the situation comes close to a controlled experiment of the effects of a demand-management policy which does not take the external constraint into account. The Norwegian experience points to the crowding out of private activity, as indicated by the evolution of competitiveness (Figures 5 and 6) as well as the pressure

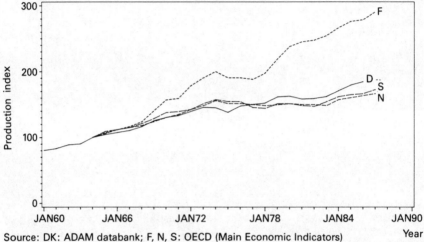

Source: DK: ADAM databank; F, N, S: OECD (Main Economic Indicators)

Fig. 5. Manufacturing production (index 1964 = 100).

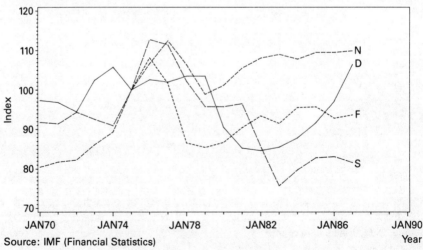

Source: IMF (Financial Statistics)

Fig. 6. Relative labor unit costs (1975 = 100).

for selective industrial support (see below). It also motivated a reorientation of economic policy in the early 1980s. Something similar occurred in
Sweden.

Monetary policy has also been designed to achieve selective objectives.
It has therefore been under pressure in the sense that it was supposed to
fulfill quite a number of objectives: (i) finance current-account deficits, (ii)
reduce consumption and imports, (iii) promote investments and (iv)
eventually facilitate and cheapen the financing of public deficits. Obviously, it was impossible to achieve all these goals by a market conform
monetary policy, and selective instruments have been widely used. The list
includes restrictions on borrowing for private consumption, favorable
terms for loans to firms and attempts to twist the term structure of interest
rates. The latter was intended — if possible — to maintain reserves by a
high short-term interest rate while keeping down long-term interest rates
relevant for investments and public borrowing. It should also be noted that
restrictions on international capital movements implied low substitutability between domestic and foreign securities.

As a consequence, the policy mix has usually been such that fiscal policy
was more expansionary than monetary policy. This implies a different
channel through which financial crowding out develops in small and open
economies as compared to a closed economy. In the latter, expansion of
domestic demand pushes up prices so that the supply of real balances
declines and interest rates increase, thereby reducing demand sensitive to
the interest rate. In an open economy, this process works in the way that
fiscal expansion tends to worsen the current account, and monetary policy
is tightened to maintain a fixed exchange rate (see also below).

Exchange Rate Policy

In the 1970s all four countries followed a fixed exchange-rate policy by
participating in a formal exchange-rate cooperation or by fixing the
exchange rate relative to some kind of trade weighted basket of currencies.
Finland has pursued the latter policy since 1973, while the other three
countries initially joined the exchange rate cooperation, known as the
"snake", set up between a number of European countries in 1972. Sweden
left this arrangement in 1977 and Norway in 1978, whereas Denmark
remained a member and later joined the EMS. A number of discrete
devaluations have taken place in all four countries throughout this period
to reverse the tendency for competitiveness to deteriorate. To the extent
that this was caused by the expansion of demand for nontradeables
according to the sheltering strategy (cf. Section II), the devaluations should
not be expected to have any long-term real effects since they were inconsistent with the overall policy stance. Accompanying policies often
involved price controls so that temporary effects were usually attained, but

policy initiatives were seldom taken to make it likely that devaluation would signal permanent real changes.

Supply Policies

Supply policies in a sheltering strategy usually consist of selective industrial policies and employment programs.

Selective industrial policies focused on industries which faced difficulties and usually took the form of subsidies to particular activities such as construction and shipyards, regional subsidies and stock building. An important reason for pursuing such policies was to avoid too much dispersion in the geographical distribution of unemployment. This was particularly relevant in Finland, Norway and Sweden which have low population density. All four countries also pursued investment-promoting policies in regard to the selective objectives which underlie the sheltering strategy. The key instruments were so-called firm-specific investment funds that allow firms to reduce their tax bill by reserving a certain fraction of current surplus for future investments and generous tax depreciation rules.

Employment programs were aimed at either preserving or creating jobs. The former objective was, of course, partially fulfilled by selective industrial policies, but also by employment subsidies. Employment programs were usually dominated by public initiatives, e.g. relief and environmental work as well as increased activities in the public sector. In Sweden, such programs were rather elaborate, amounting to some 3–4 per cent of the labor force. In terms of present-day terminology, job-preserving policies avoid an increase in outsiders, with the implied possibility of persistence, while keeping intact the human capital of employees, whereas initiatives to create new jobs primarily affect the human capital dimension. These active labor-market policies must be related to more passive policies such as unemployment insurance systems. Denmark, Finland and Sweden offered a high replacement ratio. The entitlement period was fairly long in Denmark, but very short in Sweden. Benefits in Finland were duration dependent. Norway provided a somewhat lower replacement ratio. Combined with the relative importance of employment programs, we thus find that unemployment policies vary between a very generous passive policy in Denmark to an active policy in Sweden. A comparison of these two countries suggests that the entitlement period is more crucial than the replacement ratio.

Selective supply policies predominated in Norway and Sweden during the 1970s. They were less important in Denmark, although they were included in the policy of the late 1970s. Finland refrained the most from embarking on selective supply policies, relying instead on market adjustment. Interestingly, this ranking of the importance of selective policies is reflected rather clearly in the development of manufacturing production in the four countries; cf. Figure 5. Note that Finland pursued a production strategy rather than a sheltering strategy in the late 1970s; cf. above and Section VI.

Empirical Evaluation

A crucial determinant of the success of the demand management policies implied by the sheltering strategy is the extent to which private activities are crowded out. Crowding out via the labor market may work through either the terms-of-trade effect or an accommodative employment policy, as outlined in Section III. The latter hypothesis is difficult to test for a number of reasons, and it should also be noted that signals of employment guarantees are usually made in relation to cooperative settlements between labor market organizations and the government. Some evidence regarding the importance of the terms-of-trade hypothesis can be gained from studies of wage formation in the Nordic countries. Table 5 reports the effects on the product real wage due to changes in producer prices relative to consumer prices according to a number of country-specific and international studies of wage formation in the Nordic countries.

The impact effect of increased demand for domestically produced goods is higher prices of such goods, and since consumers also purchase

Table 5. *Elasticities of product real wages with respect to producer prices relative to consumer prices*

	Short run	Long run
Denmark		
Andersen and Risager (1989)	−0.23	+0.51
Bean et al. (1986)	+0.22	+0.27
Finland		
Eriksson, Suvanto and Vartia (1989)	−0.10	−0.10
Bean et al. (1986)	−0.17	−0.57
Norway		
Holden and Rødseth (1989)[1]	−0.58	**
Hoel and Nymoen (1987)[1]	**	−0.30
Bean et al. (1986)	+0.13	+0.28
Sweden		
Calmfors and Forslund (1989)	−0.30	−0.51
Holmlund and Pencavel (1988)[2]	−0.67	−0.22
Bean et al. (1986)	−0.48	**

**Not available.
[1] Elasticity of product wages in tradeables w.r.t. tradeables prices relative to consumer prices.
[2] Elasticity of product real wages w.r.t. producer prices.

foreign goods, it follows that producer prices increase relative to consumer prices.[9] Wages respond to these price changes; the question is by how much, and thus whether the product real wage is reduced and profitability enhanced as a consequence of higher output prices. If wages increase by less than prices of domestically produced goods, the product real wage declines and incentives for firms to produce increase. In this case, greater demand for domestically produced goods translates into more domestic supply, i.e., the aggregate supply curve has a positive slope (cf. Section III). The elasticity of the product real wage with respect to the relation between producer and consumer prices is thus crucial to the slope of the aggregate supply curve and to the question of whether increased demand for domestically produced goods implies a higher level of domestic activity. The higher the elasticity, the higher wage responsiveness and wage crowding out. The critical value is zero; if the elasticity is negative, some gains in profitability accrues, whereas if it is positive, supply incentives are reduced.

Table 5 shows that wage crowding out is potentially important in all four countries. It has been relatively moderate in Sweden, but more important in Finland. Substantial wage crowding out is found in the cases of Denmark and Norway, which both exhibit more crowding out in the long run than in the short run. Some of the findings indicate that in the short run there might even be more than 100 per cent crowding out. Although this cannot be ruled out on theoretical grounds, it is probably an overstatement.[10] However, all the results reported above suggest that wage crowding out is important. This is also reflected in the evolution of industrial production in Denmark, Norway and Sweden; cf. Figure 5. Casual empirical evidence also reveals that inflationary impulses originated in nontradeable sectors rather than tradeable sectors in periods where the focus was on aggregate demand management. Wage increases have thus exceeded those predicted by the Scandinavian model of inflation, as should be expected given the domestic origin of the demand pressure; cf. Section III.

VI. Production Strategy

During the 1970s the nontradeable sectors in Denmark, Norway and Sweden grew stronger relative to the tradeable sectors, which — as

---

[9] Since the empirical studies do not explicitly distinguish between tradeables and nontradeables, we speak loosely about the demand for domestically produced goods without specifically relating it to a particular sector.

[10] It is not possible in any single case to reject that the long-run elasticity is zero, implying 100 per cent crowding out in the long run and thus a vertical aggregate supply curve.

predicted by theory — made it difficult to achieve internal and external balance in the medium to long run. As a consequence, attempts were made to reorient policies towards ensuring expansion through the private sector in general and the tradeables sector in particular. Efforts were also made to signal a nonaccommodative policy strategy so as to discipline labor-market organizations. The policy shift in Denmark was signalled by a policy program introduced by the minority coalition government which took over in late 1982. In Norway the change in policy priorities was announced by the minority government which came to power in 1986. The stabilization program (the "third way") accompanying a large discrete devaluation in October 1982 reflected a similar policy shift in Sweden. By focusing to a much greater extent on the need for expansion of the private sector in the past, Finland did not undergo such a policy shift, although demand management policies were reoriented from external to internal objectives.

Demand Policies

The few degrees of freedom left in the use of fiscal instruments made a policy shift almost compulsory in the Nordic countries. Public-sector deficits continued to rise, the overall tax burden was about 50 per cent in all of the countries except Finland, and the public sector had grown to a substantial size. Interestingly, policy reorientation in Denmark, Norway and Sweden succeeded in reversing the increasing trend in the share of public consumption in gross domestic product; cf. Figures 3 and 4. Attempts to implement restrictive fiscal policies revealed a coordination problem between state and local authorities, since targets for the overall development of government expenditures were often violated by excessive local expenditures. This was due to the discretionary power granted to local fiscal authorities combined with potential conflicts of interest which may have been reinforced wherever local authorities had a different political majority than parliament.

The production strategy was also supplemented by a savings strategy intended to increase the overall savings ratio and, in particular, the private savings ratio, since the current-account deficit was viewed as a savings deficit and caused by a low savings ratio. A reduction in demand was also contemplated to speed up the adjustment process by moving resources from nontradeables' to tradeables' sectors and giving firms in the trade-ables' sector an incentive to become more aggressive in export markets. Such policies took the form of subsidies to savings for particular purposes such as pensions and education or reduced tax subsidies to borrowing. Savings policies were also pursued to smoothen aggregate demand through e.g. countercyclical depository schemes for firms (e.g. in Finland).

Supply Policies

Common to all four countries was an effort to increase the supply responsiveness of the economy — a term which has developed into a political phrase to signal a break with previous policy views. In practice, it has mostly come to mean deregulation of both industrial policies and financial markets as well as less emphasis on employment programs. More recently, substantial changes in taxation of incomes have also been envisaged. Reorientation of industrial policies in Norway and Sweden occurred against a background of elaborate systems of selective policies. Priority was given instead to general measures which provided a favorable industrial climate, including tax incentives for investments. Financial deregulation meant not only that quantity restrictions and selective interest rate policies were abandoned, but also that restrictions on transactions between foreign and domestic financial markets were reduced. This reorientation reflected the fact that constraints in financial markets tended to be circumvented by market forces (grey markets). Financial deregulation has triggered an increase in debt-financed private consumption in all four countries. This is in accordance with intertemporal theories of consumption which predict that restrictions on borrowing reduce possibilities of moving consumption forward in time.

Owing to international integration of capital markets, monetary policy has begun to focus more on external objectives. This works through the impact of exchange-rate expectations on interest-rate determination and the need to stabilize financial flows so as to maintain a fixed exchange rate. These influences are perhaps especially apparent in Denmark and Finland where hard-currency options have been taken and capital flows have been liberalized the most.

Stabilization Programs

Although the objectives were fairly identical, quite different policy instruments were used in each of the Nordic countries. The differences are brought out very clearly by comparing the policies pursued in Denmark and Sweden.

Denmark and Sweden: Exchange-rate policies constitute an important difference between the stabilization program proposed in Denmark and Sweden in 1982. Sweden undertook a large discrete devaluation (16 per cent, following a 10 per cent devaluation in 1981), whereas Denmark pursued a fixed exchange-rate policy. In both cases the aim was to improve competitiveness and ensure expansion of the private sector. Underlying the Swedish policy was a "once-and-for-all" strategy which signalled that the devaluation was undertaken to restore competitiveness and exchange-rate changes would not be used to this end in the future. The Danish exchange-rate policy was guided by a "no more" philosophy according to which any discrete devaluation would signal a willingness to accommodate wage increases. In order to avoid this and ensure that labor-market organizations perceived a responsibility for employment and competitiveness, the fixed exchange-rate policy had to be made credible; cf. Section III. The pros and cons of the two strategies can be summarized as follows. The "once-and-for-all" policy ensures an immediate change in the right direction but encounters credibility problems in the medium term because it fuels inflation, implying that policymakers might be forced to devalue again. The "no more" policy causes heavy strain in the short term when the credibility of the low inflation policy is established, implying output losses and the like, but eventually it is very effective in curbing inflationary expectations.

The credibility of a given exchange-rate policy depends critically on the overall stabilization program. The change in relative prices induced by a devaluation will not materialize in the medium term unless they are supported by real changes. Hence, the credibility of both the "once-and-for-all" and the "no more" exchange-rate policies depends not only on the announced objectives but also on the overall stabilization program. Both Denmark and Sweden undertook a restrictive fiscal policy, but monetary policy was probably more expansionary in Denmark than in Sweden. Moreover, incomes policies were part of the Danish policy in the form of guidelines for wage increases and removal of indexing clauses. The latter was important in eliminating the hangover from the previous high inflation period; on the other hand, it increased the short-run gain from a surprise devaluation; see Andersen and Risager (1988b).

Both policies were highly successful in the very short run. Credibility was established fairly quickly in the Danish case, which is evident from the remarkable reduction in nominal interest rates within a very short period of time; cf. Andersen and Risager (1988b). The private sector expanded, unemployment declined and the balance of payments improved in 1983.[11] The Swedish economy experienced an improvement in the double balance problem induced by expansion of the private sector. In a medium-term perspective the Swedish policy experiment seems to have worked better than the Danish. Although Denmark had a falling unemployment rate, the balance of payments deficit soon went out of control. Success in bringing down inflation and balancing the public budget should be noted, however. Development of the current account was crucial in the sense that elimina-

---

[11] Although in part due to reasons unrelated to the stabilization program, it did contribute to the establishment of credibility, however.

tion of the deficit was the primary objective of the stabilization program. Hence, the credibility of the exchange-rate policy declined and problems in keeping wage increases under control were intensified.

What accounts for the difference? It is tempting to point to the obvious difference in exchange-rate policies. This might be part of the explanation, but it is not obvious that Denmark would have replicated the results of Sweden if a large discrete devaluation had been undertaken in late 1982. First, empirical evidence suggests that wage formation in Sweden may be characterized by some nominal rigidities, indicating that a devaluation would succeed in bringing down product wages, see Calmfors and Forslund (1990), whereas no such effect can be found in the Danish case; see Andersen and Risager (1990). Alternatively, there may have been a general understanding in the Swedish labor market that the step was necessary to maintain jobs in the medium run. Second, the Danish fixed exchange-rate policy did gain credibility, and the implied noninflationary policy resulted in a substantial reduction in nominal wage increases, from about 10 per cent to 5 per cent. The incomes policy may thus have served the signalling role which could otherwise have been accomplished by a devaluation. Furthermore, the overall shift to a nonaccommodative policy seems to have had a significant effect on wages; see Andersen and Risager (1990).

Hence, the explanation is likely to be found elsewhere. In light of the theoretical considerations in Section III, it seems that the success and adequacy of the accompanying policies are crucial in validating the desired relative-price changes through aggregate demand-management as well as the supply potential of the two countries. The growth rates of domestic demand in the Nordic countries from 1981 to 1987 are given in Table 6. Domestic demand increased more in Denmark than in Sweden over this period. The evolution in Sweden immediately after the policy change thus seems broadly consistent with the changes signalled by the devaluation, i.e., relative price changes were vindicated by the tight evolution of domestic demand; cf. Section III.

Although the importance of public consumption was reduced in Denmark, aggregate demand did not decline so as to make room for

Table 6. *Growth of domestic demand in the Nordic countries, 1981–86*

	1981	1982	1983	1984	1985	1986	1987
Denmark	−4.1	3.5	1.4	5.1	5.7	5.4	−3.2
Finland	−0.6	4.4	2.3	2.0	2.8	2.4	5.5
Norway	0.9	2.0	1.1	6.1	1.6	9.9	−1.1
Sweden	−2.8	0.8	−0.8	3.2	4.0	1.8	3.7

Source: OECD, National Accounts.

expansion of the tradeables sector and hence improvement in the trade balance. First, monetary policy was much more expansionary than anticipated due to the effects of deregulation and the credibility of the exchange-rate policy. Private consumption rose due to both the effects of increased wealth brought about by the sharp reduction in interest rates and the removal of liquidity constraints. Second, the supply capacity of the private sector was eroded after a period of very low investment, cf. Andersen and Overgaard (1989), and expansion of the private sector had to be accompanied by increased investments (1984: 12.5 per cent and 1985: 14.1 per cent); see Figure 7. It also turned out that expansion soon induced a shortage of specific types of labor despite double-digit official unemployment figures. This may reflect the fact that these figures are poor indicators of labor-market slack, perhaps due to hysteresis effects, and that there is substantial dispersion in unemployment among different trade groups. Boosting demand, combined with the need to restore relative wages between public and private employees and an upcoming election help explain the high wage increases resulting from the 1987 settlement, which can be said to mark the end of the 1982 experiment. Perhaps the policy experiment was destroyed by its own success in the sense that the establishment of credibility created a boom which eventually produced a very substantial current-account deficit which, in turn, eroded the credibility closely linked to the current account. This implies, of course, that the use of instruments and the announcement of policy goals were not internally consistent.

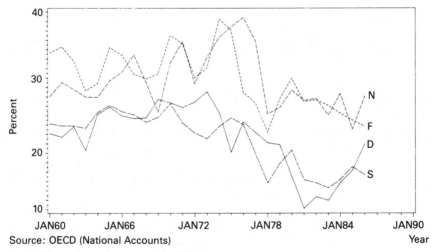

Source: OECD (National Accounts)

Fig. 7. Share of gross investments in GDP.

As a result of reasonably high capital accumulation in preceeding years and a more active labor-market policy, Sweden did not suffer to the same extent from supply-side problems. It cannot be ruled out that the selective industrial policy and active labor-market policy pursued in the 1970s, despite the implied inefficiencies, were important in keeping the supply capacity intact and therefore provide the basis for a successful devaluation. With the benefit of hindsight it may thus be concluded that the devaluation was well timed. Subsequent developments illustrate the difficulties in keeping wage growth under control and thus maintaining internal and external balance in a situation characterized by strong growth in domestic demand (as also implied by the empirical results reported in Table 5). Demand management policies have therefore not been consistent with the "once-and-for-all" philosophy in the most recent years.

Norway: The shift towards a production strategy is less clear cut in Norway. Oil and gas revenues (in some periods about 20 per cent of GDP) permitted the government to pursue an ambitious employment policy without incurring severe current-account deficits. This was reflected by booming domestic demand in the mid-1980s along with low unemployment and a current-account surplus (NOK 27 billion in 1985). With exports of oil and gas yielding revenue of around NOK 85 billion in 1985, it was apparent that the underlying situation was worse than indicated by the gross figures. It has thus been questioned whether it was wise to reap all the benefits from exploitation of natural resources in the very short term and whether the consequent squeeze on the traditional tradeables sectors impaired fulfillment of the employment goal in the medium run. The collapse of oil prices in 1985/86 made it imperative to come to grips with this issue, and the minority labor government that took over in early 1986 announced a policy strategy with many similarities to those pursued in Denmark and Sweden. The main ingredients were a tight fiscal and monetary policy, a 10 per cent devaluation and incomes policies. Use of the devaluation instrument may suggest a similarity between Norway and Sweden, but two differences should be noted. First, the Norwegian devaluation was a defensive reaction to the oil-price increase, whereas the Swedish devaluation was of a more aggressive nature in line with the production strategy. Second, the once-and-for-all aspect was not stressed in Norway, although more recent policy statements may be regarded as an attempt to make the fixed exchange-rate policy credible. The Norwegian strategy was thus more defensive; it removed the effects of the boom and brought the economy back to trend. In contrast, demand began to grow in Denmark and Sweden as a result of increased activity in the private sector. Hence, significant movement of resources from nontradeable sectors to nonoil tradeable sectors is still expected.

Finland: A production strategy was emphasized in Finland in the late 1970s. The overall aim was to ensure a recovery based on the private sector while restraining the growth of the public sector. A few discrete devaluations and, in particular, substantial tax reductions to firms were intended to improve profitability. These measures help account for the high investments in Finland (see Figure 7) and the large increases in labor productivity. Since increases in public sector employment were explicitly avoided as a means of reducing unemployment, the nonaccommodative policy stance was signalled, which probably facilitated the necessary adjustments. This is reflected in the remarkable increase in manufacturing production (see Figure 5), the constant share of public employment in total employment (see Figure 3) and the fall in the share of public consumption in gross domestic product (see Figure 4). However, as revealed by Table 6, domestic demand (particularly private and public consumption) played an important role in the 1980s. The policy experience of Finland in the 1970s indicates that the production strategy did succeed in making the tradeable sector the growth center of the economy.

VII. Concluding Remarks

Although stabilization policies in the Nordic countries have a great deal in common, there are also substantial variations which reflect the different problems faced by these countries and different approaches to solving problems of internal and external balance. This helps account for the differences in economic performance of the four Nordic countries considered in this study despite roughly similar institutions, at least when measured in terms of the degree of centralization; see Calmfors and Driffill (1988).

The problem of combatting unemployment has led a number of authors to advocate expansion of aggregate demand; see e.g. McCallum (1986) and Alogoskoufis and Manning (1988). The experience of the Nordic countries shows that this certainly works — at least in the short run — but it also explains why policymakers are reluctant to pursue such policies. The primary reasons are negative effects on the external balance and crowding out of the tradeables sector which diminishes the possibilities of attaining internal and external balance in the medium run.

References

Alogoskoufis, G. S. & Manning, A.: Unemployment persistence. *Economic Policy 6,* 427–69, 1988.
Andersen, T. M.: Demand management towards internal and external balance in open economies with centralized wage setting. Memo, Institute of Economics, University of Aarhus, 1989.

Andersen, T. M. & Overgaard, P. B.: Demand and capacity constraints on Danish employment, 1989. In C. Bean et al. (eds.), Europe's Unemployment Problem, MIT Press,
forthcoming.
Andersen, T. M. & Risager, O.: The role of credibility for the effects of a change in exchange
rate policy. Seminar paper 373, IIES, University of Stockholm, 1988a.
Andersen, T. M. & Risager, O.: Stabilization policies, credibility and interest rate determina-
tion in a small open economy. European Economic Review 32, 669–79, 1988b.
Andersen, T. M. & Risager, O.: Wage formation in Denmark, In Calmfors (1990).
Anderson, S. & Devereux, M.: Trade unions and the choice of capital stock. Scandinavian
Journal of Economics 90, 27–44, 1988.
Bean, C., Layard, R. & Nickell, S.: The rise in unemployment: A multicountry study.
Economica (supplement) 53, 1–22, 1986.
Calmfors, L.: Employment policies, wage formation and trade union behaviour in a small
open economy. Scandinavian Journal of Economics 84, 345–73, 1982.
Calmfors, L.: Stabilization policies and wage formation in economies with strong trade
uninos. In M. Emerson (ed.), Europe's Stagflation, Oxford University Press, 1984.
Calmfors, L. (ed.): Wage Formation and Macroeconomic Policy in the Nordic Countries. SNS
and Basil Blackwell, 1990.
Calmfors, L. & Driffill, J.: Bargaining structure, corporatism and macroeconomic perform-
ance. Economic Policy 6, 14–61, 1988.
Calmfors, L. & Forslund, A.: Wage setting in Sweden. In Calmfors (1990).
Calmfors, L. & Horn, H.: Accommodation policies and the adjustment of real wages.
Scandinavian Journal of Economics 87, 234–61, 1985.
Eriksson, T., Suvanto, A. & Vartia, P.: Wage formation in Finland. In Calmfors (1990).
Hersoug, T.: Union wage responses to tax changes. Oxford Economic Papers 36, 37–51,
1984.
Hoel, M. & Nymoen, R.: Wage formation in Norwegian manufacturing. An empirical
application of a theoretical bargaining model. European Economic Review 32, 977–98,
1987.
Holden, S. & Rødseth, A.: Wage setting in Norway. In Calmfors (1990).
Holmlund, B. & Pencavel, J.: The determination of wages, employment and work hours in
an economy with centralized wage setting: Sweden 1950–83. Economic Journal, 1988.
Horn, H. & Persson, T.: Exchange rate policy, wage formation, and credibility. European
Economic Review 32, 1621–36, 1988.
Jackman, R.: Wage formation in the Nordic countries viewed from an international
perspective. In Calmfors (1990).
Lindbeck, A. & Snower, D. J.: The Insider–Outsider Theory of Employment and Unemploy-
ment. MIT Press, 1989.
Marston, R. C.: Stabilization policies in open economies. In R. W. Jones & P. B. Kenen (eds.),
Handbook of International Economics, Vol. II, North-Holland, 1985.
McCallum, J.: Unemployment in the OECD countries in the 1980s. Economic Journal 96,
942–60, 1986.
OECD: Economic Surveys, Denmark, Finland, Norway and Sweden, various issues.
Söderström, H. T.: Exchange rate strategies and real adjustment after 1970 — The
experience of the smaller European economies. In T. Peeters, P. Praet & P. Reding (eds.),
International Trade and Exchange Rates in the Late Eighties, North-Holland, 1985.
Söderström, H. T. & Viotti, S.: Money wage disturbances and the endogeneity of the public
sector in an open economy. In A. Lindbeck (ed.), Inflation and Employment in Open
Economics, North-Holland, 1979.
Sørensen, J. R. & Andersen, T. M.: Exchange rate variability and wage formation in open
economies. Economics Letters 28, 263–8, 1988.

Comment on T. M. Andersen, "Macroeconomic Strategies towards Internal and External Balance in the Nordic Countries"

Lars Calmfors

Institute for International Economic Studies, Stockholm, Sweden

Main Contents of the Paper

The purpose of the paper is to discuss and evaluate the different macro-economic policy strategies for combining high employment and external balance in the main Nordic countries. In view of the great similarities in institutional structures and policy priorities, this is a worthwhile exercise: comparing the policy strategies of the Nordic countries is probably as close to a controlled experiment as one can come in this area.

The main contribution of the paper is an insightful account of the various policies followed. I find the distinction between "bridging", "sheltering" and "production strategies" very illuminating. I also agree with Andersen's classifications of policies in the various countries. Policies in all four countries were designed to "bridge" what was believed to be a temporary recession in the mid-1970s. In Denmark, Norway and Sweden, the late 1970s were characterized by defensive attempts to maintain employment through targeted policies (public-sector expansion, employment programs, or selective subsidies) that would minimize the demand spillovers to imports. In the 1980s, policies in these countries have instead focused on achieving "export-led" growth via improvement in the relative cost position *vis-à-vis* foreign competitors. In Finland, these policies were followed in reverse order; the supply-side policies of the 1970s have given way to more Keynesian demand policies in the 1980s.

The main analytical preoccupation of the paper concerns the possibilities of affecting employment via aggregate demand policies and the tradeoff between employment and external balance. The aim is to combine the traditional open-economy analysis of the 1970s with more recent models of wage setting and equilibrium unemployment. This is a worthwhile undertaking since the latter models have usually been developed in a closed-economy framework and open-economy aspects are often added in

72   L. Calmfors

a rather unsatisfactory way; Alogoskoufis (1989) is a nice exception, however.

I will attempt to systematize Andersen's discussion with the help of a simple diagram. In Figure 1, the upward-sloping curve is a *wage-setting schedule* relating the consumption wage (the after-tax real wage in terms of the consumer price index) to employment. A standard outcome of union and bargaining models is that the higher the employment, the higher the consumption wage. The downward-sloping curve may be regarded as a *labor-demand relation* if we, like Andersen, assume perfect competition in the goods market. The exact interpretation of the labor-demand relation depends on the underlying open-economy model. It is common to think in terms of either a model with one domestically produced good, which is an imperfect substitute for the foreign good, or a model with domestic production of both nontradeables and tradeables, in which the latter are perfect substitutes for foreign tradeables and thus have their price exogenously given from the world market. Under reasonable assumptions, in both cases we get a downward-sloping relation between the consumption wage and labor demand, the location of which will depend on the relative price between the two goods in question (since labor demand in any sector depends on the product wage — the money wage cost deflated by the output price — and the relative goods price affects the wedge

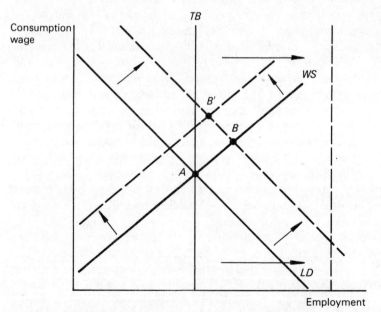

Fig. 1. WS = Wage-setting schedule; LD = labor-demand relation; TB = trade-balance equilibrium.

between product and consumption wages). The intersection of the two curves at A gives the equilibrium consumption wage and equilibrium employment. This diagram can now be used to illustrate the effects of the government demand policies discussed by Andersen.

In the domestic-foreign goods model, an increase in government expenditure on domestic goods clearly shifts the labor-demand relation to the right. The increase in demand for domestic goods raises their relative price. Hence the product wage falls for any given consumption wage. But the increase in the relative price between domestic production and output may also raise the consumption wage at each given level of employment, i.e., shift the wage-setting curve to the left, because workers choose to take out part of their improved opportunities in the form of higher wages. The resulting consumption-wage increase may partially or fully offset the tendency towards increased employment. This is one of the offsets to aggregate demand policies of increased employment that Andersen discusses.

Another offset may occur in the model with tradeables and nontradeables. There it is no longer clear that an increase in government purchases of nontradeables will increase employment even at a given consumption real wage, i.e., it is not clear in which direction a domestic demand expansion will shift the labor-demand relation. The reason is that fiscal expansion raises the price of nontradeables relative to tradeables so that the product wage falls in the nontradeables sector and rises in the tradeables sector. Hence the employment increase in the nontradeables sector is offset by the crowding-out of employment in the tradeables sector. The net result is ambiguous. Although not mentioned by Andersen, this is a well-known result from standard open-economy macro models from the 1970s, such as Helpman (1977) and Rödseth (1979). If there is a shift to the right in the labor-demand relation, the endogenization of the consumption wage via a union/bargaining model will, as above, further offset the tendency towards an employment increase.

The third possible offset to a positive employment effect from fiscal expansion discussed by Andersen emanates from the external-balance constraint. According to the absorption approach, we can view the trade balance as the difference between domestic income ($=$output) and domestic expenditure. If we use the model with only one domestically produced good and make the simplistic assumption that domestic real expenditure depends on domestic real disposable income only, we can write the trade balance (here equal to the current account) as

$$TB = Y - D((1-t)Y) - G,$$

where $TB =$ the trade balance in terms of domestic goods, $Y =$ output, $D =$ total domestic private expenditure in terms of domestic goods, $t =$ the tax rate, and G = government expenditures on domestic goods (= total government expenditures). With this formulation, the trade balance depends on output, the tax rate, and government expenditure. Given the two latter variables, there is only one output level that equilibrates the trade balance. Inverting the production function, the locus which gives a zero trade balance can therefore be drawn as a vertical line in Figure 1.[1] I have drawn the line through the original equilibrium at A. However, an increase in government purchases of domestic goods will shift this locus as well, to the right and, under reasonable assumptions, more than the labor-demand relation. Hence the new equilibrium at B will involve a negative trade balance. Such an external deficit has often induced governments in the Nordic countries (as elsewhere) to abandon fiscal expansion in order to keep up employment in a classical stop-and-go cycle, as argued by Andersen.

By and large, I agree with Andersen's analytical distinctions between various reasons why fiscal expansion may not be a way of stimulating employment. I have two main objections to his analysis. The *first* is that he discusses the external balance, which should reflect savings and investment decisions, without any proper intertemporal model (as I did, too). Moreover, no reasons are given as to why governments should care about the external balance; a more relevant variable would be *total* net savings of the country (including both financial savings and net investment in physical capital) and the associated distribution of welfare over time and across generations. However, in a positive analysis, in which government fears of current-account deficits are taken merely as a stylized fact, a simplistic approach to trade-balance determination of the type discussed could perhaps serve as an acceptable empirical approximation. *Second*, the empirical analysis is somewhat too casual for my taste. The most convincing part deals with how the relative-price changes induced by fiscal policies affect wage setting, i.e., the question of how the wage-setting schedule shifts. But there is not much firm evidence on which to judge the relevance of crowding-out effects between traded and nontraded goods: nor is there much evidence on the tradeoff between employment and external balance, which is the main topic of the paper.

---

[1] I have neglected the difference between the current account and the trade balance due to interest payments on foreign debt. Taking this into account still leads to the conclusion from the above simplistic model that only one level of output is consistent with a zero current account at each point in time, although the level will, of course, change slowly over time if there is accumulation or decumulation of foreign debt.

Accommodation versus Nonaccommodation Policies

The key question that emerges from Andersen's analysis, but on which he remains agnostic, is how we should assess demand policies in order to stabilize employment in connection with negative employment shocks of the type that occurred in the mid- and late 1970s. Two polar views can be held. One is that accommodative policies should be avoided because they eliminate the incentives for real wage adjustment and may therefore even harm employment in the long run; cf. e.g. Calmfors and Horn (1985). The other is that employment stabilization policies may prevent unnecessary unemployment from emerging during the period in which real wages adjust to the unexpected shocks; cf. e.g. Jackman (1990). With unemployment persistence (hysteresis), such policies will also maintain employment in the longer run.

Support can be found for both views from the Nordic experiences. Wage explosions occurred in the mid-1970s in connection with very accommodative policies and the subsequent real wage adjustments have coincided with shifts to more nonaccommodating fiscal policies. For Denmark, Sweden and Finland, there is firm econometric evidence that can be interpreted in favor of this view; cf. Calmfors (1990) for a survey.

But the Nordic experiences also seem to provide strong *prima facie* evidence in favor of unemployment persistence. The two countries that permitted a strong rise in unemployment in the mid-1970s, Denmark and Finland, have not been able to return to earlier low levels. On the other hand, Sweden, which relied heavily on extensive employment stabilization programs in the mid- and late 1970s, has managed to maintain low unemployment. The same has held for Norway up until the last two years of strong fiscal restraint.

For Denmark, it is tempting to draw a stylized diagram which "explains" both unemployment persistence and external-balance disequilibrium. Assume that wages are set in the interest of "insiders" so as to preserve the existing level of employment. The wage-setting curve is vertical as in Figure 2. In the diagram, the initial wage-employment equilibrium at *A* is assumed to be consistent with a certain external-balance disequilibrium (a persistent feature of the Danish economy since the early 1960s). In the case of an *unexpected* labor demand shock, real wages do not adjust and employment falls. Hence the wage-setting curve moves to the left in the next period, and *B* becomes a new wage-employment equilibrium. Because of lower output, the deficit in the trade balance is worsened. An *anticipated* increase in government expenditure, shifting the labor-demand schedule to the right again, only raises wages but does not affect employment and output. From our trade-balance equation, it follows that it will only worsen the external imbalance. The economy is locked into a situation of unemployment and external-balance deficit.

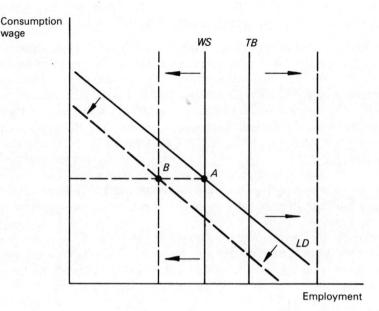

Fig. 2. Hysteresis and external disequilibrium.

Of course, this example is based on extreme assumptions. For instance, the wage-setting curve is not likely to be vertical, as I have drawn it. Less extreme assumptions will provide less extreme results. Still, the example highlights the danger of permitting a considerable increase in unemployment for a substantial period of time. The Nordic macroeconomic experiences of the last 15 years would seem to indicate that the art of demand management consists of cruising between the danger of unemployment persistence and the danger that too much accommodation may remove incentives for real wage restraint. It remains an open question whether any of the Nordic countries has been able to strike a compromise that is sustainable in the long run.

References

Alogoskoufis, G. S.: *The Rise and Fall of European Unemployment*. CEPR and Birkbeck College, London, 1989.

Calmfors, L. & Horn, H.: Classical unemployment, accommodation policies and the adjustment of real wages. *Scandinavian Journal of Economics 87*(2), 234–61, 1985.

Calmfors, L.: Wage formation and macroeconomic policy in the Nordic countries: A summary, 1990. In L. Calmfors (ed.), *Wage Formation and Macroeconomic Policy in the Nordic Countries*, SNS and Oxford University Press, forthcoming.

Helpman, E.: Nontraded goods and macroeconomic policy under a fixed exchange rate. *Quarterly Journal of Economics*, August 1977.

Jackman, R.: Wage formation in the Nordic countries viewed from an international perspective. 1990. In L. Calmfors (ed.), *Wage Formation and Macroeconomic Policy in the Nordic Countries*, SNS and Oxford University Press, forthcoming.

Rødseth, A.: Macroeconomic policy in a small open economy. *Scandinavian Journal of Economics 81* (1), 48–59, 1979.

Comment on T. M. Andersen, "Macroeconomic Strategies towards Internal and External Balance in the Nordic Countries"

Peter Englund

Uppsala University, Sweden

In recent years it has become common to regard macroeconomic policies not as being chosen by an omnipotent policymaker but as resulting from the interplay among various groups in society. By viewing economic policy as endogenous, differences in macroeconomic performance across countries are explained by institutional arrangements rather than by policy "choices". One example of such an approach is the game-theoretic literature on the interplay of monetary and fiscal policy which stresses the degree of independence of the central bank and the role of a "conservative" governor of the central bank. Another example is the literature on the impact of the degree of centralization of wage bargaining, and yet a third example is the literature on the relation between macroeconomic performance and support for the government in parliament. Torben Andersen notes that while institutional factors may explain some differences in performance, see for example Calmfors and Driffill (1988) or Roubini and Sachs (1989), there is certainly a great deal left unexplained. A comparison of the Nordic countries provides a case in point. Despite very similar institutional arrangements, recent macroeconomic performances have differed considerably, indicating the relevance of the "old-fashioned" approach, where policy choices are regarded as largely autonomous and the choices of macroeconomic strategy as an interesting question *per se*. Torben Andersen's paper gives a nice example of such a study.

The paper starts by stating that a primary concern for economic policy in a small open economy is to strike a balance between unemployment and the external deficit. This may be a natural point of departure, since it is certainly true that these are commonly perceived by policymakers as two prime intermediary targets, and a large literature following Mundell and Fleming analyzes how both targets can be attained simultaneously. Nevertheless there are only very indirect links from the current account to any ultimate welfare-related goals. Perhaps focus on the current account as an intermediary target could be part of an optimal two-stage policy in the same way as it is optimal to focus monetary policy on the money supply under some circumstances, even though the ultimate goals are, say, production and inflation.

However, I know of no studies which derive a key role for the current account as an intermediary target. There would be two main issues in such an analysis: Do contemporaneously available current account figures convey useful information? Can the current account be reliably controlled by available instruments? I think the answer is basically negative to both questions. The quality of current account statistics is notoriously poor, particularly the figures available in the short run, and we know very little about the determinants of the current account; Rose and Yellen (1989) fail to find any influence from terms of trade, and Englund and Vredin (1987) find no evidence of Granger causality in a four-variable vector autoregression on Swedish data of terms of trade, real wages, government consumption and the current account. Disregarding the unlikely possibility that the lack of dynamic relations follows from an optimal economic policy, I conclude that the current account is not an attractive intermediary target for macroeconomic policy.

In line with the focus on unemployment and the current account, Andersen calculates an open economy version of the Okun performance index by adding the two perceived policy targets. According to this index, Sweden is the success story and Denmark the big failure in terms of both the average level of the index and the change between the periods before and after the first oil crisis. But this ranking certainly cannot be taken to reflect overall macroeconomic performance; indeed the ranking would be reversed by looking instead at the other two indicators given in Table 1 of Andersen's paper. If an index is created by subtracting growth from inflation, Sweden is found to have the largest deterioration in "macroeconomic performance" between the two subperiods.

Nevertheless, it cannot be disputed that policymakers appear to be obsessed with current account figures, both in the very short run and as a guide for macroeconomic strategy in the medium run. Hence, in a positive analysis aimed at clarifying policy strategies chosen it is highly natural to focus on the current account. From what angle should the current account be analyzed? The answer obviously depends on the mechanisms to be highlighted.

Torben Andersen chooses to disaggregate into traded and nontraded goods, thereby viewing the current account as the supply minus demand for tradeables. This illuminates the relation between sectoral reallocation and the external account, and allows an analysis of the interplay of macroeconomic policies and wage formation. It also serves as a background for classifying the macroeconomic strategies pursued after the first oil crisis into three categories: bridging strategies, sheltering strategies and production strategies. This classification has intuitive appeal, but perhaps clearer empirical definitions could have been given. I have some difficulties in distinguishing between bridging and sheltering. My interpretation is that the former refers to a *temporary* response to a particular shock, whereas the latter is a more *permanent* policy for dealing with adverse external disturbances. The former entails a combination of general demand management with strongly selective policies, whereas the latter consists of a general reallocation towards the sheltered sector of the economy. Empirically this should show up in a pronounced shift of resources towards the public sector (the empirical counterpart of the nontraded goods sector) when a sheltering policy is pursued. Indeed this is what we see in Denmark after 1977, but not in Sweden where the rate of increase in public consumption was highest between 1974 and 1977 when a bridging policy was pursued.

The focus on sectoral composition conceals the intertemporal perspective on the current account which many have found useful in interpreting the development following the oil crisis. According to Sachs (1981) differing current account experiences are explained mainly by differences in investment. This pattern is also found by Englund and Vredin (1989) in a study of yearly postwar data for the Nordic countries, Great Britain, West Germany and the United States. For these countries, the sample correlation coefficients between the percentage change in investment and the current account range between -0.44 and -0.82, whereas the correlation with savings in most countries is very close to zero.

Table 1. *Average yearly rates of change in savings* (S) *and investment* (I)

	1972–77	1977–82	1982–87
Denmark			
S	− 2.9	− 7.1	+ 11.0
I	+ 1.3	− 4.8	+ 7.9
Finland			
S	+ 2.2	+ 3.3	− 1.4
I	+ 2.3	+ 5.1	+ 1.4
Norway			
S	+ 0.8	+ 8.0	+ 3.4
I	+ 10.7	− 2.9	+ 6.2
Sweden			
S	− 3.1	− 2.7	+ 6.4
I	+ 0.7	− 0.4	+ 3.2

Source: OECD National Accounts.

82   P. Englund

Table 1 summarizes the development of savings and investment of the four Nordic countries divided into three five-year periods dominated in turn by bridging, sheltering and production strategies. Bridging policies after the first oil crisis are clearly reflected in decreased savings rates in Denmark and Sweden, but not in Norway and Finland where the policy stance was more expansionary prior to the oil crisis. The drop in savings resulted in deterioration of the current account in both Denmark and Sweden, but the deterioration was considerably stronger in Norway due to the investment boom. In the second period the sheltering strategies of Denmark, in particular, and Sweden show up in very poor savings *and* investment performance with further deterioration of the current account. The change in strategy in both countries after 1982 is very evident, particularly in Denmark, with rather parallel increases in both savings and investment.

Differences in savings and investment performances suggest a distinction between short- and long-run success of macroeconomic policies. It is beyond dispute that Sweden has recently done well in the short run, perhaps due to a combination of active labor market policies and reallocation of resources away from nonprofitable industries which has managed to keep employment up and the current account in approximate balance. But modest investment performance is one indicator of problems ahead. The Danish situation is the opposite with obvious failures in terms of employment and the external account. But recent deficits may be largely accounted for by rapid investment growth, which entails a potential for production and employment in the future.

References

Calmfors, L. & Driffill, J.: Bargaining structure, corporatism and macroeconomic performance. *Economic Policy 6*, 14–61, 1988.
Englund, P. & Vredin, A.: The current account, supply shocks and accommodative fiscal policy. Interpretations of Swedish data. Institute for International Economic Studies, Seminar Paper No. 399, Stockholm, 1987; revised version forthcoming in *Finnish Economic Papers*.
Englund, P. & Vredin, A.: Mönster i bytesbalansen. Sverige i en internationell jämförelse (Current account patterns. Sweden in an international comparison). Seminar Paper No. 7, National Institute for Economic Research, Stockholm, 1989.
Rose, A. K. & Yellen, J. L.: Is there a J-curve? *Journal of Monetary Economics 24*, 53–68, 1989.
Roubini, N. & Sachs, J. D.: Political and economic determinants of budget deficits in the industrial democracies. *European Economic Review 33*, 903–31, 1989.
Sachs, J. D.: The current account and macroeconomic adjustment in the 1980s. *Brookings Papers on Economic Activity* 1:1981, 201–68, 1981.

The Wage Curve*

David G. Blanchflower and Andrew J. Oswald

Dartmouth College, Hanover NH; NBER, Cambridge MA, and London School of
Economics, London, England

Abstract

This paper, which follows in an LSE tradition begun by Phillips and Sargan, examines the
role of unemployment in shaping pay. In contrast to most of the literature, it (i) uses microeconometric data on individuals and workplaces, (ii) examines a variety of data sets as a
check on the robustness of results, and (iii) studies the effects of unemployment on the real
wage level (not on the rate of change of pay or prices). Evidence is found — on British and
U.S. data — of a wage curve. The curve has a negative gradient at low levels of unemployment, but becomes horizontal at relatively high levels of unemployment.

I. Introduction

There exists much evidence that capitalist economies periodically suffer
from high and persistent unemployment. Many economists have argued
that, in a way not yet fully understood, normal wage adjustment
mechanisms fail to operate when unemployment is high.

The object of this paper is to provide microeconomic evidence related
to this failure and how it occurs. A *wage curve*, defined more precisely
below, is estimated which describes the way in which unemployment acts
to depress the level of pay. Unlike the large literature stemming from the
work of Phillips (1958), the estimation is done on microeconomic data,

---

*This work has benefited from discussions with Joe Altonji, Charlie Bean, David Card,
Meghnad Desai, Kevin Denny, Bill Dickens, Bob Gibbons, Nils Gottfries, George Johnson,
Larry Katz, Karl-Gustaf Löfgren, Richard Freeman, Bertil Holmlund, Richard Jackman,
Richard Layard, Assar Lindbeck, Barry McCormick, Steve Nickell, Martin Paldam, Torsten
Persson, Hashem Pesaran, Edmund Phelps, Chris Pissarides, Asbjørn Rødseth, Dennis
Snower, Bob Solow, David Soskice, Mark Stewart, Sushil Wadhwani and Ian Walker.
Helpful comments were also received from the referees and editors of this journal, and from
participants in presentations at Cambridge, Labour Institute (Helsinki), Hamilton, Keele,
LSE, Oxford, NBER (Boston), Stockholm, and Surrey. Mario Garrett provided excellent
research assistance. The normal disclaimer applies.

and the focus is on the relationship between unemployment and the wage level rather than between unemployment and wage inflation. The paper uses one U.S. and three British data sets — each to provide a check against the others.

A central finding of the empirical analysis is that there is a wage curve which becomes flat at moderately high levels of unemployment. At such levels, therefore, the equilibrating forces of the labour market can break down. Similar wage curves emerge from the four data sets, which suggests that the statistical results are robust.

It is also argued that one well-known explanation for persistent British unemployment appears to be incorrect. The Layard and Nickell (1987) hypothesis, that it is a high proportion of long-term unemployment which nullifies downward wage adjustment in a slump, is tested. It is found that the effect of long-term unemployment disappears once non-linear unemployment terms are included. This suggests that the role found for long-term unemployment in previous wage equations — all estimated on short time-series data sets — may have been the result merely of a correlation between high unemployment and high long-term unemployment.

Section II of the paper concerns new work on the unemployment elasticity of pay (the proportional responsiveness of the real wage to the level of unemployment). Section III outlines a model of wage determination. It suggests that unemployment depresses pay by weakening workers' bargaining power, and that the exact shape of the resulting wage function cannot be determined on theoretical grounds. Section IV examines microeconomic data and, after adjustment for many individual and workplace control variables, reveals evidence of a wage curve linking workers' pay to the unemployment rate in their local area or industry. The estimated wage curve becomes flat at relatively high levels of unemployment. Section V concludes, and the Appendix provides background information.

II. Earlier Work on the Unemployment Elasticity of Pay

The work of Phillips (1958) has produced an unusually large literature.[1] Although Phillips' empirical evidence was greeted enthusiastically by many economists, observers became progressively more sceptical. The

[1] See, for example, Lipsey (1960), the survey by Laidler and Parkin (1975), Wadhwani (1985), the debate between Desai (1975, 1984) and Gilbert (1976), and the work on cross-country Phillips Curves in Grubb, Jackman and Layard (1983), Paldam (1980), Newell and Symons (1985) and Grubb (1986).

Phillips Curve is generally thought of as a fragile empirical relationship; see, for example, the recent negative results of Christofides *et al.* (1980) and Beckerman and Jenkinson (1986). The work of Phelps (1967) and Friedman (1968) exposed the theoretical weaknesses of early formulations. A long-run Phillips Curve, according to modern theory, is vertical.

Sargan (1964) was one of the first economists to point out that the Phillips Curve could be thought of as an adjustment mechanism around a long-run relationship in which the wage level depends upon the unemployment level. Sargan saw this as a function calibrating the way in which wage bargainers' demands are shaped by the extent of joblessness in the whole economy. In Sargan (1964), which has been widely overlooked by all but a small group of (time-series) econometrics specialists, the author estimated the average long-run elasticity of pay at − 0.03.

This intellectual tradition is carried on today in work such as Layard and Nickell (1986). The authors estimate a real wage equation on British data between 1950 and 1983. Their estimate of the unemployment elasticity of pay is − 0.06. Carruth and Oswald (1987, 1989) and Holly and Smith (1987) obtain slightly larger elasticities of − 0.1 or over. In contrast to these British results, Sneesens and Drèze (1986) find a statistically insignificant elasticity for Belgium. Very small elasticities emerge from studies of Scandinavian pay, such as Hoel and Nymoen (1988) and Andersen and Risager (1988).

A difficulty with these kinds of studies is that small numbers of degrees of freedom are inevitable. Time series analysis based on highly aggregated data has other well-known limitations. In an attempt to apply a different empirical method Section IV of this paper uses cross-section data to explore the connections between unemployment and the wage level. This builds upon work reported in Blanchflower, Oswald and Garrett (1990).

The last few years have seen an expansion in the numbers of cross-section inquiries into the effect of unemployment upon pay. However, few attempts[2] have been made to draw together and compare the various estimates. Table 1 does this. First, it reveals that there is extensive evidence that unemployment depresses the real wage level. Second, it suggests that the unemployment elasticity of pay is small. Numbers close to − 0.1 are the norm but estimates insignificantly different from zero exist. Adams (1985) and Beckerman and Jenkinson (1988) even obtain a positive elasticity on one unemployment rate and a negative one on another (when two rates are entered simultaneously). Third, fairly similar estimates of the unemployment elasticity of pay emerge from studies of the U.S., Britain, Sweden and Canada.

---

[2] Oswald (1986b) discusses some of the literature and concludes that the unemployment elasticity of pay is around − 0.1.

Table 1. Estimates of the unemployment elasticity of real wages from cross-section and panel data

Study	Data	Notes	Unemployment elasticity
1. Bils (1985)	U.S. NLS Panel, 1970s, 5,000 young males.	Aggregate annual U.S. unemployment used as independent variable. Few annual observations.	− 0.1 (approx.)
2. Rayack (1987)	U.S. PSID Panel, 1968–80, 27,000 white males.	Aggregate annual U.S. unemployment rates.	− 0.1 (approx.)
3. Adams (1985)	U.S. PSID Panel, 1970–76, various samples.	State and industry unemployment rates.	− 0.02 to − 0.11 (industry rates) 0.13 to 0.20 (state rates)
4. Beckerman and Jenkinson (1986)	Panel of 12 OECD countries, 1963–83.	National unemployment rates.	Approx. zero
5. Beckerman and Jenkinson (1988)	Panel of 14 U.K. manufacturing industries 1972–86.	Unemployment by industry and nationally. Data on 1983–86 constructed by authors.	− 0.13 (aggregate rates) + 0.18 (industry rates)
6. Blanchflower (1989)	British BSA, 1983–86, 3,800 adult workers.	Regional unemployment.	− 0.1
7. Blackaby and Manning (1987)	British General Household Survey, 1975, 7,300 white males.	Regional unemployment.	− 0.16
8. McConnell (1988)	U.S. union contract data, 1970–81, 3,000 contracts.	State unemployment.	Approx. zero
9. Holmlund and Skedinger (1988)	Panel on Swedish timber industry, 70 regions, 1969–85.	Regional and national unemployment.	Zero to − 0.04

10. Blanchflower, Oswald and Garrett (1990)	British 1984 WIRS, manual workers in 1,200 establishments.	County unemployment.	Zero to −0.14
11. Blanchflower and Oswald (1990)	British 1984 and 1980 WIRS. Non-manual workers in 800 establishments.	Regional unemployment. Regional wage included as a control.	Zero to −0.08
12. Nickell and Wadhwani (1987, 1988)	Panel of 219 U.K. firms. 1974–82.	Industry and national unemployment.	−0.05 (industry) −0.05 (national)
13. Christofides and Oswald (1988)	Canadian union contract data.	Provincial unemployment.	−0.03 to −0.12
14. Card (1988)	Canadian union contract data, 1,293 contracts, 1966–83.	Provincial unemployment. National unemployment for some provinces.	−0.05 to −0.1
15. Freeman (1988)	U.S. state data. British county data. Changes from 1979–85.	State and county unemployment.	Zero to −0.1 (approx.)
16. Symons and Walker (1988)	British FES data, 6,500 married males, 1979–84. Various samples.	Monthly regional unemployment.	Zero to −0.2

Notes:

We are grateful to Mark Bils for calculating for us the elasticity implicit in Bils (1985). Rayack (1987) does not report an elasticity explicitly. We have calculated the figure " − 0.1 approx." by inserting our best estimate of the unemployment rate in his data set. Similarly for Card (1988). We thank Ian Walker for helpful discussions about the elasticities in Symons and Walker (1988), and David Blackaby for the same on Blackaby and Manning (1987).

It is not possible to calculate the elasticity in Freeman (1988) so we have inserted our estimate of the British and U.S. means. The U.S. elasticity is insignificant at 5 per cent confidence, which is why the table gives zero as the lower bound.

III. Theoretical Issues

To place our statistical results in context, a theoretical framework is required. Although this paper does not attempt to test one specific model against another, it suggests a way to rationalize the correlations observed in the data.

Consider the following model. Assume that a profit maximizing firm bargains with a utility maximizing trade union.[3] Assume that the firm has a maximum profit function

$$\pi(w, p) = \max_{n} pf(n) - wn, \qquad (1)$$

where w is the wage, p is the (exogenous) price of output, n is employment and $f(n)$ is a well-behaved production function. Assume that the union's utility function can be described locally by $u = w$, so that the union is risk neutral and assigns no weight to employment.[4] These assumptions are stronger than necessary for later results.

Assume that wage determination may be modelled as a Nash bargain. This may be justified axiomatically, as in Nash (1953), or strategically, as in Binmore, Rubinstein and Wolinsky (1986), and might even be used as a model of rent-sharing in the non-union sector.

Let the firm's and union's fall-back or delay utilities be, respectively, π^* and u^*. The former may be thought of as profit during a strike; the latter can be seen as a worker's income while on strike. The value of u^* will depend upon the availability of, and wage paid in, temporary work.[5] By the assumption of risk neutrality, the expected utility of a worker on strike may be assumed to be

$$u^* = w^* = s(U) y + (1 - s(U)) z, \qquad (2)$$

where $s(U)$ is the probability of finding temporary work, U is the unemployment rate in the economy, y is the income paid in the temporary

---

[3] Among the early studies, both Sargan (1964) and Desai (1973) rely implicitly on a bargaining framework. Recent empirical work on bargaining models includes Nickell and Andrews (1983), Blanchflower, Oswald and Garrett (1990), Hoel and Nymoen (1988), Holmlund and Skedinger (1988), Nickell and Wadhwani (1987) and Rowlatt (1987). Empirical work on the simpler monopoly union model includes Farber (1978), Pencavel (1984), Carruth and Oswald (1985), Pencavel (1985) and Hersoug, Kjær and Rødseth (1986).

[4] This is a special case of the seniority model in Oswald (1987); a state-contingent version is contained in Oswald (1986a). The flat indifference curve model is criticized in Holmlund and Skedinger (1988). The model of Section III can be generalized to a union utility function such as that in Drèze and Modigliani (1981), McDonald and Solow (1981) or Oswald (1982), by allowing unemployment to affect the worker's alternative income.

[5] During a strike the worker may derive income from other sources, such as spouse's earnings. This income is likely to depend upon the availability of jobs in the outside labour market.

job, and z is the income — equivalent value of leisure if no temporary work can be found. It is assumed that $y - z > 0$.

The function $s(U)$ is of some importance. It captures the probability that the striking employee will be successful in finding a temporary source of income. The function is assumed to be declining and convex in unemployment, U, and to have the characteristics

$$\lim_{U \to U'} s = 0 \tag{3a}$$

$$\lim_{U \to 0} s = 1. \tag{3b}$$

Thus when unemployment is U' the individual is certain to be unable to find temporary work, whereas when unemployment is zero the individual is always able to find such work. Once unemployment reaches U', therefore, a striking worker has no chance of obtaining additional income from the labour market. The worker's bargaining power reaches a minimum at this level, and remains there as unemployment rises above U'.

The Nash bargain solves the problem

$$\max_{w}(\pi(w, p) - \pi^*)(w - w^*), \tag{4}$$

so that an interior optimum requires that the wage be given by

$$w = w^* + \frac{\pi - \pi^*}{n}. \tag{5}$$

This presupposes that the problem is concave (it can be checked that the second-order condition relies on the restriction that the elasticity of labour demand be lower than 2). It should be stressed that equation (5) is easily generalized.

Equation (5), the wage formula, states that the outcome of the wage negotiations depends upon the sum of two components. The first, w^*, is the delay wage, namely, the level of income the individual earns during a breakdown in wage negotiations. By equation (2) this is taken to be a convex combination of the wage in temporary work and the value of leisure. The second component, $(\pi - \pi^*)/n$, is the level of (adjusted) profit per employee. Put loosely, the equilibrium level of pay is shaped by a mixture of external and internal forces.[6]

The next issue is that of how the unemployment rate affects wage determination. The first-order condition for the Nash maximization may

[6] This is consistent with industrial relations surveys of managers' views on the forces determining pay; see, for example, Blanchflower and Oswald (1988).

90   D. G. Blanchflower and A. J. Oswald

be written

$$\pi(w, p) - \pi^* + (w - s(U) y - (1 - s(U)) z) \pi_w = 0. \tag{6}$$

By differentiation, at this optimum,

$$dw\{2\pi_w + (w - s(U) y - (1 - s(U)) z) \pi_{ww}\} - dU\{\pi_w s'(U) (y - z)\} = 0. \tag{7}$$

At a maximum the first term within curly brackets is negative. The second of the terms in curly brackets is positive.

Equation (6) defines an equation linking the price of labour to the level of unemployment. Intuitively, higher unemployment in the outside labour market weakens the union's bargaining strength, because it reduces workers' chances of finding temporary income during a delay (such as a strike) in reaching a wage agreement.

The wage function described by (6) is, in general, nonlinear in the level of unemployment. The properties of this wage curve matter at the macroeconomic level; see e.g. Layard and Nickell (1986).

Define the elasticity of labour demand as

$$\alpha = - w \pi_{ww} / \pi_w. \tag{8}$$

Then

$$\frac{dw}{dU} = s'(U) (y - z) / \left\{ 2 - \left(1 - s(U) \frac{y}{w} - (1 - s(U)) \frac{z}{w} \right) \alpha \right\} < 0. \tag{9}$$

Under these assumptions, the wage curve has a negative gradient.

Beyond this it is difficult to make clear predictions about the structure of the wage curve. However, by assumptions made earlier about the $s(U)$ function, and the monotonicity of the curve, it is necessary that

$$\lim_{U \to U'} w = w^{\min} = z + \frac{\pi - \pi^*}{n} \tag{10}$$

$$\lim_{U \to 0} w = w^{\max} = y + \frac{\pi - \pi^*}{n}. \tag{11}$$

Beyond unemployment levels of U', therefore, the wage curve is flat. A somewhat similar argument has been made recently by Manning (1988).

Differentiation of equation (9) produces a complicated mixture of positive and negative terms. Even under the restriction that α, the labour demands elasticity, is a constant, there appears no way to sign unambiguously the second derivative of the wage curve.[7]

---

[7] We would like to thank David Soskice and Meghnad Desai for detailed suggestions on the theory of the wage curve, which will be explored in our forthcoming book.

The wage curve is bounded below. No matter how high the level of unemployment, the individual employee on strike enjoys some positive value from leisure. This imparts a minimum degree of bargaining power.

The thrust of this approach is different from that associated with papers stemming from Hall (1972), such as Marston (1985) and Topel (1986), in which wages and unemployment are positively correlated in equilibrium. Under the assumption of imperfectly competitive labour markets the traditional compensating wage differential argument need not apply.

IV. Estimating the Wage Curve on Micro Data

The possibility of complicated nonlinearities has rarely been considered in empirical work. However, both Carruth and Oswald (1987, 1988) and Nickell (1987) find that, on British time series data, the best equation is more complex than a loglinear function. Nickell (1987), for example, shows that the wage equation reaches a minimum, in unemployment space, at 19 per cent unemployment (male rate, pre-1982 definition). Similar evidence is presented in Layard and Nickell (1987), where the authors argue that it is high long-term unemployment which pushes up wage pressure at large levels of total unemployment. Carruth and Oswald (1987) report wage equations in which the coefficients of both the natural logarithm of unemployment and its cube are statistically significant. Whilst these studies find evidence of a highly nonlinear wage curve, they suffer inevitably from a shortage of observations. This is liable to be a particular difficulty when the object is to estimate nonlinearities.

An alternative approach is to use microeconomic data sets which allow for effects from outside unemployment. In contrast to the macroeconomic Phillips Curve tradition, an aggregate link from unemployment to wages can be investigated by studying the existence of such a relationship at the microeconomic level.

The method adopted in this paper is to use data on unemployment rates by geographical area or industry. These are inserted into microeconomic wage equations. The underlying assumption is that — if imperfectly — unemployment in the firm's local area or particular industry can be used to proxy external labour market forces.

The empirical work uses four microeconomic data sets:

(1) The Workplace Industrial Relations Survey of 1980 (WIRS), which provides information on approximately 2,000 British establishments.

(2) The National Child Development Study (NCDS) of 1981, which provides information on approximately 6,000 British 23 year old employees.

(3) The British Social Attitude (BSA) Surveys of 1983–87, which when pooled provide information on approximately 5,000 British adult employees.

(4) The International Social Survey Programme (ISSP) data for 1985–87, which when pooled provide information on approximately 2,000 U.S. employees.

Details of surveys 1–3 are given in Blanchflower and Oswald (1989b), and of survey 4 in Blanchflower and Oswald (1989a).

For WIRS and NCDS, county unemployment rates (across approximately 65 countries) were grafted onto the data sets. For BSA, regional unemployment rates across 11 regions by 5 years were added to the survey data. In the case of the ISSP survey, 30 industry unemployment rates by 3 years were added. In all cases the unemployment variables were total unemployment rates. To allow an examination of the Layard and Nickell (1987) hypothesis that long-term unemployment influences wage pressure, long-term unemployment rates were also entered, by geographical area, into the British data sets.

For each data set the wage equation

$$w = f(x, U)$$

was estimated, where x is a vector of individual or establishment variables, and U is the unemployment percentage in the relevant county or region. The x variables are of a kind conventional in the literature on cross-section wage equations.

In all four data sets there is evidence of a nonlinear association between pay and unemployment. This was investigated by fitting different polynomial structures in unemployment. After some experimentation it was found that two specifications worked well:

(i) $w = g(x, U, U^2)$
(ii) $w = h(x, \log U, (\log U)^3)$

In general these give similar results. Checks using a series of dummy variables confirmed that the curvature was not being forced on these data by the functional forms.

The detailed wage equations are set out in Tables 2–5.[8] As these and Table 6 show, there is a well-defined wage curve which becomes horizontal between 9 per cent and 15 per cent unemployment.[9] This is the paper's

---

[8] This paper reports wage equations which include very large numbers of control variables. Given the focus of the paper, and constraints of space, it is not possible to provide a proper discussion of them here. The tables are constructed to be as self-explanatory as possible — Blanchflower and Oswald (1989b) report the complete results. A full description of the variables' effects will be given in a forthcoming book.

[9] The wage is at a minimum at somewhat different levels of unemployment across the four data sets. Current work is concerned with explanations of the different minima.

Table 2. *British WIRS1 wage equations, 1980*

	(1)	(2)	(3)	(4)	(5)	(6)
Log unemployment				-0.0827	-0.2353	-0.2442
				(4.35)	(2.65)	(2.75)
(Log unemployment)[3]					0.0129	0.0162
					(1.76)	(2.10)
Unemployment	-0.0096	-0.0387	-0.0371			
	(3.88)	(3.00)	(2.87)			
Unemployment²		0.0017	0.0019			
		(2.29)	(2.52)			
Long-term unemployment			-0.0044			-0.0037
			(1.50)			(1.30)
Constant	4.0560	4.1646	4.2202	4.1432	4.3353	4.3932
	(118.50)	(71.30)	(60.97)	(90.96)	(36.68)	(34.79)
Adjusted R²	0.4915	0.4930	0.4935	0.4929	0.4936	0.4939
F	26.542	26.252	25.867	26.680	26.312	25.907
Degrees of freedom	1,449	1,448	1,447	1,449	1,448	1,447

Notes: The following control variables were also included:

(1) Per cent part-time employees; (2) per cent female manuals; (3) per cent manuals; (4) per cent skilled; (5) shiftworking dummy; (6) financial performance dummies; (7) quadratic in establishment size; (8) age of plant dummies; (9) union and closed shop dummies; (10) private sector dummy; (11) 60 industry dummies.
The equation uses 65 county unemployment rates. For full details of these equations see Blanchflower and Oswald (1989b).

Table 3. *British NCDS wage equations, 1981*

	(1)	(2)	(3)	(4)	(5)	(6)	(7)	(8)	(9)
Log unempt.	-0.246130 (8.81)	-0.111986 (2.82)	-0.086468 (2.25)	-0.223615 (8.27)	-0.039634 (1.27)	-0.081034 (2.34)		-0.309471 (2.58)	-0.755016 (6.75)
(Log unempt.)³								0.014042 (2.00)	0.032134 (4.88)
Unemployment							-0.029279 (2.89)		
(Unemployment)²							0.000983 (2.50)		
Long-term unempt.	0.004220 (2.46)	0.002097 (1.00)	0.001784 (0.89)	0.004130 (2.49)	0.000789 (0.42)	0.001819 (0.95)	0.000209 (0.10)	0.000604 (0.30)	0.002432 (1.45)
South East	*	*			0.066016 (5.00)	0.041895 (2.64)	0.035944 (2.22)	0.038938 (2.46)	
Greater London		0.108234 (6.72)	0.107189 (6.88)		0.180265 (11.99)	0.149586 (8.02)	0.146926 (7.85)	0.148973 (8.07)	
Regional dummies (9)	No	Yes	Yes	No	No	No	No	No	No
"Worst" regions†	No	No				-0.029829 (2.77)	-0.024511 (2.28)	-0.021808 (2.01)	
Industry dummies	No	No	Yes	Yes	Yes	Yes	Yes	Yes	Yes
Constant	4.618071 (62.92)	4.366995 (49.33)	4.282714 (46.65)	4.516647 (57.15)	4.131207 (48.63)	4.229183 (45.99)	4.343349 (45.52)	4.679752 (22.36)	5.449024 (28.54)
Adjusted R²	0.47720	0.48916	0.53101	0.52037	0.53088	0.53137	0.53419	0.53418	0.52473
F	114.06192	100.47902	60.29091	62.84190	64.38182	63.96073	64.66702	63.71940	62.97289
D. of freedom	6,389	6,379	6,318	6,328	6,326	6,325	6,323	6,282	6,285

Notes:
*Excluded category.
†Category includes E. Anglia, S. West, E. Midlands, Yorkshire and Humberside, and Scotland.

The following control variables were also included:
(1) Fourteen qualification dummies; (2) 2 numeracy/literacy problems dummy variables; (3) 4 health dummies; (4) 8 dummies for workers' attitudes to jobs; (5) gender, marital status, children dummies; (6) dummies for second job, previous unemployment, unsocial hours; (7) no. of jobs since leaving school; (8) tenure current job; (9) 2 unionization dummies; (10) dummy for a move of location between 1974/81; (11) 5 plant size dummies; (12) branch office and limited company dummies; (13) 63 industry dummies.
The equations use 65 county unemployment rates. For full details of these equations see Blanchflower and Oswald (1989b).

principal result. It suggests that, when unemployment is sufficiently large, downward pressure on pay reaches a maximum. A further increase in unemployment then has no depressive effect on wage rates. At low levels of unemployment, however, the unemployment elasticity of pay is negative rather than zero.

The empirical evidence presented here suggests that the recent literature on real wage equations has been wrong to assume constancy of the unemployment elasticity of pay. This assumption has rarely been tested. The paper's results seem to imply that it is only at low levels of unemployment that the real wage is flexible.

Table 2 reports wage equations for semi-skilled manual workers using data from the 1980 Workplace Industrial Relations Survey (WIRS), which are based upon our earlier work in Blanchflower (1984) and Blanchflower and Oswald (1990). The dependent variable is the "gross (weekly) pay of the typical semi-skilled employee". The wage data are grouped and open-ended. We follow the standard practice of allocating midpoints to the wage bands. A series of sensitivity tests were undertaken which showed that the results were stable to changes in the values allotted to the end categories.

Table 3 presents wage equations using data on approximately six thousand young people — all of whom were born between March 3 and. March 9, 1958 — who were interviewed in 1981. They form part of a large scale cohort study — the National Child Development Study (NCDS). In this case the respondent reported to the nearest £ his or her "gross (weekly) pay before deductions for tax and National Insurance including any overtime, bonus, commission and tips" on the last occasion they were paid.

Table 4 reports wage equations using a pooled set of cross-sections from the British Social Attitude Surveys of 1983–86. The dependent variable is "gross annual earnings before deductions of income tax and National Insurance". Once again the wage data are grouped and open-ended — in this case into 13 categories. The same method described in the paragraph above was used to allocate values to each of the wage bands.

A difficulty with the results on WIRS, BSA and NCDS is that it is not possible to control adequately for region specific fixed effects. It is only in BSA that a full set of area dummies can be entered, and — perhaps unsurprisingly given the small number of data points — when this is done (see equations (4) and (8) of Table 4) the unemployment rates become insignificant. The NCDS results do allow for region-level fixed effects: for example equation (7) of Table 3 reveals that the wage curve is robust to the inclusion of regional dummies.[10]

---

[10] The 10 regional dummies in column 3 of Table 5 are grouped in 3 categories, on the basis of F-tests.

Table 4. *British BSA wage equations, 1983–87*

	(1)	(2)	(3)	(4)	(5)	(6)	(7)	(8)
Log unemployment	-0.1128	-1.0184	-1.0212	-0.3186				
	(4.03)	(2.80)	(2.81)	(0.52)				
(Log unemployment)^3		0.0520	0.0506	0.0533				
		(2.50)	(2.42)	(1.48)				
Unemployment					-0.0094	-0.0791	-0.0840	-0.0205
					(3.79)	(2.99)	(3.09)	(0.33)
(Unemployment)^2						0.0030	0.0031	0.0014
						(2.64)	(2.71)	(0.64)
Long-term unemployment			0.0017				0.0021	
			(0.68)				(0.83)	
Regional dummies	No	No	No	Yes	No	No	No	Yes
Constant	6.5900	8.0270	7.9875	6.5853	6.4248	6.8120	6.7763	6.1511
	(57.74)	(13.69)	(13.56)	(6.50)	(67.24)	(38.94)	(37.60)	(15.83)
Adjusted R^2	0.6764	0.6767	0.6767	0.6781	0.6762	0.6766	0.6766	0.6781
F	342.86	332.69	322.59	261.56	342.67	332.58	322.50	261.60
Degrees of freedom	5,040	5,039	5,038	5,030	5,040	5,039	5,038	5,030

Notes:
The following control variables were also included:

(1) Dummies for employment expected to rise/fall; (2) previous unemployment dummy; (3) dummy for redundancy expected; (4) dummies for gender, part-time and marital status; (5) a quadratic in age; (6) years of schooling; (7) dummies for private sector, unionization, supervisor, manual and workers' attitudes; (8) dummy for self-employment history; (9) 3 year dummies; (10) 9 industry dummies.
The equations use 11 regional unemployment rates by 5 years. For further details of these equations see Blanchflower and Oswald (1989b) and Blanchflower (1989).

The difficulty of controlling for region-specific fixed effects is circumvented in Table 5, which presents new and separate evidence for the U.S. In this case the regressions include not area unemployment but (2-digit) industry unemployment rates. Remarkably, despite this difference, and the fact that these data are from a different country, a similar wage curve is found.[11]

Table 5. *United States ISSP wage equations, 1985–87*

	(1)	(2)	(3)	(4)
Log unemployment	−0.2426	−0.7865		
	(5.26)	(3.90)		
(Log unemployment)^3		0.0583		
		(2.77)		
Unemployment			−0.0346	−0.1333
			(4.58)	(3.79)
(Unemployment)^2				0.0070
				(2.87)
Constant	6.4131	7.1411	6.2178	6.6332
	(9.48)	(9.99)	(9.28)	(9.69)
Adjusted R^2	0.3789	0.3809	0.3769	0.3791
F	38.19	37.44	37.87	37.16
Degrees of freedom	2,039	2,038	2,039	2,038

Notes: The following control variables were also included:

(1) Three marital status dummies; (2) dummies for part-time, union, male, supervisor, manual and manufacturing; (3) years of schooling; (4) quadratic in age; (5) 9 regional dummies; (6) 5 highest qualification dummies; (7) 6 city size dummies; (8) 2 year dummies. The equations use 30 industry unemployment rates by 3 years.

Table 6. *The unemployment percentage at which estimated wage curves minimize*

	Log cubic specification	Quadratic specification
(1) Great Britain		
WIRS	12%	12%
NCDS	15%	15%
BSA	13%	14%
(2) United States		
ISSP	9%	10%

Note: Based upon columns (2) and (5) of Table 2, columns (7) and (8) of Table 3, columns (2) and (6) of Table 4, and columns (2) and (4) of Table 5.

---

[11] This is reassuring for another reason. Data on area prices were unavailable for the British data sets, so the estimation implicitly imposes a national price deflator. The evidence of a U.S. wage curve suggests that the result is not being generated by some geographical misspecification of this type.

Figures 1 and 2 sketch the wage curves that emerge from the individual adult equations from BSA for Great Britain and ISSP for the U.S.[12] The British wage curve minimizes at 13 per cent compared with 10 per cent for the U.S. The other two British wage curves are not presented: they have the same shape.

The idea that the wage curve turns up significantly, and so takes a positive gradient, is not predicted by the earlier theoretical model and appears to go against commonsense. It may be that, because few unemployment observations occur over that range, the results there are unreliable.

The addition of long-term unemployment (as a proportion of total unemployment) to the British wage equations contributes nothing once nonlinear unemployment effects are incorporated. On its own, however, long-term unemployment is occasionally positive and significant, as predicted by Layard and Nickell (1987). See column 4 of the NCDS results in Table 3, for example. In column 9, the inclusion of a cubic term in unemployment, itself highly significant, halves the coefficient on long-term unemployment and drives it insignificant. Once regional dummies are

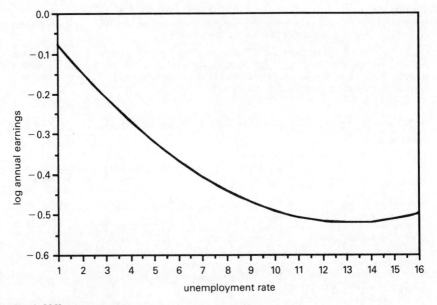

Fig. 1. U.K. wage curve.

---

[12] Whilst the WIRS, BSA, and NCDS data sources do not generate identical wage curves, they produce similar ones. In the figures we plot the level of unemployment and its square rather than the log formulation.

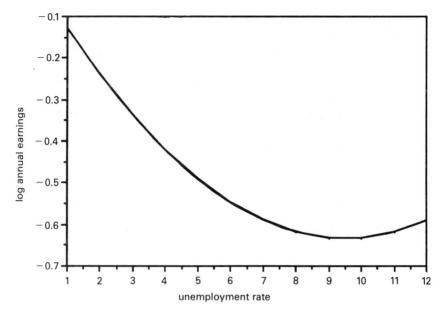

Fig. 2. U.S. wage curve.

incorporated, the long-term unemployment statistic goes down to 0.03, and the unemployment variables remain highly significant.

Across the first three data sets the statistical performance of long-term unemployment is consistently weak. Although the possibility of Type II error exists, the results suggest that long-term unemployment does not play an independent role in wage formation.

V. Conclusions

The purpose of this paper has been to estimate the shape of the wage curve linking pay to the level of unemployment. It uses British microeconomic data sets on establishments, adults and young workers, and a U.S. data set on individuals. They produce comparatively similar wage curves. These curves were estimated by fitting unrestricted polynomials and were not forced on to the data.

The paper should be seen as an attempt to identify an empirical regularity in microeconomic data on wages and unemployment in the 1980s. Various theoretical interpretations are possible, but we favour one based upon a bargaining framework.

Two major conclusions emerge from the empirical analysis. First, in both Britain and the U.S. there is a wage curve which has a negative gradient over low levels of unemployment. However, these curves become flat once sufficiently large unemployment rates are reached.[13] Second, contrary to the argument in Layard and Nickell (1987), the British evidence does not support the view that long-term unemployment[14] is an important element in the wage determination process.[15]

These findings have implications for macroeconomics. If the wage curve flattens out at moderate to high levels of unemployment, shocks to the economy over this range can produce little or no wage adjustment but substantial changes in unemployment. Wage flexibility is greatest when unemployment is low.

Appendix.   Variable Definitions in the Four Data Sets

Great Britain

(1) WIRS		*Mean*
Wages	Log of weekly earnings — semi-skilled workers.	4.161
Unemployment rate	Total unemployment rate in the county, 1980. Data supplied by the Department of Employment.	7.106
Long-term unemployment	Proportion of the unemployed in the county who had been continuously unemployed for at least one year. Data supplied by the Department of Employment.	17.793
(2) BSA		
Wages	Log of annual earnings.	8.59
Unemployment rate	Unemployment rate in the Standard Region.	2.44
Long-term unemployment	Proportion of the unemployed who had been registered as unemployed and claiming benefit for at least one year.	43.22

---

[13] This accords well with Nickell's (1987) time-series results, despite the differences in data and methodology. The results are also consistent with Carruth and Oswald's (1987) conclusion that the cube of the log of unemployment enters a wage equation.

[14] A referee has pointed out that the lack of a long-term unemployment effect may be because the variable should be entered in a different way. This is plausible, so we do not rule out the possibility that future research will uncover positive evidence.

[15] This possibility was anticipated in Nickell's (1987) closing caveat.

(3) NCDS

Wages	Log of weekly earnings.	4.508
Unemployment rate	Unemployment rate by county. Data supplied by the Department of Employment.	11.012
Long-term unemployment	Proportion of the unemployed in the county continuously unemployed for at least one year. Data supplied by the Department of Employment.	20.208

United States

(4) ISSP

Wages	Log of annual earnings.	9.410
Unemployment rate	Unemployment rate by industry. Source *Employment and Earnings*, 1988, 1989 U.S. Bureau of Labour Statistics.	6.130

References

Adams, J. D.: Permanent differences in unemployment and permanent wage differentials. *Quarterly Journal of Economics 100*, 29–56, 1985.

Andersen, T. M. & Risager, O.: Wage formation in Denmark. IIES Paper 414, Stockholm, 1988.

Beckerman, W. & Jenkinson, T.: What stopped the inflation? Unemployment or commodity prices? *Economic Journal 96*, 39–54, 1986.

Beckerman, W. & Jenkinson, T.: The wage-profit relationship: A disaggregated analysis. Mimeo, Oxford, 1988.

Bils, M. J.: Real wages over the business cycle: Evidence from panel data. *Journal of Political Economy 93*, 666–89, 1985.

Binmore, K., Rubinstein, A. & Wolinsky, A.: The Nash bargaining solution in economic modelling. *Rand Journal of Economics 17*, 176–88, 1986.

Blackaby, D. H. & Manning, D. N.: Regional earnings revisited. *Manchester School 55*, 158–83, 1987.

Blanchflower, D. G.: Union relative wage effects: A cross-section analysis using establishment data. *British Journal of Industrial Relations 22*, 311–32, 1984.

Blanchflower, D. G.: Fear, unemployment and pay flexibility. DP No. 344, Centre for Labour Economics, LSE, 1989.

Blanchflower, D. G. & Oswald, A. J.: Internal and external influences on pay settlements. *British Journal of Industrial Relations XXVI*, 363–70, 1988.

Blanchflower, D. G. & Oswald, A. J.: International patterns of work. In R. Jowell, S. Witherspoon & L. Brook (eds.), *British Social Attitudes: The International Report*, Gower Press, Aldershot, 1989a.

Blanchflower, D. G. & Oswald, A. J.: The wage curve. DP No. 340, Centre for Labour Economics, LSE, 1989b.

Blanchflower, D. G. & Oswald, A. J.: The determination of white collar pay. *Oxford Economic Papers*, forthcoming, 1990.

Blanchflower, D. G., Oswald, A. J. & Garrett, M. D.: Insider power in wage determination. *Economica*, forthcoming, 1990.

Card, D.: Unexpected inflation, real wages and employment determination in union contracts. Mimeo, Princeton University, 1988.

Carruth, A. A. & Oswald, A. J.: Miners' wages in post-war Britain: An application of a model of trade union behaviour. *Economic Journal 95*, 1003–20, 1985.

Carruth, A. A. & Oswald, A. J.: Wage inflexibility in Britain. *Oxford Bulletin of Economics and Statistics 49*, 59–78, 1987.

Carruth, A. A. & Oswald, A. J.: Testing for multiple natural rates of unemployment in the British economy: A preliminary investigation. In R. Cross (1988).

Carruth, A. A. & Oswald, A. J.: *Pay Determination and Industrial Prosperity.* Oxford University Press, Oxford, 1989.

Christofides, L. N. & Oswald, A. J.: Real wage determination in collective bargaining agreements. Mimeo, LSE, 1988.

Christofides, L. N., Swidinsky, R. & Wilton, D. A.: A microeconometric analysis of the Canadian wage determination process. *Economica 47*, 165–78, 1980.

Cross, R. (ed.): *Unemployment, Hysteresis and the Natural Rate Hypothesis.* Basil Blackwell, Oxford, 1988.

Desai, M.: Growth cycles and inflation in a model of the class struggle. *Journal of Economic Theory 6*, 527–45, 1973.

Desai, M.: The Phillips Curve: A revisionist interpretation. *Economica 42*, 1–19, 1975.

Desai, M.: Wages, prices and unemployment a quarter century after the Phillips Curve. In Hendry and Wallis (1984).

Drèze, J. H. & Modigliani, F.: The trade-off between real wages and employment in an open economy (Belgium). *European Economic Review 15*, 1–40, 1981.

Farber, H. S.: Individual preferences and union wage determination: The case of the United Mine Workers. *Journal of Political Economy 68*, 923–42, 1978.

Freeman, R. B.: Evaluating the European view that the United States has no unemployment problem. *American Economic Review.* Papers and Proceedings, 294–99, 1988.

Friedman, M.: The role of monetary policy. *American Economic Review 54*, 1–17, 1968.

Gilbert, C. L.: The original Phillips Curve estimates. *Economica 33*, 51–7, 1976.

Grubb, D.: Topics in the OECD Phillips Curve. *Economic Journal 96*, 55–79, 1986.

Grubb, D., Jackman, R. & Layard, R.: Wage rigidity and unemployment in OECD countries. *European Economic Review 21*, 11–39, 1983.

Hall, R. E.: Turnover in the labor force. *Brookings Papers on Economic Activity III*, 709–64, 1972.

Hendry, D. & Wallis, K. (eds.): *Econometrics and Quantitative Economics.* Basil Blackwell, Oxford, 1984.

Hersoug, T., Kjær, K. N. & Rødseth, A.: Wages, taxes and the utility-maximizing trade union: A confrontation with Norwegian data. *Oxford Economic Papers 38*, 403–23, 1986.

Hoel, M. & Nymoen, R.: Wage formation in Norwegian manufacturing: An empirical application of a theoretical bargaining model. *European Economic Review 32*, 977–97, 1988.

Holly, S. & Smith, P.: A two sector analysis of the U.K. labour market. *Oxford Bulletin of Economics and Statistics 49*, 79–102, 1987.

Holmlund, B. & Skedinger, P.: Wage bargaining and wage drift: Evidence from the Swedish wood industry. Mimeo, Uppsala University and FIEF, Stockholm, 1988.

Laidler, D. & Parkin, M.: Inflation: A survey. *Economic Journal 85*, 741–809, 1975.

Layard, R. & Nickell, S. J.: Unemployment in Britain. *Economica 53*, S121–S170, 1986.

Layard, R. & Nickell, S. J.: The labour market. In R. Dornbusch & R. Layard (eds.), Oxford University Press, Oxford, 1987.

Lipsey, R. G.: The relation between unemployment and the rate of change of money wage rates in the United Kingdom: A further analysis. *Economica 27*, 1–31, 1960.

The wage curve 103

McConnell, S.: Strikes, wages and private information. DP No. 323, Centre for Labour Economics, LSE, 1988.

McDonald, I. M. & Solow, R. M.: Wage bargaining and employment. *American Economic Review 71*, 896–908, 1981.

Manning, A.: Imperfect competition, multiple equilibria and unemployment policy. Mimeo, Birkbeck College, 1988.

Marston, S. T.: Two views of the geographic distribution of unemployment. *Quarterly Journal of Economics 79*, 57–79, 1985.

Nash, J. F.: Two-person cooperative games. *Econometrica 21*, 128–40, 1953.

Newell, A. & Symons, J. S.: Wages and unemployment in the OECD countries. DP No. 219, Centre for Labour Economics, LSE, 1985.

Nickell, S. J.: Why is wage inflation in Britain so high? *Oxford Bulletin of Economics and Statistics 49*(1), 103–29, 1987.

Nickell, S. J. & Andrews, M.: Unions, real wages and employment in Britain, 1951–79. *Oxford Economic Papers 35*, 507–30, 1983.

Nickell, S. J. & Wadhwani, S.: Insider forces and wage determination. Mimeo, LSE, 1987.

Nickell, S. J. & Wadhwani, S.: Unions, wages and employment: Tests based on U.K. firm-level data. *European Economic Review 32*, Papers and Proceedings, 727–34, 1988.

Oswald, A. J.: The microeconomic theory of the trade union. *Economic Journal 92*, 576–95, 1982.

Oswald, A. J.: Unemployment insurance and labour contracts under asymmetric information: Theory and facts. *American Economic Review 76*, 365–78, 1986a.

Oswald, A. J.: Wage determination and recession: A report on recent work. *British Journal of Industrial Relations XXIV* (2), 181–94, 1986b.

Oswald, A. J.: Efficient contracts are on the labour demand curve: Theory and facts. DP No. 284, Centre for Labour Economics, LSE, 1987.

Paldam, M.: The international element in the Phillips Curve. *Scandinavian Journal of Economics 82* (2), 216–39, 1980.

Pencavel, J. H.: The trade-off between wages and employment in trade union objectives. *Quarterly Journal of Economics 99*, 215–32, 1984.

Pencavel, J. H.: Wages and employment under trade unionism: Microeconomic models and macroeconomic applications. *Scandinavian Journal of Economics 87*(2), 197–225, 1985.

Phelps, E. S.: Phillips Curves, expectations of inflation and optimal unemployment over time. *Economica 34*, 254–81, 1967.

Phillips, A. W.: The relation between unemployment and the rate of change of money wage rates in the United Kingdom, 1861–1957. *Economica 25*, 283–99, 1958.

Rayack, W.: Sources and centres of cyclical movement in real wages: Evidence from panel data. *Journal of Post-Keynesian Economics 10*, 3–21, 1987.

Rowlatt, P. A.: A model of wage bargaining. *Oxford Bulletin of Economics and Statistics 49*, 347–72, 1987.

Sargan, J. D.: Wages and prices in the United Kingdom: A study in econometric methodology, 1964. Reprinted in Hendry and Wallis (1984).

Sneessens, H. R. & Drèze, J. H.: A discussion of Belgian unemployment combining traditional concepts and disequilibrium econometrics. *Economica 53*, S89–S119, 1986.

Symons, E. & Walker, I.: Union/non-union wage differentials, 1979–84: Evidence from the U.K. family expenditure surveys. Mimeo, Keele University, 1988.

Topel, R.: Local labor markets. *Journal of Political Economy 94*, S111–S143, 1986.

Wadhwani, S.: Wage inflation in the United Kingdom. *Economica 52*, 195–208, 1985.

Comment on D. G. Blanchflower and A. J. Oswald, "The Wage Curve"

Martin Paldam

University of Aarhus, Denmark

Introduction: The Wage Curve and the Phillips Curve

It is nice, indeed, for an old proponent[1] of the Phillips Curve to attend a conference which seems to be devoted to the resurrection of this good old tool — it is surely a modest tool, but as such deserves its modest place. As an aside, I think future historians of thought will find that the main reason why the Phillips Curve fell into disrepute to such an extent was that there was a time when it had been appointed the King of Macroeconomics — hence a great disappointment.

The empirical study by Blanchflower and Oswald (BO) provides considerable help in giving the Phillips Curve back the modest, but respectable role it deserves. The data sets analyzed by BO are cross sections taken at (or calculated to be at) a certain fixed time. Therefore, the model estimated has to have two characteristics:

(C1) It is void of dynamics   and   (C2) All results are in fixed prices.

BO analyze $w = w(u)$, where w is the wage level and u the rate of unemployment, while the simple Phillips Curve — of the 1958 vintage of A. W. Phillips himself — is $\dot{w} = \dot{w}(u)$, where $\dot{w}$ is the rate of wage increases. As BO's explained variable is wages (not the rate of growth for wages), and as the analysis is in fixed time, they call the estimated curve the Wage Curve. However, it is clear that the two curves are closely related.

Think of the effect of a general change in u on a Wage Curve, from one year to the next, in a world where productivity — and hence wages — grow at a rate of 3 per cent per year. Clearly the effect will be a change in the rate of wage increases. And, of course, BO themselves argue several times in their paper that they have provided a new microfoundation for the Phillips Curve. It is well known that the simple Phillips Curve suffers from

---

[1] My findings and interpretations as regards the Phillips Curve are found in Paldam (1980, 1983 and 1989).

two main defects:

(i) It is quite inadequate, as it only explains about 25 per cent of the variation in wage increases. The remaining variation is highly dynamic and has proved difficult to account for by a stable explanation.[2]

(ii) The Phillips Curve tends to disintegrate when disaggregated, so it appears to be a purely macro phenomenon.

The BO paper is an ambitious and rather successful attempt to address the second problem, by estimating a disaggregate Phillips Curve/Wage Curve on three different data sets from the U.K. and one from the U.S. But the curve found is surely the good old Phillips Curve. The results can be summarized as follows:

(R1) A very significant Wage Curve is found in all four data sets. BO also explain why everybody else has failed to find a cross-section Phillips Curve — their findings hinge crucially on the nonlinearity of the model used.

(R2) The results are rather similar across the sets.

(R3) The curve found has two characteristics: It is linear for small to medium values of u. For higher values of u the curve flattens out so that the tradeoff disappears.[3] The sizes of these key characteristics are shown in Table 1.

I encounter three problems in discussing the paper:

(1) The paper is only the top of a major iceberg, from which several hundred more pages will later emerge.

(2) The data are cross-section data sets, which are, no doubt, fraught with problems. I suspect that the major part of the research carried out for the paper consisted of forcing these data sets to tell their story. I have no comments on that major part of the work.

The third problem is general — and perhaps twofold. It follows from the unfortunate fact that while our profession has developed a standard for the

---

[2] The main explanation of the dynamics of $\dot{w}$ is, of course, inflationary expectations, where the instability of the models can conveniently be ascribed to rational explanations. In the papers referred to in footnote 1, I have found that the dynamics is very similar across countries — one average "$\dot{w}$-series" for the OECD area takes care of almost all of the dynamics in all of the countries. The same trick can also be performed in most of the countries, by using the number of industrial conflicts as a dynamics proxy.

[3] The mathematical form used even forces the curves to turn upwards after the minimum; but that (unreasonable) result of the BO study appears insignificant.

Table 1. *Main quantitative results*

Survey	Year(s)	Table (model)	(w, u)-tradeoff	
			Linear[a]	Zero tradeoff[b]
UK, WIRS1	1980	2(3)	−1.0	12
UK, NCDS	1981	3(7)	−0.7	15
UK, BSA	1983−86	4(6)	−1.3	13−14
US, ISSP	1985−87	6(4)	−1.3	9−10

[a] Effect in per cent on wage of belonging to group with 1 per cent higher unemployment c.p. for small u's. Giving a well-defined tradeoff between real wages and unemployment, the figures are difficult to calculate from the curves as the coefficients to u given in BO's Tables 2 to 5 are somewhat unstable.
[b] The unemployment rate where the tradeoff has fallen to zero — from BO's Table 6.

presentation of time-series results, it has failed to develop a standard for the presentation of regressions on micro data. This problem is confounded by the fact that while time-series data are generally public goods, micro data are generally private goods (even if they are available on request there are large starting costs before we can even begin to work with them). BO present their results better than many others, but nevertheless:

(3) The cross-section data sets used are not public property, they are difficult to look at, very few test statistics are given, no graphs of the data are provided. We have to believe that the two fishermen, who have access to hidden ponds, have caught the biggest fish.

With these qualifications I am, however, still fascinated by the BO study. I would like to concentrate on two main comments. The first is that the paper, as it stands, provides a strong policy conclusion of particular interest for Sweden.

A Policy Conclusion about an Active Labor Market Policy

Many countries — and Sweden in particular — pursue an "active labor market policy". This policy consists of systematic (and large-scale) retraining of unemployed workers. The policy has two goals: (G1) increase growth by adjusting the labor supply to labor demand, i.e., remove bottlenecks; (G2) improve the aggregate w/u-tradeoff — i.e., reduce the average w rate for the same average u, so that it becomes possible to reduce u without getting a higher w. We only discuss (G2).

The policy assumes a segmented labor market with, say, two groups. We assume that unemployment is higher in group 1. We term the rates of unemployment and wage increases for the two groups $(u_1, \dot{w}_1)$ and $(u_2, \dot{w}_2)$, respectively. We further take BO to be right, so that there is a separate, but similar, wage curve for each group: $w_i = w_i(u_i)$.

108 *M. Paldam*

The policy "takes" unemployed workers from group 1 and trains them to join group 2, where they start as unemployed, but with an improved chance of finding work. Hence, the policy reduces the (high) unemployment u_1, thereby increasing $\dot{w}_1$. When training is completed, it increases u_2, thereby decreasing $\dot{w}_2$. If, and only if, the $(\dot{w}_1, u_1)$-tradeoff is different from the $(\dot{w}_2, u_2)$-tradeoff, there is a change in the total $\dot{w}$ for a given u. We term this the C-effect (where C denotes composition) of the policy. We say the C-effect is positive if $\dot{w}$ falls for a given u. As the curves are similar according to BO, the possibility of obtaining a C-effect hinges exclusively on the nonlinearity of the curve.

However, the policy also has a negative effect — the A-effect (where A denotes aggregate). By keeping a part (such as 2 per cent) of the labor force in retraining, u is reduced. Hence, there is an aggregate effect which reduces u, thereby increasing $\dot{w}$.

Figure 1A shows BO's findings as regards the nonlinearity — "translated" into a wage-increase result (perhaps this is somewhat of an over-interpretation). Figure 1B gives the good old Phillips case, where wages "explode" as unemployment falls towards zero, the capacity limit. The standard drawing has already been rendered theoretically plausible in Lipsey's (1960) discussion of the Phillips Curve. The same pattern also follows easily from the simple 45-degree Keynes model, which played such an important role in policymaking in the 1960s.

It is clear that the proponents of an active labor market policy believe that the Wage Curve looks like Figure 1B. The key policy is then to educate people to fill in bottlenecks, so that the really wild nonlinearities fail to become operational. However, if BO are right, the scope for an active labor market policy turns out to be much more limited, as the curve is linear all the way from zero to about 10 per cent. Any reshuffling of the unemployment between groups with unemployment rates below 10 per

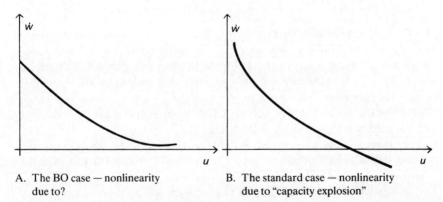

A. The BO case — nonlinearity due to?

B. The standard case — nonlinearity due to "capacity explosion"

Fig. 1. The nonlinearity of the Wage Curve: Two cases.

cent will have no effect whatsoever on wages. However, once unemployment is as high as 15 per cent, the Wage Curve is flat. The policy of taking people out for retraining will then have no effect, so with these high unemployment rates an active labor market policy will be very efficient. Hence, it is important to study the nonlinearity very carefully.

The Conversion to Aggregate Time-Series Results

Nearly everything else we (used to) use the Phillips Curve for takes place within a time-series framework. We therefore need a conversion of BO's fix-price disaggregated results into an aggregate time-series framework. This is well known to be a very difficult conversion.

My own results, when considering nominal $\dot{w}$'s and long series for many OECD countries, is that the tradeoff is 0.6, so that if u goes down by 1 per cent (of the labor force) then $\dot{w}$ rises 0.6 per cent more than would otherwise be the case. BO's corresponding fix-price results are about 1 per cent, so we are in the same neighborhood.

BO seem to believe that their result can be read as representing the steady state; when everything is fully adjusted, then those who belong to a group with one more per cent employment will end up getting a 1 per cent lower wage. It is not easy to see how such a result can be reconciled with the standard theory of the dynamic Phillips Curve.[4] So a great deal of theory will have to be rethought.

However, there is a problem in that the cross-section data used do not necessarily represent the steady-state relations. They represent a mixture of the short and longer run as all cross sections must necessarily do. A high unemployment rate for a certain group may be due to a short-run crisis for a particular firm. Since firm x failed to obtain a certain order, it had to lay off its workers for a month; but then everyone is back in business again. Alternatively, a high unemployment rate may be a permanent situation. We observe the same cross-section pattern; but surely the effect on wages must be different in the two cases?

To summarize: it is important and interesting to study the cross-section Wage Curve; but for most uses the time-series relations have to be studied, and it is difficult to know how to get from the cross-section results to the time-series evidence.

Concluding Remarks

The BO study is an empiricist paper,[5] and it is important to note the empirical findings in the paper regardless of the theoretical interpretation

---

[4] I am not favorably inclined towards this theory for reasons explained in Paldam (1989).
[5] Empiricism is much maligned method in economics. It is almost as if economists believe that theory is a goal in itself. Our goal is to understand the economy — to do so we need to

given by the paper. Theoretical interpretations are presented; but they are clearly peripheral to the main message. Perhaps they even detract from the main message, as we easily come to discuss the theories instead of the findings. This is not a paper which tests a theory. BO, and everyone else, know that there is likely to be "something" in these data — now they have tried very hard to find out exactly what this "something" looks like. If they are right, this is already a great deal — forcing us to rethink the basis for the whole family of active labor market policies.

Let me conclude by saying that I find the paper to be an important building block in research on the Phillips Curve. It is very reassuring, indeed, for us who work with macro Phillips Curves, to know that there exists a simple stable micro Phillips Curve on which we can build.

Perhaps we have now reached the reverse situation from the one we used to confront. We all believed that there was a macro Phillips Curve, but we had no micro Phillips Curve. Now many discard the macro Phillips Curve, but Blanchflower and Oswald have provided us with a micro Phillips Curve.

References

Lipsey, R. G.: The relation between unemployment and the rate of change of money wage rates in the United Kingdom, 1862–1957: A further analysis. *Economica 27*, 1–31, 1960.

Paldam, M.: The international element in the Phillips Curve. *Scandinavian Journal of Economics 82* (2), 216–39, 1980.

Paldam, M.: Industrial conflicts and economic conditions — A comparative empirical investigation. *European Economic Review 20*, 231–56, 1983.

Paldam, M.: A wage structure theory of inflation, industrial conflict and trade unions. *Scandinavian Journal of Economics 91* (1), 63–81, 1989.

Phillips, A. W.: The relation between unemployment and the rate of change of money wage rates in the United Kingdom, 1861–1957. *Economica 25*, 283–99, 1958.

have a great deal of respect for what the data want to tell us. The more we use our theories to structure the way we look at the data, the harder it is to discover the cases where the data tell another story. I think we should behave as BO do in this paper — they follow the advice of their great countryman Sherlock Holmes: "It is a capital mistake to theorize before you have all the evidence. It biases the judgement." [Quoted from Chapter 3 of *A Study in Scarlet*].

Comment on D. G. Blanchflower and A. J. Oswald, "The Wage Curve"

Asbjørn Rødseth

University of Oslo, Norway

Blanchflower and Oswald have provided us with an impressive collection of empirical evidence on the relation between unemployment and the real wage level. The analysis shows convincingly that the wage curve in the U.K. is negatively sloped until it becomes flat at unemployment rates between 9 and 15 per cent.

As I read their results, their wage curves mainly reflect the cross-sectional correlation between unemployment and pay. Dual labor market theorists and some regional economists have believed this to be negative for a while, but Blanchflower and Oswald present a more extensive set of evidence than I have seen anywhere else.

The authors interpret their wage curve as an estimate of the first-order condition for a Nash-bargaining solution in a game between local employers and unions. The negative slope is presumed because strike threats are less effective when unemployment is high, since fewer workers will find temporary work during a strike. The explanation for the horizontal part of the curve is that when unemployment exceeds a limit, it becomes impossible for workers on strike to get temporary jobs. Before buying this explanation, it would be useful to see additional evidence on the actual importance of temporary jobs during strikes.

It is not obvious that the estimated curve is the same as its presumed theoretical counterpart in Blanchflower and Oswald's equation (6). Their interpretation of the estimated equation requires that unemployment varies due to some unmentioned, independent force, and does not respond to the wage. Producer prices and wages in temporary jobs are arguments in equation (6), but are omitted from the estimated equations. On the other hand, the estimated equations sometimes contain variables which are difficult to relate to the theory, e.g. regional dummies.

A discussant is allowed to speculate about alternative interpretations. In Scandinavia, negative correlation of unemployment and wages across regions has been explained by the existence of national agreements on minimum wages. Due to limited mobility of labor, equilibrium wages vary strongly among regions. In regions where equilibrium wages are above the minimum levels, there are high wages and full employment. In the other regions, wages are at the national minimum and levels of unemployment vary. Because of "solidary" wage policy, similar variation is obtained across industries.

Blanchflower and Oswald's observations are from two countries where nationwide agreements on wages play a more limited role. The existence of qualitatively similar wage curves for the U.K. and for Norway should call into question the traditional Scandinavian view that centralized wage bargaining and solidary wage policy are important determinants of the uneven distribution of unemployment across submarkets. On the other hand, it is difficult to see that the probability of finding a temporary job during a strike can play any role in the Norwegian case, since strikes and lockouts are prohibited in local bargaining.

An alternative explanation for the cross-sectional wage curve is efficiency wage considerations. Suppose quit rates depend negatively on wages in the firm and on unemployment in the region. Suppose firms set wages to minimize labor costs per worker, which constitute the sum of direct wage costs and turnover costs. The first-order condition for an optimum is then that the direct cost effect of a marginal wage increase should be exactly balanced by the induced reduction in turnover costs. It seems plausible that wages have a stronger effect on quit rates in regions with low unemployment than in regions with few alternative job opportunities. In this case wages will be set at lower levels in the regions with higher unemployment. It is also possible to explain the flat part of the wage curve if it can be assumed that when wages are already low as compared to wages in the leading region, quit rates become independent of unemployment in the same region. This could happen if, when wage differentials are high, people who quit are only interested in new jobs in the high-wage regions and not in alternative jobs in the regions where they happen to be. Concerns about high turnover costs due to workers leaving for the high-wage regions can limit the absolute wage difference between regions even if there is a more abundant supply of labor in some regions than in others.

Similar results could be achieved in other efficiency wage models where effort depends on relative wages and on unemployment.

Which interpretation is chosen could matter for the macroeconomic implications. Without strong theoretical presumptions, it is not possible to conclude from a cross section that there is real wage resistance to aggregate shocks. The time span of Blanchflower and Oswald's panel data is very short, and the interpretation of the time-series evidence is obscured by the use of year dummies. Year dummies remove any effect which could have arisen from aggregate shocks.

Unlike the British wage curves, the American wage curve estimated by Blanchflower and Oswald uses unemployment rates by industry, not by region. Two recent American studies, which are both referred to by the authors (Adams, 1985 and Marston, 1985), find a positive long-term relation between regional unemployment rates and wages in the U.S. Perhaps this points to a significant difference in the functioning of U.S. versus U.K. labor markets. Adams made a point of distinguishing between temporary and permanent differences in unemployment, and this distinction may be useful in further attempts to differentiate between resistance to regional wage differences and resistance to wage adjustments in response to aggregate shocks.

Measuring Unemployment and Cyclical Participation in the British Labour Market*

Gordon Hughes

University of Edinburgh, Scotland

Barry McCormick

University of Southampton, England and Trade Union Institute for Economic Research, Stockholm, Sweden

Abstract

Unemployment rates for the U.K. are ordinarily calculated using National Insurance registration data. This paper uses individual data from the Labour Force Survey to (i) determine unemployment rates on an aggregate and socioeconomic group basis using search based criteria and (ii) estimate the extent to which search is sensitive to labour market slack. We find that the probability of ILO/OECD search among the jobless is insensitive to labour market conditions, whereas the probability of employer contact search among the jobless is significantly greater in low unemployment markets. Thus measures of "discouraged" workers hinge on the search definition adopted.

I. Introduction

While it is generally agreed that the 1980s recession in the U.K. was severe, few would regard the official unemployment figure as a reliable indicator of the scope for noninflationary expansion. In this essay we illuminate two basic reservations concerning U.K. unemployment data, and construct estimates on a closer footing to those of other countries.

We first discuss the peculiarity that U.K. unemployment data are based on National Insurance registrations, and count those who are both available for work and in receipt of either unemployment or supple-

---

*We are particularly grateful to Martin Chalkley, Nils Gottfries, Bertil Holmlund, Ole Risager and Alistair Ulph for helpful criticism. We are pleased to acknowledge support from the Nuffield Foundation, and assistance with data provision from the ESCR Data Archive, the Department of Employment, and the Office of Population and Census.

mentary benefit. This definition does not provide to a measure of search among the jobless, both because some nonsearching workers are included, and because active searchers who are ineligible for benefits, are excluded. As it happens, between 1983 and 1986, total official unemployment was temporarily similar to that measured on the ILO/OECD unemployment criterion,[1] but this is not the case for certain socioeconomic groups, and will change with policy towards social security compensation. Second, we examine the widely held view that the recession has discouraged many participants from searching. While this issue is critical to the prospects for continued expansion without "overheating", the U.K., unlike many other countries, does not publish estimates of the number of discouraged workers.[2]

To pursue these objectives we use the Labour Force Surveys (LFS) of 1981 and 1983–86. In Section II we describe two measures of unemployment — each based on search criteria and disaggregated by socioeconomic group — which are contrasted with official unemployment rates. These survey based measures correspond to (a) the ILO/OECD unemployment rate criterion, and (b) an indicator of "employer contact" search. In Section III we use the survey data to estimate the extent of hidden unemployment. In contrast to the familiar approach based upon questions concerning respondents reasons for not searching, we draw upon the variation in labour market slack between survey years, and across regions, to estimate ask how far within a socioeconomic group, search rates amongst the jobless — and thus participation rates — vary with local unemployment and vacancy rates. The resulting elasticities of search — with respect to local unemployment and vacancy rates — are then used to indicate the cyclical response of participation. Section IV offers some conclusions.

II. "Claimant Count" versus Search Based Unemployment

The "claimant count" is the number receiving social security or unemployment benefit, and is the official unemployment measure. The ILO/OECD measure combines both claimants and nonclaimants who had engaged in search during a four-week reference period, and is constructed from the LFS data by using any one of the following criteria as sufficient to indicate the occurrence of search: visited a Job Centre or Government employment agency; been on a private recruitment agency's register; advertised for jobs; answered advertisements; inspected the vacancy advertisements in a

---

[1] See *Employment Gazette*, January 1987. By 1989 a wide gap had arisen with official unemployment over 2 percentage points below the ILO/OECD measure.
[2] The 1987 *OECD Employment Outlook* provides a convenient international survey of discouraged worker statistics.

newspaper; made a direct approach to a firm/employer; asked relatives or friends about vacancies; other methods.

From an economic standpoint, it is of interest to amend the ILO/OECD concept in one respect. We may identify those search activities which involve seeking or making contact with an employer — advertise the jobs, answer job advertisements, make a direct approach to a potential employer. This is interesting both because employer contact may affect how the unemployed influence wage-setting in a way in that other search will not, and also because this type of search is likely to reflect greater intensity of purpose and effectiveness, leading to shorter durations of unemployment.[3] The major categories omitted in this definition are those which involve only search by visiting a Government Job Centre or reading newspaper advertisements. We have called this alternative survey based measure the "employer contact" unemployment rate. We have added a further indicator of the significance of "employer contact" search by giving the number of unemployed (claimants or not) who regard an employer contact method as their "main" search method expressed as a percentage of the labour force on the ILO/OECD basis; see column 5 in Table 1.[4]

The sample used in Table 1 consists of individuals interviewed in the 1986 LFS, who lived in Britain one year prior to interview. Since in Section III we wish to focus on hidden unemployment without the complications of nonsearch due to retirement, we limit our study to those under 60, and in order to abstract from flows into and out of full-line education, we also restrict our sample to those over 20. For each unemployment definition, the labour force comprises those in work and those unemployed on the given criterion. All members of the armed forces are excluded, as also are those for whom occupational information is missing. This sample amounts to about 70,000 individuals per year.

The evidence in Table 1 for the official claimant count suggests that in 1986 there existed by historical standards a slack labour market: with the exception of professional/managerial workers, unemployment rates by occupation ranged from 6.6 per cent to 26.8 per cent. If nonsearching claimants are excluded and searching non-claimants added to give the ILO/OECD measure, then a broadly similar picture is obtained. However, when the criterion of search is tightened to employer contact, then with the exception of unskilled and semi-skilled workers, the scope for expansion appears significantly reduced: the relatively low unemployment rates on

---

[3] Using U.S. data, Keley and Robbins (1985) report that persons undertaking employer contact search experience significantly shorter periods of unemployment, but there is as yet no equivalent evidence for the U.K.

[4] Recent issues of the *Department of Employment Gazette* contain articles using evidence concerning search amongst the unemployed drawn from LFS data.

Table 1. *Unemployment rates in Britain on three different criteria, 1986*[a]

	Claimant (%)	ILO/OECD (%)	Employer contact Search (%)	Employer search Main method[d] (%)	Frequency[c]
AGE					
< 35 years	13.5	13.8	9.5	7.4	40
35–49 years	7.1	8.0	5.1	4.4	39
> 50 + years	11.3	8.1	4.4	4.2	21
EDUCATION					
Degree	4.0	4.7	3.6	3.1	12
"O" Levels +	7.1	7.9	5.5	4.7	32
Lower qualification	12.5	13.0	8.9	7.0	11
No qualification	15.1	13.7	8.3	6.8	45
OCCUPATION					
Professional/managerial	2.9	3.0	2.3	1.8	16
Junior nonmanual	7.8	9.0	6.0	5.7	33
Personal service	6.6	8.4	5.7	4.8	5
Skilled manual	8.2	7.6	5.5	3.6	20
Semi-unskilled	26.8	24.6	15.4	12.5	26
REGION					
South-East[e]	7.8	8.1	5.6	5.0	30
Nondepressed	9.5	9.5	6.1	5.2	28
Depressed[b]	13.2	12.7	8.1	6.1	42
Overall	10.5	10.4	6.7	5.5	—

Notes:
[a] As percentage of the labour force according to different definitions for adults aged over 20 and under 60.
[b] North, North-West, West Midlands, Wales, Scotland.
[c] Distribution of total sample including nonparticipants.
[d] Number of workers who indicate an employer contact mode of search as their main method, as a percentage of those employed plus the number with employer contact as main search mode.
[e] Including Greater London.

this criterion might reflect withdrawal from employer contact search for reasons other than having become discouraged. The importance of employer contact search varies considerably between searchers in an interesting way: about one third of job searchers engage in no employer contact, but three quarters of those contacting employers regard such contact as their main search method. Table 1 also reveals a wide regional dispersion of unemployment rates, and its concentration into those without formal education.

There has been little published study of search amongst claimants in the U.K. and no study of search among nonclaimants. To prepare the way for a disaggregation of hidden unemployment which distinguishes between claimants and nonclaimants, Tables 2 and 3 describe search behaviour in

Table 2. *Search rates among those unemployed on the official claimant count, 1986*

	Frequency	ILO/OECD search	% of the unemployed Employer contact search	Employer contact search Main method
AGE				
< 35 years	51.4	78.0	52.3	35.0
35–49 years	27.5	74.9	47.4	33.7
50 + years	21.1	52.6	27.6	24.1
EDUCATION				
Degree	5.4	79.4	59.9	48.4
"O" Levels +	24.0	78.3	54.5	40.2
Lower qualification	12.8	74.6	52.0	33.5
No qualification	57.8	67.8	39.6	27.4
OCCUPATION				
Professional/managerial	5.4	79.8	57.8	47.4
Junior nonmanual	23.9	70.7	47.3	38.2
Personal service	3.2	79.3	54.3	40.0
Skilled manual	18.7	82.0	58.4	36.5
Semi-unskilled	48.8	67.0	38.2	25.7
REGION				
South-East[c]	22.8	68.9	48.1	37.1
Nondepressed	25.4	72.2	45.1	34.1
Depressed[b]	51.8	72.8	45.0	29.3
Overall	—	71.8	45.8	32.3

Notes: See Table 1.

1986 among the jobless claimants and nonclaimants, respectively. Table 2 illustrates the importance of deciding upon an acceptable level of search intensity for interpreting the official unemployment statistics: while approximately 72 per cent of the official unemployed had engaged in some search in the four-week reference period, only 46 per cent had contacted employers. This figure differs considerably between countries. Björklund and Holmlund (1989) find that over 70 per cent of the Swedish unemployed only search via Employment Agencies. Table 2 also provides evidence concerning search patterns across U.K. regions: while the depressed areas perhaps surpisingly have marginally higher ILO/OECD search rates, they also have marginally lower "employer contact" and "employer contact main method" search rates. Employer contact search is also comparatively lower among the unqualified.

Little is known about the approximately one million nonclaimants who were searching for jobs in Britain in 1986. To which socioeconomic groups do they belong? How actively do they search? Table 3 provides some evidence. Nonclaimants are typically older workers than claimants —

Table 3. Search rates among jobless nonclaimants, 1986

	Heads of household (a)			Nonheads of household (a)		
	Frequency (%)	% rate of employer contact	% rate of ILO/OECD search	Frequency (%)	% rate of employer contact	% rate of ILO/OECD search
AGE						
<35 years	27.4	11.8	20.4	41.4	7.8	12.7
35–40 years	32.1	10.1	17.7	34.3	7.2	12.1
> 50 years	40.5	3.6	6.9	24.3	2.3	4.7
EDUCATION						
Degree	5.4	19.6	24.6	5.7	10.2	12.7
"O" Levels +	16.1	14.4	24.0	25.3	8.2	12.7
Lower qualification	8.8	10.6	20.6	11.3	7.8	14.3
No qualification	70.7	5.2	10.1	57.7	4.7	8.7
OCCUPATION						
Professional/managerial	5.0	24.0	29.3	2.0	13.7	16.6
Junior nonmanual	22.4	10.9	19.0	40.0	7.3	12.0
Personal service	2.6	12.6	27.6	3.2	14.8	21.7
Skilled manual	7.8	15.0	25.0	2.2	14.6	20.4
Semi-unskilled Manual	62.2	4.5	9.1	52.6	4.2	8.1
REGION						
South-East (incl. Greater London)	25.5	11.1	18.3	29.5	6.4	10.3
Nondepressed	25.7	6.6	12.5	28.3	6.5	10.2
Depressed	48.8	7.0	12.6	42.2	5.9	11.0

Note: (a) Frequency of the total population of jobless nonclaimants, for either HoH or non-HoH.

especially Head of Household (HoH) nonclaimants. Nonclaimants have a similar proportion of degree level individuals as the claimant count, but a higher proportion with no qualifications. Nonclaimants are slightly more likely to be in the South-East, and less likely to be in depressed regions, relative to claimants. Search rates among nonclaimants are generally much lower than among claimants, particularly on the employer contact criteria but also on the ILO/OECD criteria.

While a recession might reduce serious search efforts, and thereby drive a wedge between the two search measures of unemployment, a conventional labour supply argument would also suggest that recessionary conditions will prompt certain of the jobless to cease all search, and reduce participation rates. Table 4 documents in 1986 and 1981 (in parentheses) participation rates and thus the recent sharp changes. Participation is defined on both the "claimant count" (columns 1 and 3) and the ILO/OECD measure (columns 2 and 4). Since the evidence differs markedly for HoH, who are primarily male, the data are disaggregated. For HoH on both criteria, there has been a marked reduction in participation rates, which was particularly dramatic in the case of unqualified workers. However, among non-HoH there has been a sharp *increase* in participation, despite the recession. The exceptions are those either aged over 50, or unqualified. While these developments partially reflect non-cyclical long-

Table 4. *Labour participation, percentage rates, 1986* (and 1981 in parentheses)

	Heads of Household		Non-Heads of Households	
	Claimant basis	ILO search basis	Claimant basis	ILO search basis
AGE				
< 35 years	92.5 (93.8)	91.3 (94.7)	72.9 (65.8)	74.2 (68.5)
35–49 years	93.4 (94.3)	92.5 (95.2)	70.8 (67.5)	73.4 (69.9)
> 50 years	85.5 (87.5)	81.0 (95.2)	59.1 (57.5)	59.0 (59.5)
EDUCATION				
Degree	97.0 (97.3)	96.9 (98.1)	81.0 (74.9)	82.7 (77.1)
"O" Levels +	95.4 (95.6)	95.2 (96.5)	76.9 (71.1)	78.5 (73.1)
Lower qualification	91.7 (92.4)	90.2 (93.8)	71.5 (67.2)	73.5 (69.9)
No qualification	85.8 (89.7)	82.1 (90.5)	61.7 (60.3)	63.0 (63.0)
REGION				
South-East (incl. Greater London)	92.6 (93.3)	91.5 (94.6)	70.3 (65.5)	71.9 (68.1)
Nondepressed	91.9 (92.7)	90.0 (93.6)	69.4 (63.8)	71.2 (66.1)
Depressed	89.5 (91.3)	87.2 (91.9)	69.4 (65.0)	70.7 (67.3)

Note: Labour participation is the number employed plus that unemployed, on the relevant basis, as a percentage of the appropriate socioeconomic population.

term trends, it might be expected that the recession has aggravated the declining participation among HoH, and moderated the rise in non-HoH participation. At the same time, the underlying rise in participation among non-HoH may have extended the period of high unemployment.

III. Hidden Unemployment

We now ask how far an expansion will elicit either search among those not presently searching or more intensive search among those already searching. Although related issues appertaining to the measurement of unemployment have been relatively neglected in the British literature, there is a long history of such studies in the U.S. — for example, *President's Committee to Appraise Employment and Unemployment Statistics, Measuring Employment and Unemployment* (1962), (Gordon Committee), and *National Commission on Employment and Unemployment Statistics* (1979). This literature considers at length how to classify workers whose search activities do not warrant their being readily regarded as unemployed labour market participants. In particular, attention has been focused upon making meaningful the concept of "discouraged" workers, and upon whether to include these workers in the leading unemployment estimate. While in Britain this term is used rather loosely, it has a precise meaning in the labour force data for many other countries. "Discouraged workers" in the U.S. are those who would like regular employment and whose primary reason for not searching actively for work is that they are discouraged by either the unavailability of suitable work or perceived lack of education, skills or experience. Unfortunately, this definition is not a common currency among countries officially using the expression.[5]

The approach of most countries to measuring unemployment has been to restrict the classification of unemployed to those actively engaged in job search, while separately counting the number of "discouraged workers". This increment can be substantial: if added to the stock of unemployed, discouraged workers increase the U.S. unemployment rate over the past decade by about 14 per cent (to about 8 per cent of labour force) and that in Sweden by about 35 per cent (to about 3.5 per cent of the labour force).

Two considerations appear to have been important in limiting the emphasis placed upon "discouraged workers". First, the classification is based upon a subjective assessment of why the respondent is not searching. Second, it has recently been uncovered that the relationship between

---

[5] For example, in Sweden, Canada and Australia, respondents must also indicate availability for work. Furthermore, the question uncovering the reasons for not searching differs in emphasis between countries, as do reasons counted as sources of discouragement — with only the measurements in Australia and Ireland taking as broad a view as the U.S.

the unemployed and discouraged workers is not as "close" as might be thought, where by "close" we mean that discouraged workers comprise those pushed out of the labour market through lack of success, or those about to enter if the market improves. In particular, discouraged workers in the U.S. appear to behave subsequent to interview rather as other nonsearching workers who want a job, although for those that do enter the labour force (by becoming active searchers), a smaller proportion become employed compared with other groups. In contrast, the unemployed have a higher probability of entering employment in the following period, and should a job not be secured, of actively searching; cf. OECD Employment Outlook (1987).[6]

In contrast to the official U.S. discouraged worker statistics we do not draw upon questionnaire evidence concerning why workers are not searching. Instead we pool several years of survey data (the LFS, 1981 and 1983–86) in order to examine whether, among workers within a socio-economic category, the pattern of search differs with the substantial regional and time-series variation of unemployment and vacancy rates. Thus our work resembles Perry (1977) and Wachter (1977) who also study the relationship between participation rates and cyclical fluctuations. However, these studies used only time-series of aggregate data. With a sequence of individual level data sets we are able to control in much more detail for the demographic variations in the data, and the relevant unemployment/vacancy rate.[7]

Analyses of search have elaborated the "Keynesian" idea that higher unemployment may discourage search. Mortensen (1986) surveys the theoretical work,[8] while Pissarides (1986) provides both a theoretical and empirical study. In that model, workers choose both search intensity — the fraction of time allocated to search — and the reservation wage. Search intensity is increased until the marginal cost of search effort is equal to the gain from being employed relative to unemployed, multiplied by the marginal influence of search intensity upon the transition probability. For a broad class of job matching technologies, an increase in unemployment or reduction in vacancies will reduce the marginal influence of search

---

[6] Clark and Summers (1979) found that 14 per cent (16 per cent) of unemployed women (men) who subsequently left the labour force were classified as discouraged, which would not appear a sufficiently significant component of these flows to place emphasis upon the officially defined discouraged workers as the primary potential source of labour force entrants.

[7] While our data set is rich in many respects, we do not have access to a suitable panel-data series that would enable a study of transitions between search/employment states similar to that in, for example, Clark and Summers (1982).

[8] Barron and McCafferty (1979) provide an empirical study of search among the unemployed.

intensity on the probability of entering employment, and also reduce search. An increase in the utility of unemployment relative to the expected wage reduces the gain from employment and also search intensity.

We cannot examine this directly since our survey does not identify hours of search, but it does provide qualitative information concerning search effort — whether the individual searches, whether an employer is contacted, and whether an employer contact method is regarded as the main search method. There are two ways in which we might interpret analysis of these data. First, the jobless who contact employers may be assumed to allocate more time to search than others. Thus we may investigate influences upon (i) whether a worker searches, and (ii) whether a worker engages in employer contact search, to examine the marginal contribution of explanatory variables upon search at low and high level of search hours. In a second interpretation, we might regard only employer contact as search as it is formally conceived, because other search — for example, scanning newspapers or contacting friends — might be regarded as either (a) involving no opportunity cost, or (b) gathering information about the wage offer distribution. In this interpretation, variations in nonemployer contact search might be explained by variations in the demand for information about the wage distribution, which is usually assumed to be known in search models. This second interpretation implies that the determinants of employer contact search may differ qualitatively from those of nonemployer contact search.

In the following models we shall consider the binary decisions of whether (i) the jobless engage in search; (ii) the searching jobless engage in employer contact; and (iii) the jobless consider an employer contact made to be the main search method.[9] We allow the cost of search to vary between socioeconomic groups, indexed Z, and with the incomplete unemployment spell length, l. We assume that the utility of leisure may vary with these variables and also with the ratio of benefits to the expected wage, b. We also allow the lagged unemployment and vacancy rates for each individual's occupational category in the relevant region to influence the returns from search. Thus the search intensity of jobless individual i, in period t, is given by $S_{i,t}$, where

$$S_{i,t} = S(U_{i,t-1}, V_{i,t-1}, Z_i, l_i, b_i)$$

where Z_i is a vector of personal characteristics (age, education, gender, house tenure, occupation, working wife, number of dependant children, and whether ever had a job) that might influence the value of leisure or the

---

[9] There is plainly some ambiguity regarding how respondents interpret the word "main", however we shall assume that it reflects a combination of possibilities that place particular weight on the identified strategies.

matching technology. We allow for four age categories and five occupational categories (professional/managerial, junior nonmanual, personal service, skilled manual, semi and unskilled manual).

$V_{i,t-1}$ and $U_{i,t-1}$ are the vacancy and official unemployment rates lagged by one year of individual i's occupation/region/sex/year combination. For each individual we allow for five occupational groups and nine regions. These rates are lagged for two reasons. First, we wish to address the concern that causation may run counter to the conjecture (from search rates to unemployment). Second, an individual's search effort may be expected to respond with a lag to aggregate labour market conditions, either because important decisions take time for a household to process, or because labour market information is only available with a lag. We also examine below a more general pattern of lags to allow for "echo" effects of past unemployment rates on the subsequent participation.

l_i is the length of the individual's incomplete unemployment spell. It reflects both (i) the failure to obtain an acceptable offer earlier in the unemployment spell and therefore individual-specific tendencies to find leisure valuable and thus to search less actively (adverse selection), and (ii) that the matching technology may produce fewer offers for the long-term unemployed, due to discrimination, diminished skills, or screening considerations. For both of these reasons we would expect workers with longer incomplete spells to search less intensively. We allow for five categories of incomplete spell length.

b_i is the ratio of benefits whilst unemployed to expected wage. This variable cannot be constructed precisely with the information available from the survey. Instead, we use the fact that benefits are heavily dependent upon certain criteria and proxy benefits as a linear function of three socioeconomic characteristics: whether the individual is married, has a working spouse, and the number of dependant children. The relevant wage is assumed to be the gender/region/occupation/year specific rate, and is constructed in a way which is compatible with the analogous unemployment and vacancy rates. This specification can be conveniently included into the model by adding interactions between the three socioeconomic characteristics and the reciprocal of the appropriate wage. Since benefits are influenced by each of these characteristics in a potentially different way each year, each of these terms is allowed to have a differential effect for each of the five years of the data period.

In each of the following models our prime interest is the extent to which temporal and regional variations of the unemployment rate of the socioeconomic group to which the individual belongs helps to explain in participation. If lower unemployment increases search, then policies which increase the demand for labour, drawing unemployed workers into jobs, and reducing the claimant unemployment rate, will also act to increase search among the remaining jobless. Insofar as active searchers are hired first in the expansion, the consequence of lower unemployment on search among those remaining is to ameliorate the tendency for selection in the recruitment process to reduce mean search effort amongst the jobless.

One criticism of this approach is that we have reversed the line of causation by studying the influence of aggregate unemployment rates (within socioeconomic groups) on individual search behaviour, for it may be argued that less job search will to lead to higher group unemployment. Whilst this argument may carry weight in economies in which Trade Unions play a small role in wage and employment determination, we take it as more reasonable in a European context to regard regional unemployment rates on the claimant count basis as broadly independent of search effort. Under the assumption that jobs were rationed between 1981–86, we shall regard the regional claimant count unemployment rate of the relevant gender/occupation group as a determinant of search intensity.

Our findings for search among workers on the claimant count are reported separately to those workers outside the official workforce. We do this both because of the interest in establishing whether hidden unemployment may substantially differ for nonclaimants and also because it is possible that the unobserved circumstances which result in the jobless being nonclaimants may well produce a different set of search incentives. To add further homogeneity to our samples we have considered separately HoH's and non-HoH's who again experience different incentive structures. In studying jobless claimants, we report here evidence for HoH's since they are more numerous than non-HoH's; for jobless nonclaimants we report, for the same reason, evidence for non-HoH's. Our basic conclusions are not significantly modified by including these groups.

Table 5 sheds light on three aspects of participation. First, in columns 1 and 4, for claimants and nonclaimants respectively, we study the probability that a jobless individual undertakes some form of search in the four week reference period (ILO/OECD criterion). We examine, in columns 2 and 5, the probability of "employer contact" search conditional upon having undertaken some form of job search. In columns 3 and 6 we study the probability that an employer contact mode is considered the "main search method".

The models in Table 5 have the following as the nonlisted "norm" categories for each of the explanatory characteristics: male, aged 35–49, outright owner, nonworking spouse or no spouse, no dependant children, and unemployed between 24–35 months. The additional variables which are included in these models but which are not described in Tables 5 and 6 are four educational achievement dummy variables, five year dummies, five occupational category dummies, and the benefit ratio proxies.

The Findings. Amongst officially unemployed HoH, variations in regional unemployment are found to have little impact on the probability of ILO/OECD search — both in the evidence in Table 5 and in experiments that are not reported here.[10] Thus when participation is defined at a low level of search intensity — that might be characterized as information gathering — it appears that U.K. workers are not discouraged from participating by high unemployment. However, we do find that unemployment discourages more active search: an officially unemployed HoH who undertakes some form of search is significantly less likely to undertake employer contact search, all else equal, in high unemployment areas and periods. This conclusion is supported by the related finding that the probability that an officially unemployed HoH considers an employer contact strategy the main search method is also considerably lower in the high unemployment rate regions — with a high degree of statistical significance. In summary, among HoH claimants there is strong evidence that higher local unemployment discourages employer contact search, but the probability of undertaking a base level of search is unchanged.

These findings are not implausible. Those with a broad intention of returning to employment may regard vacancy advertisements, and discussing with friends, as methods of checking the distribution of wage offers, and inferring the likelihood that an application will meet with success. As an economically inexpensive activity it is also more likely to be influenced by social rather than economic considerations. Directly contacting a single employer will generally constitute a considerable investment of time and expenditure into a job opening that probably provides little information on the wage offer distribution. If unemployment rises, this may have its primary effect on the competition for jobs, and thus on the incentive to contact employers, rather than upon the willingness to learn about the availability of jobs and wage offers.

Among nonclaimant non-HoHs our findings are broadly similar, with the qualification that evidence supporting the view that employer contact search is discouraged by high unemployment is somewhat weaker. The only significant statistical finding is that the probability that employer contact is the main search method is lower in high unemployment rate regions and periods, which is consistent with the view that employer contact search is more sensitive to cyclical conditions.

---

[10] In order to keep the computational cost of the work within reasonable bounds, the actual samples used for the estimations were obtained by taking a random probability sample from the full set of cases in our data set. For all claimant HoHs this sample comprised 50 per cent of the full data set while for all nonclaimant non-HoHs the is sample comprised 30 per cent of the full data set. For manual workers the equivalent proportions were 100 per cent and 50 per cent. These proportions were chosen to ensure an adequate number of searchers in each sample.

Table 5. *Logit equations for search behaviour among the jobless, 1981–86*

Variable	Claimant HoH			Nonclaimant non-HoH		
	ILO/OECD search	Employer contact given ILO/OECD search	Employer contact Main method	ILO/OECD search	Employer contact given ILO/OECD search	Employer contact Main method
Regional unemployment rate	0.010 (1.17)	−0.022 (2.16)	−0.035 (5.43)	0.001 (0.20)	0.019 (0.94)	−0.09 (11.96)
Regional vacancy rate	−0.137 (0.85)	0.027 (0.14)	0.158 (1.36)	−0.12 (1.15)	0.15 (0.70)	−0.29 (2.56)
Female	−0.94 (3.97)	0.26 (0.83)	−0.42 (3.44)	−1.05 (8.19)	0.02 (0.10)	−0.80 (5.39)
Age < 35 years	0.07 (0.87)	0.18 (2.31)	0.03 (0.51)	−0.04 (0.66)	0.26 (1.95)	−0.05 (0.78)
50 < Age < 54	−0.76 (7.93)	−0.23 (1.93)	−0.35 (4.17)	−0.53 (4.72)	−0.11 (0.44)	−0.40 (3.14)
55 < Age < 59	−1.42 (16.20)	−0.62 (5.33)	−0.72 (8.85)	−1.26 (9.64)	−1.16 (3.35)	−1.21 (7.78)
Owner-occupier (with mortgage)	0.28 (2.59)	0.33 (2.45)	0.22 (2.74)	0.06 (0.69)	−0.22 (0.94)	−0.13 (1.30)
Council or housing association tenant	0.23 (2.49)	0.15 (1.22)	0.13 (1.89)	0.26 (2.82)	−0.14 (0.58)	−0.05 (0.45)
Private sector tenant	0.15 (1.22)	−0.06 (0.36)	0.17 (1.73)	0.09 (0.74)	0.22 (0.72)	−0.18 (1.32)

Working spouse	0.27 (2.82)	0.34 (3.36)	0.09 (1.38)	0.00 (0.00)	0.49 (2.84)	0.04 (0.45)
Unemployment duration						
<6 months	0.51 (4.54)	0.35 (3.03)	0.11 (1.40)	0.94 (8.30)	0.29 (1.09)	0.84 (6.6)
6–11 months	0.43 (3.60)	0.46 (3.57)	0.11 (1.32)	0.57 (4.57)	−0.25 (0.9)	0.53 (3.71)
12–23 months	0.36 (3.15)	0.20 (1.68)	0.05 (0.59)	0.35 (2.86)	−0.16 (0.55)	0.40 (2.87)
36+ months	−0.40 (3.98)	−0.27 (2.34)	−0.27 (3.26)	−0.51 (5.05)	−0.23 (0.97)	−0.63 (5.21)
Never had a job	−0.72 (3.94)	−0.23 (0.96)	−0.67 (3.49)	−1.27 (8.04)	0.26 (0.71)	−1.63 (7.68)
No response	−7.49 (14.8)	−2.16 (1.90)	−2.22 (1.36)	−8.5 (14.2)	(n/a)	−3.51 (18.7)
−2 log likelihood	7,591	11,336	11,900	13,965	1,628	9,664
n	9,542	4,563	9,542	22,284	1,204	22,284
Test-statistic	3.05	5.61	38.04	1.60	1.93	150.13

Notes:
(a) In addition to the listed variables, the model also includes: intercept shift variables for each year, 1983–86; three educational achievement dummies; five occupational dummies; and the wage socioeconomic group interactions described above to capture the benefit ratio.
(b) The data, which are drawn from the Labour Force Surveys, 1981 and 1983–86, concern individuals aged over 20 years and under 60 at the time of survey, and who were not employed in either the agricultural sector or the armed services.
(c) The test-statistic is the increase in minus twice log likelihood $-2(LL* - LL)$ when the restricted model is formed by excluding unemployment and vacancy rates. It has a chi squared distribution with two degrees of freedom.

Table 6. *Logit models of search among jobless manual workers, 1981–86*

Variable	Claimant HoH			Nonclaimant non-HoH		
	ILO/OECD search	Employer contact given ILO/OECD search	Employer contact Main method	ILO/OECD search	Employer contact given ILO/OECD search	Employer contact Main method
Regional unemployment rate	0.008	-0.02	-0.04	0.02	-0.01	-0.01
	(1.19)	(1.98)	(7.21)	(2.60)	(0.39)	(1.01)
Regional vacancy rate	-1.124	0.39	-0.15	0.53	0.53	0.40
	(0.62)	(1.60)	(1.18)	(2.56)	(0.97)	(1.77)
Female	-1.81	0.23	-0.44	-0.89	0.25	-0.50
	(6.01)	(0.58)	(3.35)	(6.92)	(0.84)	(3.10)
Age <35 years	0.24	0.08	0.07	0.07	0.16	0.05
	(3.68)	(1.31)	(1.55)	(1.05)	(1.02)	(0.55)
50 < Age < 54	-0.77	-0.29	-0.29	-0.69	0.04	-0.47
	(10.21)	(3.14)	(4.35)	(5.80)	(0.1)	(3.38)
55 < Age < 59	-1.27	-0.64	-0.57	-1.35	-1.34	-1.29
	(18.28)	(6.91)	(8.74)	(9.75)	(3.07)	(7.35)
Owner-occupier (with mortgage)	0.22	0.20	0.23	0.06	-0.06	-0.15
	(2.30)	(1.81)	(3.32)	(0.58)	(0.24)	(1.34)
Council or housing association tenant	0.09	0.06	0.07	0.14	-0.11	-0.19
	(1.13)	(0.55)	(1.14)	(1.43)	(0.44)	(1.72)

Private sector tenant	0.08 (0.73)	−0.13 (0.95)	0.02 (0.3)	0.18 (1.31)	−0.15 (0.40)	−0.04 (0.24)
Working spouse	0.21 (2.79)	0.31 (3.91)	0.05 (0.99)	0.16 (2.19)	0.23 (1.25)	0.19 (2.05)
Unemploymet duration						
<6 months	0.44 (4.58)	0.27 (2.88)	0.14 (2.2)	1.11 (6.97)	−0.20 (0.55)	1.04 (5.52)
6–11 months	0.51 (4.90)	0.25 (2.55)	0.08 (1.22)	0.67 (3.82)	−0.47 (1.14)	0.51 (2.37)
12–23 months	0.27 (2.83)	0.17 (1.82)	0.11 (1.64)	0.38 (2.19)	−0.61 (1.52)	0.73 (3.56)
36+ months	−0.53 (6.33)	−0.21 (2.37)	−0.11 (1.66)	−0.66 (4.71)	−0.59 (1.73)	−0.41 (2.26)
Never had a job	−1.09 (7.38)	−0.54 (2.63)	−0.61 (3.67)	−1.75 (9.38)	−0.15 (0.36)	−1.73 (6.68)
No response	−7.88 (18.89)	−2.43 (2.0)	−2.20 (6.78)	−8.16 (13.5)	(n/a)	−3.5 (15.97)
−2 log likelihood	15,648	9,052	17,856	11,380	1,158	7,571
n	14,675	6,939	14,675	21,463	840	21,463
Test-statistic	3.55	14.11	56.38	8.44	2.66	8.95

Notes: See Table 5.

These experiments may be criticized on the grounds that our sample contains a range of occupations with different search behaviour, and that if the inclusion of occupational dummies in a noninteractive way is incorrect, then the model is misspecified. To address this we consider the more homogeneous sample of manual workers in Table 6. Focusing upon manual workers does not lead to markedly different findings for the effect of unemployment upon search among claimant HoHs. However, the results for nonclaimant non-HoHs require amendment: employer contact appears to be less significantly influenced by unemployment than was implied in the larger sample, and participation on the ILO/OECD basis may even be higher among nonclaimant non-HoH in the high unemployment regions. Why might participation by non-HoH be increased when official unemployment rates amongst the occupation/gender/region relevant group are greater? One possibility is the following. First, note that the unemployment rate which we are assuming influences search is the official claimant count, and this is heavily influenced by HoHs. It is plausible that non-HoHs partially regard themselves as reserve labour, and are prompted to undertake low intensity search, when HoHs experience a slacker labour market. Thus the sharp rise in participation of non-HoHs in the 1980s is found to have been accentuated, rather than ameliorated, by the recession.

Local vacancy rates generally have an insignificant impact on the various job search rates, which is *a priori* surprising. However, the usefulness of U.K. vacancy data have come into question in the mid 1980s because there exist higher vacancy rates in the "depressed" regions of Scotland and Wales, than in the more buoyant South-East. The vacancy data refer to jobs notified to government employment offices, and the possibility that reporting rates have altered between regions during the recession, or with the changing role of the employment office, appears to require study.

Joint Hypotheses. The findings that unemployment and vacancy rates do not significantly influence ILO/OECD search might be thought to be a consequence of multicollinearity between these variables. We therefore consider whether the null hypothesis that parameters on both variables are zero, can be rejected. This test is described in the penultimate row of Tables 5 and 6 where we give the difference between -2 log likelihood values for the unrestricted and restricted models. The resulting statistic has a chi squared distribution with 2 degrees of freedom; critical value at 5 per cent level (5.99), at 1 per cent level (9.21). No major problems with collinearity emerge: the joint hypothesis is rejected strongly only when either one or both of unemployment/vacancy rates have large individual t-values. Thus our finding that ILO/OECD search is not significantly affected by local labour market conditions is unaltered. This evidence also strengthens our contention that employer contact search is inhibited by slack labour markets. There are two equations where the joint hypothesis is rejected even though the individual *t*-values are marginally significant or are insignificant. They are:

(i) employer contact given ILO search for all manual claimant HoHs — the *t*-value for the unemployment rate is just significant but the joint hypothesis is decisively rejected.

(ii) employer contact main method for manual nonclaimant non-HoHs — neither of the *t*-values is significant but the joint hypothesis is rejected at the 0.01 level.

Other Variables. The coefficients of the duration of unemployment follow a plausible pattern and suggest that the propensity to search on the ILO/OECD criterion declines quite slowly — dropping off sharply only after two years of unemployment. Employer contact conditional upon ILO/OECD search follows a similar pattern. Thus while the likelihood of search shrinks slowly with unemployment duration, a diminishing fraction of this smaller group contacts an employer. To an extent this is consistent with the Layard and Nickell (1986) view that short-term unemployment rates are a more appropriate explanatory variable in U.K. wage equations than total unemployment rates: they serve as a better proxy for variations over time in employer contact search. However, the choice of the six months as the appropriate duration of unemployment to separate those contacting employers and those not, appears to be less suitable than two years.

Several of the control variables included in Tables 5 and 6 have parameters of interest. First, perhaps surprisingly we persistently find that having a working spouse has a significant *positive* impact on both ILO/OECD search rates and upon employer contact search. This contrasts with the considerable public speculation that the long-term rise in female non-HoH participation has helped reduce the incentive for unemployed males to find work. One might speculate that having a working wife reduces the utility gained by a HoH from any additional leisure associated with unemployment. We also find that unemployed females, even when HoH, are much less likely to be searching actively. As would be expected, search efforts also decline rapidly with age, all else equal.

The motivation for allowing for house tenure is the observation that owners with mortgages have significantly lower unemployment rates than outright owners and other workers, when a list of observable characteristics — including a fine grid of age controls — are held constant, and that this largely arises because owners with mortages are less likely to enter unemployment following a job separation; see McCormick (1983). This suggests that workers with mortgage debt repayments may search more intensively. In order to study the influence on search of being a mortgagor that allows for the interactions between tenure and occupational group we focus on manual workers (Table 6). There are two main reasons why search might be thought to be correlated with house tenure, holding observed influences including local unemployment rates, equal. An unobserved characteristic may lead certain workers to be both less likely to become unemployed and more likely to opt for home ownership. Second, the pattern of incentives that accompanies a given tenure may increase the cost of being unemployed, and thus search effort. In the tables, the default category is owners outright, and throughout the various experiments these are found to search least actively. Among HoHs, the most active searchers are mortgagors. This is robust to further experiments, and consistent with the view that within a population with similar unobserved characteristics (owner occupiers), those with debt will engage in more search.

Echo Effect. In the models described above we did not experiment with the unemployment rate lag structure. However, high rates of unemployment when, or just before, an individual becomes unemployed might have echo effects — influencing the pattern of participation not only in the following year, but also subsequently. For example, at an early stage of a period of unemployment an individual may enter implicit contracts in the "underground economy". To this end, we experimented with a variety of lag structures over two and three years but without altering the implications of our original findings.

Simulation Evidence. It was pointed out above that participation rates have declined sharply amongst HoH between 1981 and 1986 — particularly for those without formal qualifications — but rose amongst non-HoH. During that time unemployment rates on the claimant count have risen steadily for adults over 20 and under 60 from 7.8 to 10.5 per cent. We now consider some simulations with the models described in Table 5 in order to estimate the extent to which current search amongst the jobless is sensitive to a return to 1981 labour market conditions, and in particular, the occupation/gender/region appropriate (a) unemployment and vacancy rates and (b) distribution of unemployment durations, prevailing in 1981.

Column 1 of Table 7 describes the predicted mean search rates on an ILO/OECD basis for 1986 using the prevailing distribution of unemployment durations and vacancy/unemployment rates. The predictions are differentiated by socioeconomic group, and are constructed using the relevant occupational vacancy/unemployment rates, and distribution of unemployment durations. The values of the other explanatory variables are set at their mean value for the group concerned. Column 2 gives predicted search rates on the same basis using the 1981 unemployment and vacancy data. Columns 3 and 4 give projections of the probability of

Table 7. *Search rates: simulation evidence*

	ILO/OECD Search rates		Employer contact conditional upon ILO/OECD search	
	1986 estimate	1986 Simulation (1981 data)	1986 estimate	1986 Simulation (1981 data)
HoH claimants				
Professional/managerial	73.4	76.2	78.5	80.4
Clerical	67.3	72.2	70.5	75.9
Skilled manual	83.3	84.2	73.0	75.2
Unskilled/semiskilled manual	65.6	66.6	56.1	67.6
Non-HoH nonclaimant				
Clerical	11.0	12.0	64.3	68.3
Unskilled/semi-skilled manual	7.2	7.6	57.3	65.0

Notes:
(a) The 1986 estimates give estimated search rates, using the models in Table 5, based upon (i) the mean unemployment and vacancy rates prevailing for the occupation in question; (ii) the distribution of unemployment durations in 1986 for these occupations, and (iii) mean values for the other explanatory variables. The 1986 simulation search rates are constructed by using the models in Table 5 but with 1981 data concerning; (i) the mean unemployment and vacancy rates, and (ii) the distribution of unemployment durations.
(b) For non-HoH nonclaimants we give only clerical and Unskilled/Semi-skilled workers since these are by far the most numerous occupational categories.

employer contact search conditional upon ILO/OECD search, using 1986 and 1981 data in an analogous way to that in columns 1 and 2.

If 1981 unemployment/vacancy conditions were to prevail then ILO/ · OECD search rates increase for all occupations. This is because the mean individual unemployment duration among the jobless was much lower in 1981, and the large positive consequence of this for search more than off-sets the slight tendency for lower regional unemployment rates in 1981 to marginally increase ILO/OECD search rates. In other words, increased mean duration is much more significant than higher mean unemployment rates. Overall, when occupations are weighted by their proportion in the ILO/OECD measure of the unemployed, search rates on the basis of 1981 data are forecast to increase by about 2.5 per cent on the ILO/OECD basis. In 1986 there were about 3.2 million unemployed on the ILO/OECD basis, and so we would forecast an increase in the order of 80,000 in the working population on this same basis. Thus in contrast to the larger Swedish and U.S. estimates of discouraged workers, we would anticipate an increase in U.K. unemployment rates, were dicouraged workers included, of 2.5 per cent, from 10.4 per cent to 10.7 per cent of the labour force; see column 2 in Table 1.

The introduction of policies to return labour market circumstances to those in 1981 bring about a considerably larger predicted rise in the employer contact search rate. Under such policies we would expect employer contact search rates to rise by about 10 per cent, which reflects the increase in ILO/OECD search rates of 3 per cent, and an increase in the probability of employer contact search conditional upon ILO/OECD search by about 7 per cent on average, when occupations are weighted by their proportion in employer contact search. In 1986 slightly over two million workers were unemployed on the employer contact basis, and we would predict an extra 10 per cent or 200,000 workers engaging in employer contact search as labour market conditions become similar, in the sense described above, to those in 1981. This implies an increase in employer contact unemployment rates from 6.7 per cent to 7.4 per cent; see column 3 in Table 1.

IV. Summary and Conclusions

In Section II, official unemployment in Britain is contrasted with that on two search based measures which are constructed from the 1986 LFS. In 1986 aggregate unemployment on the ILO/OECD measure if 10.4 per cent, which is similar to the official unemployment rate in Britain of 10.5 per cent. However, only 72 per cent of the officially unemployed search, with a corresponding group of searchers who are excluded from the official unemployment data. Various stylized facts characterizing the search behaviour of these two groups are described.

Section III describes a method of estimating hidden unemployment where unemployment is defined either on the ILO/OECD basis or on an employer contact basis. In Britain ILO/OECD search rates are largely insensitive to local unemployment and vacancy rates, holding constant demographic factors and incomplete spell length. However, employer contact search increases significantly in a more buoyant labour market. It follows that we are (a) pessimistic about the potential of a conventional expansion — which we assume will draw active searchers into jobs — to bring about the eventual employment of nonsearching official claimants. Given the substantial number of nonsearching official unemployed, we would therefore add our voices to those emphasizing the importance of (i) direct training and (ii) special employment policies — along the lines, for example, of the U.K. Community Programme, or the Swedish Public Labour Programme — to reintegrate nonsearchers wanting work. At the same time we are optimistic that expansion will prompt a significant number who presently only search on a causal basis, to commence contacting employers, and thereby moderate wage inflationary pressures. In this important sense, hidden unemployment may play a significant role during U.K. cyclical fluctuations, reducing the tendency for the recovery to prompt inflation. It would be interesting to learn whether the distinction that we have found between the considerable sensitivity of employer contact search to cyclical conditions, relative to the sensitivity of search that on the ILO/OECD basis, carries over to other economies.

References

Barron, J. M. & Mellon, W.: Search effort in the labour market. *Journal of Human Resources*, 389–404, 1979.
Björklund, A. & Holmlund, B.: Effects of extended unemployment compensation in Sweden. In B. Gustafsson & A. Klevmarken (eds.), *The Political Economy of Social Security*, North-Holland, 1989.
Clark, K. B. & Summers, L. H.: Unemployment insurance and labour market transitions. In M. N. Bailey (ed.), *Workers and Jobs*, Brookings Institution, 1982.
Clark, K. B. & Summers, L. H.: Labour market dynamics and unemployment: A reconsideration. *B.P.E.A.*, No. 1, 13–60, 1979.
Keeley, M. C. & Robbins, P. K.: Government programs, job search requirements and the duration of unemployment. *Journal of Labour Economics*, No. 3, 337–62, July 1985.
Layard, R. & Nickell, S.: The U.K. labour market. Ch. 5 in R. Dornbusch & R. Layard (eds.), *The Performance of the British Economy*, 1987.
McCormick, B.: Housing and unemployment in Great Britain. *Oxford Economic Papers*, 283–305, December 1982.
Mortensen, D.: Job search and labour market analysis. In O. Ashenfelter & R. Layard (eds.), *Handbook for Labour Economics*, 1985.
Perry, G. I..: Potential output and productivity. *B.P.E.A.*, No. 1, 11–47, 1977.
Pissarides, C.: Unemployment. *Economic Policy*, 500–59, October 1986.
Wachter, M. L.: Intermediate swings in labour force participation. *B.P.E.A.*, No. 2, 543–76, 1977.

Comment on G. Hughes and B. McCormick, "Measuring Unemployment and Cyclical Participation in the British Labour Market"

Bertil Holmlund

Uppsala University, Sweden

Hughes and McCormick (HM) address important issues related to measurement and interpretation of unemployment. Measuring unemployment is not unproblematic; the borderline between unemployment and out-of-the-labor-force is diffuse, as has been pointed out by for example Clark and Summers (1979). Recent Swedish revisions of labor force surveys offer striking illustrations. Only minor and seemingly unimportant changes in the questionnaire are estimated to have reduced the measured unemployment rate by some 0.5 percentage points in 1987.

HM argue that employer contact may be a particularly relevant search method "because this type of search is likely to reflect greater intensity of purpose and effectiveness, leading to shorter durations of unemployment". The data used by HM do not allow tests of this particular hypothesis, however. Keeley and Robbins (1985) report some favorable evidence on U.S. data, and it may be asked whether similar relationships hold for a labor market where job search is to a large extent subsidized through a nationwide employment exchange system. Sweden is the obvious example here. It is compulsory for firms to notify employment exchange offices of all new vacancies. The offices also enforce the work test and implement most labor market policy measures for the unemployed.

I have used a Swedish longitudinal data set to provide some evidence on the links between job search and unemployment duration. The data are based on interviews with a number of youths (aged 16–24) registered as unemployed with employment exchange offices in the county of Stockholm at the end of January 1981. They were interviewed twice in 1981, once in 1982, and a fourth interview was conducted in 1985.[1] The data contain information on the number of hours and methods of job search. The average number of hours of job search is around six, and there

---

[1] The data are described in Holmlund and Kashefi (1987) and have been analyzed by, for example, Albrecht *et al.* (1989).

is a marked correlation between hours of search and number of methods. No information on "main method of search" was available, however.

Estimates of Weibull duration models are shown in Table 1, where (log) duration is explained by a set of personal characteristics, labor market tightness measured by the regional vacancy/unemployment ratio, and variables capturing search effort. The variables include hours of search, number of methods used and a dummy for employer contact search. The results confirm conventional wisdom concerning variables such as age, work experience, education and labor market tightness. More surprising, perhaps, is the finding of positive duration dependence.[2] We also find that search effort, measured either as hours of search or as number of methods, matters significantly for duration. But employer contact does not seem to have any additional explanatory power; the variable enters with insignificant coefficients in columns (2) and (4). The results thus differ from what has been found in the U.S. and it is tempting to speculate that the different results reflect varying degrees of institutionalized labor market search in the two countries.

HM find that a labor market improvement (more vacancies and lower unemployment) increases employer contact search, whereas there is no significant connection between the probability of search and labor market tightness. A similar picture emerges in the Swedish data set referred to above. The probability of employer contact search is significantly higher when the vacancy/unemployment ratio is higher, whereas this ratio does not seem to influence the number of hours of search. (The search regressions included personal characteristics used in the duration analysis as well as measures of income.)

Then what does search theory predict concerning the links between search effort and job availability? Burdett and Mortensen (1978) developed a sophisticated general search model, allowing for endogenous search effort and involuntary job separations. The model produces an unambiguous positive relationship between job availability and search intensity. This result is sensitive to the assumption about search technology, however, as shown by Albrecht et al. (1990). The relationship between search intensity and labor market tightness has to be determined by empirical analysis.

---

[2] The scale parameter is equal to the inverse of the duration parameter α in the Weibull hazard model

$$h(t) = \alpha t^{\alpha-1}\exp(X\beta)$$

so a scale parameter less than unity implies $\alpha > 1$, and thus positive duration dependence. Positive duration dependence is also reported by Edin (1989), who used a different longitudinal Swedish data set.

Table 1. *Unemployment duration and search effort. Weibull model with log* (duration) *as dependent variable*

	(1)	(2)	(3)	(4)
Constant	1.514	1.516	1.490	1.495
	(0.441)	(0.441)	(0.430)	(0.430)
Age	0.109*	0.109*	0.111*	0.111*
	(0.021)	(0.021)	(0.020)	(0.020)
Woman (DV)	−0.009	−0.008	−0.006	−0.006
	(0.079)	(0.080)	(0.077)	(0.077)
Foreign citizen (DV)	0.224	0.222	0.144	0.144
	(0.113)	(0.114)	(0.108)	(0.108)
Work experience	−0.091*	−0.091*	−0.094*	−0.094*
	(0.031)	(0.031)	(0.030)	(0.031)
Education: high school (DV)	−0.352*	−0.352*	−0.340*	−0.340*
	(0.089)	(0.089)	(0.087)	(0.087)
Education: university (DV)	−1.082*	1.080*	−1.110*	−1.111*
	(0.201)	(0.201)	(0.194)	(0.195)
Vacancies/Unemployment	−0.573*	−0.571*	−0.561*	−0.561*
	(0.091)	(0.092)	(0.089)	(0.089)
Search variables				
Hours of search per week	−0.022*	−0.022*		
	(0.005)	(0.005)		
# search methods			−0.061*	−0.064*
			(0.022)	(0.031)
Employer contact (DV)		−0.016		0.013
		(0.087)		(0.107)
Scale	0.89	0.89	0.89	0.89
Log likelihood	−728.14	−728.12	−769.73	−769.72
# spells	529	529	559	559

Notes:
DV is short for Dummy Variable. Standard errors are in parentheses.
Coefficients whose estimated values are more than twice their standard errors are denoted by an asterisk. A scale parameter less than unity implies positive duration dependence.

The possibility of "perverse" links between search effort and job vacancies is indicated by several empirical studies of labor market transitions. Björklund and Holmlund (1981) used CPS data from the U.S. and disaggregated the exit rate from unemployment into exits to employment and exits from the labor force. Labor force exits turned out to show strong procyclical fluctuations; the higher the vacancy rate, the higher the transition rate from unemployment to out-of-the-labor-force. Edin (1989) reports similar evidence based on individual data for a sample of laid-off Swedish workers. Heikensten (1984) used Swedish labor force survey data on unemployed individuals and found that labor force exits from unemployment increased in the vacancy/unemployment ratio.

To the extent that transitions from unemployment to nonparticipation reflect reduced search, there is thus some evidence that an increase in the demand for labor will reduce unemployment duration, by both inducing more transitions to employment and increasing exits from the labor force. This aspect of unemployment dynamics is not well understood, however, and it is unclear whether labor force exits really capture any fundamental behavioral changes.

References

Albrecht, J., Holmlund, B. & Lang, H.: Job search and youth unemployment. Analysis of Swedish data. *European Economic Review 33*, 416–25, 1989.

Albrecht, J., Holmlund, B. & Lang, H.: Comparative statics in dynamic programming models with an application to job search (1990). *Journal of Economic Dynamics and Control*, forthcoming.

Björklund, A. & Holmlund, B.: The structure and dynamics of unemployment: Sweden and the United States. In G. Eliasson, B. Holmlund & F. P. Stafford (eds.), *Studies in Labor Market Behavior: Sweden and the United States*, IUI Conference Reports 1981:2, Stockholm, 1981.

Burdett, K. & Mortensen, D.: Labor supply under uncertainty. In R. G. Ehrenberg (ed.), *Research in Labor Economics*, Vol. 2, JAI Press, Greenwich, CT, 1978.

Clark, K. B. & Summers, L. H.: Labor market dynamics and unemployment: A reconsideration. *Brookings Papers on Economic Activity*, No. 1, 1979.

Edin, P. A.: Unemployment duration and competing risks: Evidence from Sweden. *Scandinavian Journal of Economics 91* (4), 1989.

Heikensten, L.: *Studies in Structural Change and Labour Market Adjustment.* Economic Research Institute, Stockholm School of Economics, 1984.

Holmlund, B. & Kashefi, B.: Frågeformulär och variabelförteckning för undersökningen om arbetslösa ungdomar i Stockholm. (Questionnaire and list of variables for a study of unemployed youth in Stockholm.) Mimeo, 1987.

Keely, M. C. & Robbins, P. K.: Government programs, job search requirements and the duration of unemployment. *Journal of Labor Economics 3*, 337–62, 1985.

Comment on G. Hughes and B. McCormick, "Measuring Unemployment and Cyclical Participation in the British Labour Market"

Ole Risager

University of Aarhus, Denmark

In the first part of this paper, the distribution of unemployment in Britain for 1986 is estimated using search-based criteria. The purpose is to obtain a more relevant economic picture of the unemployment problem in various regions, occupations, and age groups than is provided by official unemployment statistics, which count those who receive unemployment benefits without taking into account whether or not these persons engage in any search activity. Moreover, active searchers who are ineligible for benefits are not included. The second part estimates the extent to which search activity of the unemployed is sensitive to unemployment and vacancy rates — among other things. Following the presentation of the results, which are based on logit regressions on individual data for 1981 to 1986, the authors briefly discuss policy strategies for reducing unemployment.

This very interesting work may be placed in perspective by drawing on Pissarides (1986), who showed that almost all changes in unemployment in Britain up until the mid-1980s can be accounted for by changes in the flow out of unemployment. It is solely in the period 1980 to 1981 that a rise in the flow into unemployment played a role. But even during this period, the fall in the flow out of unemployment is quantitatively the most important. In order to understand the unemployment problem, and to come up with efficient policies against it, it thus seems important to study (i) the determinants of the job search behavior of the unemployed, (ii) the conditions which determine firms' labor demand behavior, and (iii) the relationship between unemployment (and employment) and wage demands in the short and longer term under alternative policy regimes (accommodating versus nonaccommodating), i.e., the conditions under which a fall in unemployment leads to the lowest (largest) rise in wage inflation (employment) in the longer term; cf. below. This paper provides a valuable analysis of the first issue and touches on the third issue in the conclusion. The number of (recession) discouraged workers is also estimated.

In the analysis of jobless individuals' search behavior, the authors reverse the causality between search and unemployment as compared to theory, since they assume that it is unemployment which determines search behavior. However, as the opposite line of causation cannot be ruled out, the explanatory variable is the lagged unemployment rate within the relevant region, occupation, sex, etc. This seems all right on *a priori* grounds, but the analysis is less satisfactory in terms of the empirical specification as last year's (and previous years') unemployment rates are assumed to determine whether a currently jobless individual decides to advertise for a job today, contact a potential employer, etc. A more sophisticated lag structure seems desirable, but I suppose that the required data are unavailable. In this respect the analysis suffers from the same limitations as time-series analyses based on annual data. Similarly, it is regrettable that the available vacancy data are apparently poor indicators, as also mentioned by the authors, since vacancy rates could be expected to have a significant positive effect on search efforts. The result that vacancy rates are insignificant is hard to digest. A third variable that should matter for jobless individuals' search is unemployment benefits relative to the expected reward from moving from unemployment to employment. Unfortunately, the correct benefit data are not available. Instead, as a proxy for benefits, the authors sensibly use certain socioeconomic characteristics which appear to be the major determinants of unemployment benefits. But information on the exact role of unemployment benefits is lost.

Despite these limitations of the analysis, I find that the authors have produced an interesting paper on the relationship between search and unemployment. The finding that high unemployment — temporal and regional — disrupts the allocation process via the tendency to discourage active search (involving direct employer contact) is important. It lends support to the Keynesian view that high unemployment does not easily disappear. Discouraged search may thus lead the persons involved to take less care in maintaining and improving their qualifications. Moreover, it may result in less wage flexibility as it strengthens the bargaining position of insiders. Finally, it causes some people to drop out — although the authors' quantitative assessment of this problem suggests that only 80,000 persons left the labor force due to the unemployment increase between 1981 and 1986.

Another finding concerns the substantial number of nonsearching officially unemployed. In order to reintegrate these people, the authors emphasize the importance of special employment policies and focus attention on the Swedish Public Labor Program. The good thing about these policies is that they have helped to maintain and improve human capital. However, according to an empirical study by Calmfors and

Forslund (1989), these labor market programs also seem to have had a strong wage-raising effect. One explanation is probably that large-scale initiatives of this kind signal willingness on the part of the government to play an accommodating role in the economy; see also Driffill (1985). This gives the trade unions incentives to be more aggressive in their wage demands. Hence, large-scale public employment initiatives may have important social costs which should be weighed against the benefits of such programs.

References

Calmfors, L. & Forslund, A.: Wage setting in Sweden. In L. Calmfors (ed.), *Wage Formation and Macroeconomic Policy in the Nordic Countries.* Blackwell, Oxford, 1990.
Driffill, J.: Macroeconomic stabilization policy and trade union behaviour as a repeated game. *Scandinavian Journal of Economics 87*(2), 300–26, 1985.
Pissarides, C.: Unemployment. *Economic Policy 3*, 500–59, 1986.

II. POLICY ALTERNATIVES AND EQUILIBRIUM UNEMPLOYMENT

Demand- and Supply-side Policies and Unemployment: Policy Implications of the Insider–Outsider Approach*

Assar Lindbeck
Institute for International Economic Studies, Stockholm, Sweden

Dennis Snower
Birkbeck College, London, England

Abstract

This paper explores variety of government policies that can stimulate employment when unemployment is generated through conflicts of interest between insiders and outsiders. It also provides guidelines for identifying policies that may be ineffective. We show how supply-side policies can stimulate employment by raising worker productivity or reducing labor costs. Our analysis indicates that when wages and prices are flexible, product demand policies have no significant effect on employment unless these policies simulate labor productivity, the entry of firms, capital utilization or investment.

I. Introduction

This paper examines what a government can do to stimulate employment in an economy where unemployment arises out of a conflict of interest between insiders and outsiders. For this purpose, we construct a simple insider–outsider model in which nominal wages are the outcome of bargaining between firms and their insiders. This model extends the scope of previous insider–outsider models, e.g. Blanchard and Summers (1986), Lindbeck and Snower (1984, 1988, 1989a), in which nominal wages are assumed to be set unilaterally by the insiders. In this context we seek to identify channels whereby macroeconomic policies can influence employment and unemployment and to assess the effectiveness of demand- and supply-side policies in this regard.

---

*We wish to express our gratitude for insightful comments by Olivier Blanchard, Michael Hoel and Edmund Phelps.

The paper may also be seen as a link in a chain of research projects exploring the implications of labor turnover costs and insider market power for labor market activity. In a static context, some of our previous work, e.g. Lindbeck and Snower (1984), (1987a) and (1989a), has examined the simultaneous operation of three causal effects: (i) how "lumpy" labor turnover costs (i.e., costs that remain finitely large as labor turnover rates approach zero) affect firms' employment decisions, at predetermined wages, (ii) how these costs generate market power for the insiders, and (iii) how insider market power affects wages and employment. These effects have also been analyzed in isolation, but not in unison, within dynamic settings. In particular, Blanchard and Summers (1986), Gottfries and Horn (1987), and others have investigated the effect of insider power on employment, relationship (iii), presupposing that insiders have market power. Bentolila Bertola (1988), Bertola (1989) and (informally) Lindbeck and Snower (1989a, Ch. 11, Section 1, 2) examine the effect of labor turnover costs on employment, relationship (i), in the absence of insider power. This paper explores the comparative static effects of government policies under the influence of all three effects.

"Insiders" are taken to be experienced incumbent employees whose positions are protected by labor turnover costs. "Outsiders" are workers who have no such protection — they are either unemployed or hold jobs with little job security in the informal sector of the economy. We focus attention on the "formal sector", where employment is covered by job security legislation and where incumbent employees have the opportunity to exploit labor turnover costs by engaging in rent-creating activities. Both the job security legislation and the rent-creating activities generate labor turnover costs that fall on the firms, i.e., they make it costly for the firms to fire the incumbent employees and hire other workers in their place. In this setting incumbent workers are able to attain insiders status.

As the insider–outsider theory suggests, these labor turnover costs give the insiders market power, which they may use to pursue their own interests in wage negotiations. For simplicity, we assume that the insiders do not take the interests of the outsiders into account (but our qualitative conclusions could also be derived from the less extreme assumption that the insiders take their own interests more into account than those of the outsiders in the wage bargaining process). Since the outsiders have little (if any) market power themselves, they are "disenfranchised" in the wage determination process — although (as we shall see below) they do exert an indirect influence on this process.

Our model of the labor market assumes that wage and employment decisions are made in sequence: first each firm and its insiders bargain over nominal wages, given perfect information about the employment implications, then each firm makes its pricing and employment decisions, taking nominal wages as given. It is convenient to begin by considering the firm's decision problem (in Section II) and then to describe the wage setting process (in Section III). Section IV incorporates this microeconomic behavior in an aggregative analysis of the labor market. Sections V and VI examine the effectiveness of supply- and demand-side policies in this context. Section VII concludes.

II. Employment and Pricing Decisions

Our model of the firms' employment and pricing decisions is quite conventional. It presupposes that, after the nominal wage bargain has been struck, each firm makes its employment, production and pricing decisions.

We assume that there is a fixed number (M) of identical firms in the economy, all producing a homogeneous product.[1] The aggregate product demand function may be expressed as

$$P = P(Q, A) \tag{1}$$

where P is the price of the product, Q is the aggregate product demand, $-\eta$ is the price elasticity of product demand, and A is a shift parameter of the product demand function. We assume that this parameter can be influenced by demand-side policies.

Each firm's total employment (n) comprises n_I insiders and n_E entrants:

$$n = n_I + n_E. \tag{2}$$

Let m be the stock of insiders which the firm has inherited from the previous time period. This stock is historically given. It depends on last period's stock of insiders (m_{-1}), the quit rate (σ), and the proportion of last period's entrants who become insiders in the current period (δ):[2]

$$m = (1 - \sigma) \cdot m_{-1} + \delta \cdot (1 - \sigma) \cdot [n_{-1} - m_{-1}]. \tag{3}$$

Entrants are assumed to turn into insiders after one period of employment. Thus, the firm's insider employment cannot exceed its current insider stock: $n_I \leq m$.

Assuming — for simplicity — that insiders and entrants are equally

---

[1] The assumption of homogeneous products is made only for expositional simplicity. It is straightforward to extend our analysis to the case of differentiated products.

[2] The first right-hand term denotes the number of last period's insiders who have not quit. The second refers to either (a) the number of last period's entrants who have not quit (if $n_{-1} > m_{-1}$) or (b) the number of insiders who were fired in the last period and who would not have quit (if $n_{-1} < m_{-1}$). For simplicity, we assume that δ and σ are constants.

152   A. Lindbeck and D. Snower

productive,[3] we let the firm have the following production function:[4]

$$q = B \cdot n^\alpha, \qquad 0 < \alpha < 1, \tag{4}$$

where q is the quantity of output produced by the firm, and B and α are constants.

Since each firm is an imperfect competitor in the product market, its behavior depends on how it expects its rivals to respond to its decisions. We summarize these expectations by the conjecture function:

$$Q = b + v \cdot q, \tag{5}$$

where b and v are constants, and v specifies the expected response of aggregate output to a change in the firm's output. (In other words, when the firm changes its output by Δq, it expects its rivals to increase their output by $(v-1) \cdot \Delta q$). This conjecture function allows us to consider the following special cases from the literature on bargaining games: (a) cartel behavior: $v = M$, so that the firms behave like joint profit maximizers, (b) Cournot behavior: $v = 1$, and (c) Bertrand behavior: $v = 0$, so that the firms behave like perfect competitors.

We assume that each firm takes the nominal wage, W, and the payroll tax, τ, as given when it makes its pricing and employment decisions.[5] For simplicity, we assume that once a nominal wage agreement has been reached, the firm faces only one type of labor turnover cost: a firing cost, which may take the form of, say, legally mandated severance pay or the firm's expected cost of implementing agreed firing procedures. Let $\bar{F}$ be the magnitude of the firing cost per insider fired. The firm's total cost of firing is $F \cdot (m - n_1)$, where $F = \bar{F}$ for $m > n_1$, and $F = 0$ for $n_1 \geq m$. The real marginal firing cost, $\bar{f} = \bar{F}/P$ is assumed constant.

---

[3] This is not an assumption of substance. Our conclusions would also hold if we assumed insiders to be more productive than entrants, say, in a production function $q = B \cdot (\xi \cdot n_1 + n_E)$ where ξ is a positive constant greater than unity.

[4] Cobb-Douglas form of the production function merely permits us, in the analysis that follows, to derive a particularly simple aggregate labor demand relation, equation (16), and wage setting function, equations (9) and (11). Our qualitative results would still hold if we made the more general assumption that $q = f(n)$, where $f' > 0$ and $f'' < 0$. By contrast, the product demand function (1) is given in terms of a more general functional form, in order to enable us to inquire under what general conditions it is possible for demand management policies to affect labor market activity.

[5] All workers within a firm are assumed to receive the same nominal wage (W). This is not an assumption of substance; our only reason for making it is that it provides a simple channel whereby insider-induced wage increases lead to reductions in employment. To see this, suppose instead that the new entrants to the firm receive a wage which is independent of the insider wage. In that case, the firm's overall level of employment is such as to equate the entrants' marginal revenue product with their wage, and consequently this employment level cannot be affected by changes in the insider wage.

Given the nominal wage agreement W, the firm's decision-making problem is to maximize its profit subject to the constraints described above:

$$\max \pi = P \cdot q - W \cdot (1 + \tau) \cdot n - F \cdot (m - n_1) \tag{6}$$

subject to $P = P(Q, A)$
$$Q = b + v \cdot q$$
$$q = B \cdot n^{\alpha}.$$
$$n = n_1 + n_E.$$
$$n_1 \leq m,$$

where the firm's decision variables are q, P, n, n_1, and n_E.

The solution to this problem[6] may be expressed as a relation between the firm's total labor demand and the real wage, which we call the "labor demand relation", pictured in Figure 1. The three segments of this relation correspond to the following scenarios:

The "Hiring Scenario"

Here the nominal wage is low enough to induce the firm to set its employment level above its initial insider workforce. Thus, some entrants are

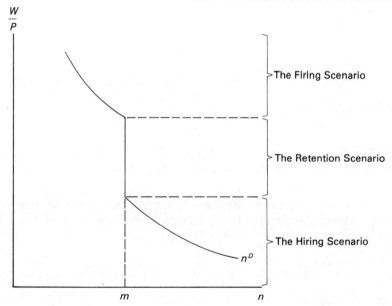

Fig. 1. The firm's labor demand relation.

---

[6] For an algebraic solution to an analytically similar problem, see Lindbeck and Snower (1987b).

hired and no insiders are fired.[7] Consequently firing costs do not arise. The firm sets its total employment so that the marginal value product of labor is equal to the nominal labor costs:

$$\alpha \cdot B \cdot (1-e) \cdot P \cdot (n^D)^{\alpha-1} = W \cdot (1+\tau), \qquad \text{for } n^D > m, \tag{7}$$

where n^D is the firm's profit-maximizing level of employment. The parameter e is Lerner's index of monopoly power (i.e., the price-cost margin):[8]

$$e = v/(\eta \cdot M), \tag{8}$$

where the conjectural variations coefficient (v), the elasticity of product demand (η), and the number of firms in the economy (M) are assumed to be taken as exogenously given by the firm when it makes its pricing and employment decisions.

Condition (7) obviously implies the following labor demand relation[9] in the Hiring Scenario:

$$n^D = \left[\frac{W \cdot (1+\tau)}{P \cdot \alpha \cdot (1-e) \cdot B}\right]^{-1/(1-\alpha)}, \qquad \text{for } n^D > m. \tag{9}$$

Since the Hiring Scenario occurs only when $n^D > m$, the nominal wage must then be less than a critical level:

$$W < K_1, \tag{9a}$$

where the constant K_1 is

$$K_1 = [1/(1+\tau)] \cdot m^{-(1-\alpha)} \cdot P[(b+v \cdot B \cdot m^\alpha), A] \cdot \alpha \cdot (1-e) \cdot B, \tag{9b}$$

by equations (4), (5), and (9).

The "Firing Scenario"

Here the nominal wage is high enough to induce the firm to set its employment level beneath its initial insider workforce. Thus, no entrants are hired and some insiders are fired, at a firing cost of $\bar{F}$ per insider. By implication, total employment is set so that the nominal wage is equal to

---

[7] On account of the firing cost, the firm never has an incentive to fire an insider when it hires entrants.
[8] By the first-order condition (7), the firm's marginal cost of production is

$$C = W/(\alpha \cdot B \cdot n^{\alpha-1}) = P \cdot (1-e).$$

Thus, the price-cost margin, $(P-C)/P$, is e.
[9] Note that equation (9) is not a labor demand curve in the perfectly competitive sense, since both n and P are endogenous to the firm.

the sum of the marginal value product of labor and the marginal firing cost:

$$\alpha \cdot B \cdot (1-e) \cdot P \cdot (n^D)^{\alpha-1} + \bar{F} = W \cdot (1+\tau), \qquad \text{for } n^D < m. \tag{10}$$

This condition implies the following labor demand relation:

$$n^D = \left[\frac{W \cdot (1+\tau) + \bar{F}}{P \cdot \alpha \cdot (1-e) \cdot B} \right]^{-1/(1-\alpha)}, \qquad \text{for } n^D < m. \tag{11}$$

Since the Firing Scenario occurs only when $n^D < m$, the nominal wage must exceed the folowing critical level:

$$W > K_2, \tag{11a}$$

where the constant K_2 is given by

$$K_2 = [1/(1+\tau)] \cdot m^{-(1-\alpha)} \cdot P[(b + v \cdot B \cdot m^\alpha), A] \cdot \alpha \cdot (1-e) \cdot B + [\bar{F}/(1+\tau)], \tag{11b}$$

by equations (4), (5) and (11).

The "Retention Scenario"

Here the nominal wage is such as to induce the firm to retain its initial insider workforce, but to hire no entrants.

$$n^D = m. \tag{12}$$

By equations (9b) and (11b), it is clear that this happens whenever the nominal wage falls into the following range:

$$K_1 \leq W \leq K_2. \tag{12a}$$

Equations (9)–(12a) will serve as our description of the firm's employment and pricing decisions. We now turn to the wage-setting process, where these decisions are taken into account.

III. Wage Determination

As noted, the nominal wage (W) is taken to be the outcome of a Nash bargain between each firm and its insiders. We proceed to describe the bargaining objectives of the firm and its insiders and then specify the bargaining problem.

The Firm's Objective

We let the firm's objective be the maximization of the "firm surplus", which is the difference between the profit earned under agreement in the wage negotiations (π) and under disagreement (π_0). As shown below, the firm's insiders have an incentive to engage in rent-creating activities when there is disagreement, but not when there is agreement. These rent-creating activities come in many guises. For instance, the insiders may work-to-rule, be uncooperative in team production, engage in litigation, or go on strike.[10] For simplicity, this paper does not consider the employment effects of government policies operating via the influence of these policies on insiders' rent-seeking activities under disagreement. Accordingly, we make the assumption that when the insiders engage in these activities, the firm earns a constant fraction $1 - \chi$ (where $0 \leq \chi < 1$), of its profit under agreement.[11] The parameter χ may be understood as a measure of the magnitude of insiders' rent-creating activities under disagreement.

Thus, the firm's surplus may be expressed in the following simple way:

$$\phi = \pi - \pi_0 = \chi \cdot \pi. \tag{13a}$$

The Insiders' Objective

The insiders seek to maximize the "insider surplus", which is the difference between the real wage income that the insiders receive under agreement and their threat-point income.

The real wage relevant to the insiders is the consumption wage: (W/P_a), where P_a is the consumer price index. We assume that each individual firm exerts a negligible influence on the consumer price index, and thus P_a is exogenous to the insiders' decision-making.

The insiders' real "threat-point wage" is denoted by w_0. For simplicity, we take w_0 to be a constant that depends on all the various determinants of the insiders' incomes in the case of disagreement in the wage negotiations: the magnitude of strike fund payments, the level of support forthcoming from family and friends during the dispute, the opportunity of finding temporary, informal work during the dispute, the reservation wage, and so on.[12]

We assume that each firm has a seniority system (viz. an ordering whereby it fires employees), and that a proportion λ $(0 \leq \lambda \leq 1)$ of the firm's

---

[10] For a discussion of these activities in the context of the insider–outsider theory, see Lindbeck and Snower (1984, 1988).

[11] This is an assumption of substance. In general we would expect that one channel whereby demand- and supply-side policies may affect wages and employment is by influencing the magnitude of insiders' rent-creating activities. However, our assumption that χ is a constant implies that its value does not affect the outcome of the Nash bargain over the nominal wage.

[12] Note that the insiders' threat-point wage (w_0) is not necessarily equal to their reservation wage (w_r). In fact the threat-point wage must be greater than or equal to the reservation wage: $w_0 \geq w_r$, for otherwise the insiders would quit the firm.

most senior insiders are actually involved in the wage negotiation process. These senior insiders use their market power to maximize just their own surplus, rather than the surplus of other workers as well. We assume that they seek to drive their nominal wage as high as possible, subject to the constraint that none of them is fired. This constraint, which we call the "relative profitabiliy constraint", specifies that the nominal wage must not exceed the sum of the outsiders' reservation wage (R) and the labor turnover cost (F):

$$W \leq R + F, \tag{14}$$

for otherwise the firm would have an incentive to replace its insiders by outsiders. Since the firm retains all its senior insiders, $\lambda \cdot m$, the surplus of the senior insiders is

$$\omega = (W - w_0 \cdot P_a) \cdot \lambda \cdot m, \tag{13b}$$

where λ and m are exogenously given for each nominal wage negotiation and thus do not affect the outcome of this negotiation.

Wage Determination

The bargaining problem of the firm and its insiders is

$$\max_{W} \omega^a \cdot \phi^{1-a}, \tag{15}$$

subject to $W \leq R + F$, where ω is the insiders' objective in the negotiations (equation 13b), ϕ is the firm's objective (equation 13a), and "a" is a constant $(0 < a \leq 1)$ that represents the bargaining strength of the insiders relative to that of the firm.

The first-order condition for an interior solution to the Nash bargaining problem (15) is

$$[(\partial \omega / \partial W) \cdot (W^*/\omega)] = -[(1-a)/a] \cdot [(\partial \phi / \partial W) \cdot (W^*/\phi)], \tag{16}$$

where W^* is the nominal wage that emerges from the negotiation process. This condition simply states that the relative elasticities of the insiders' and firm's objectives with respect to the wage must be equal to their relative bargaining strengths. Substituting the firm's objective $(13a)$ and the workers' objective $(13b)$ into (16), we obtain

$$(1 + \tau) \cdot [(W^*/P) - w_0 \cdot (P_a/P)] = [a/(1-a)] \cdot \left[\frac{(\pi/P)}{n} \right]. \tag{17a}$$

which states that the difference between real labor remuneration (inclusive of payroll taxes) under agreement and disagreement is proportional to the real profit per employee (with the factor of proportionality being the ratio of the bargaining strengths).

We may now derive the microeconomic "wage setting function", which describes the negotiated wage at any given level of employment by the firm. In the Hiring and Retention Scenarios, the firm's real profit per employee is

$$(\pi/P)/n = B \cdot n^{\alpha-1} - (W/P) \cdot (1 + \tau). \tag{17b}$$

Substituting equation (17b) into (17a), we obtain the following expression for the real product wage that is the outcome of the firm's price setting and the nominal wage negotiations between the firm and its insiders under the Hiring and Retention Scenarios:

$$(W^*/P) = a \cdot \{[B/(1+\tau)] \cdot n^{-(1-\alpha)}\} + (1-a) \cdot \{w_0 \cdot (P_a/P)\}. \tag{18a}$$

Analogously, in the Firing Scenario the firm's real profit per employee is

$$(\pi/P)/n = B \cdot n^{\alpha-1} - [(W/P) \cdot (1+\tau) + (F \cdot (m-n))/n]. \tag{17c}$$

Substituting (17c) into (17a), we find the following expression for the real product wage under the Firing Scenario:

$$(W^*/P) = a \cdot [1/(1+\tau)] \cdot [B \cdot n^{-(1-\alpha)} - (F \cdot (m-n))/n] + (1-a) \cdot w_0 \cdot (P_a/P). \tag{18b}$$

Observe that, in all three scenarios, the above real product wage (for any given level of employment by the firm) is greater, the larger the insiders' bargaining strength (a), the real threat-point wage (w_0), the productivity coefficient B, and the lower the payroll tax rate (τ). For the Firing Scenario, the above real wage is positively related to the magnitude of the firing cost per worker. Equations (18a) and (18b) comprise the microeconomic wage setting function.

Our model of real wage and employment determination at the microeconomic level of the firm is given by equations (9)–(12a) and (18a)–(18b). We now proceed to incorporate this analysis into a simple model of the aggregate labor market.

IV. The Aggregate Labor Market

Recalling that there are a fixed number (M) of identical firms in the economy, the reduced form relation between aggregate labor demand (N^D) and the real wage (W/P) — which we call the "aggregate labor demand relation" — is

$$N^D = M \cdot \left[\frac{W \cdot (1 + \tau)}{P \cdot a \cdot (1 - e) \cdot B} \right]^{-1/(1-\alpha)} \qquad \text{in the Hiring Scenario,} \tag{19a}$$

$$N^D = M \cdot m \qquad\qquad \text{in the Retention Scenario, and} \qquad (19b)$$

$$N^D = M \cdot \left[\frac{W \cdot (1 + \tau) + F}{P \cdot \alpha \cdot (1 - e) \cdot B} \right]^{-1/(1-\alpha)} \quad \text{in the Firing Scenario.} \qquad (19c)$$

(by equations (9), (11), and (12)). This aggregate labor demand relation is pictured in Fig. 2.

The labor supply function is assumed to be upward sloping,[13] i.e., the reservation wage (w_r) is positively related to the level of employment. This supply curve is denoted by N^S in Figure 2.

Now turn to the wage setting function for the aggregate labor market. As the microeconomic wage setting function, equations (18a) and (18b), shows, the negotiated wage (W^*/P) depends positively on the threat-point wage, w_0. We now assume that the threat-point wage is positively related to the employment rate:[14]

$$w_0 = w_0(N), \qquad w_0' > 0. \qquad (20)$$

This assumption seems plausible: the greater the employment rate, the greater the probability of finding a new job (and thus the greater the reservation wage), hence the greater the insiders' chances of finding temporary employment or receiving support from family and friends during a breakdown in wage negotiations, and thus the greater the threat-point remuneration w_0.

The relation between the threat-point wage and the aggregate level of employment illustrates how labor market conditions external to the firm may influence the wage setting process when insiders have market power. In short, our description of the labor market is based on an "insider–outsider" model, not merely an "insider" model.

For simplicity, suppose that each firm hires a representative sample of the labor force, so that all firms face the same exogenous real threat-point labor remuneration, w_0. Figures 2a and 2b depict the Hiring and Retention Scenarios, respectively. Here, the aggregate wage setting

---

[13] This assumption is not one of substance. Our analysis of unemployment is equally compatible with a downward-sloping aggregate labor supply curve. What is crucial to our policy results, in terms of Figures 2, is that employment be determined by the intersection of the wage setting curve and the aggregate labor demand relation. This is the case whenever the above intersection occurs to the left of the full-employment point (given by the intersection between the aggregate labor demand relation and the aggregate labor supply curve), so that there is unemployment.

[14] By implication, the wage setting function may be upward sloping in real wage – employment space, as shown in Figures 2. This upward slope is not essential to our analysis which merely requires that the slope of the wage setting function be flatter than that of the aggregate labor demand relation.

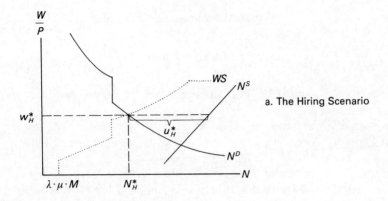

a. The Hiring Scenario

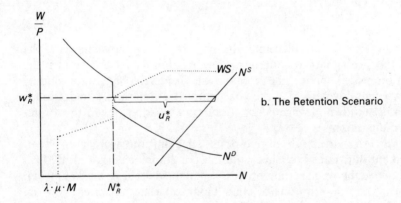

b. The Retention Scenario

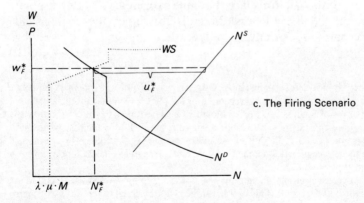

c. The Firing Scenario

Fig. 2.

function (represented by the *WS* curve in the figures) is

$$(W^*/P) = a \cdot [B/(1 + \tau)] \cdot [N/M]^{-(1-\alpha)} + (1 - a) \cdot w_0(N) \cdot (P_a/P), \qquad (21a)$$

by equations (18a) and (20), and recalling that $n \cdot M = N$.

In the Hiring Scenario, this function crosses the bottom segment of the aggregate labor demand relation (19a), so that the equilibrium real wage is w_H^* and equilibrium employment level is N_H^*. The equilibrium level of unemployment[15] (u_H^*) is the difference between the aggregate labor $N^s(w_H^*)$ and the equilibrium employment level: $u_H^* = N_s(w_H^*) - N_H^*$.

In the Retention Scenario (portrayed in Figure 2b), the aggregate wage setting function crosses the vertical segment of the aggregate labor demand curve. The equilibrium real wage, employment, and unemployment levels are denoted by w_R^*, N_R^*, and u_R^*, respectively.

Finally, in the Firing Scenario the aggregate wage setting function is

$$(W^*/P) = a \cdot [1/(1 + \tau)] \cdot \{B \cdot (N/M)^{-(1-\alpha)} - F \cdot [(m \cdot N/M) - 1]\}$$
$$+ (1 - a) \cdot w_0(N) \cdot (P_a/P) \qquad (21b)$$

by equations (18b) and (20). In Figure 2c the *WS* curve crosses the top segment of the aggregate labor demand relation (N^d). The equilibrium levels of the real wage, employment, and unemployment are denoted by w_F^*, N_F^*, and u_F^*, respectively.

By the second-order conditions for an interior optimum of the Nash bargain over the wage, $[d(W/P)/dN]|_{WS} > [d(W/P)/dN]|_{N^D}$, i.e., the slope of the wage setting function must be greater than the corresponding slope of the aggregate labor demand function. In fact, for the policy analysis which follows, we assume that the wage setting function is upward sloping.

By equations (18)–(21), it is easy to show how the level of unemployment depends on the insiders' bargaining power (given by the parameter "a"). The lower their bargaining power, the lower the wage setting function, by (18) and (19), and consequently the greater the equilibrium level of employment.[16]

Observe that, in contrast to some highly simplified insider–outsider models, our model does *not* imply that a positive quit rate among insiders necessarily leads to a progressive decline of firms' insider work forces with the passage of time. This is so because insiders do not set their wages

---

[15] Provided that the equilibrium real wage, w_H^*, exceeds the reservation wage, R — as illustrated in Figure 2 — this unemployment is involuntary in the sense that the unemployed workers are without jobs even though they would be willing to work for less than the negotiated wage.
[16] In the extreme case where insiders have no bargaining power at all ($a = 0$), the negotiated real product wage is equal to the real threat-point wage: $(W^*/P) = w_0 \cdot (P_a/P)$.

162   *A. Lindbeck and D. Snower*

unilaterally, but rather participate in wage negotiations with firms, which exert downward pressure on wages.[17]

In the context of the aggregate labor market described above, we now inquire how government policies can affect labor market activity.

V. Supply-side Policies

It is convenient to group the supply-side policies under the following three headings:

   (i) policies designed to make all workers — insiders, entrants, and outsiders alike — more profitable to the firms, to be called "employment-promoting policies",
  (ii) policies which reduce the insiders' market power, which we call "power-reducing policies", and
 (iii) policies designed to enfranchise outsiders in the process of wage negotiations, to be called "enfranchising policies".

Although these policies may ultimately have similar influences on some labor activities,[18] their proximate effects are different. The immediate impact of the employment-promoting policies is to raise the productivity or reduce the labor costs associated with all workers. (In doing so, outsiders may become "enfranchised", but that is only a by-product of these policies.) The power-reducing policies' proximate effect is to give the insiders less economic rent to exploit — though indirectly the employment of outsiders may indeed be stimulated. The immediate impact of the enfranchising policies is to make outsiders more profitable to the firms and thereby give more workers insider status. (In the process, the market power of the previous incumbents may — but need not — fall.)

Before describing the effects of each of these policies on employment and the real wage, a few general — and obvious — remarks about policy effectiveness will help set the scene. First, as noted, the analysis above indicates that whenever a firm faces labor turnover costs even under

---

[17] Of course, other reasons are conceivable as well. Insiders may have an incentive to set wages sufficiently low to permit the entry of new employees when there are increasing returns to labor, when insiders and entrants are engaged in complementary production activities, or when insiders cannot predict the precise position of the labor demand curve when wages are set; see Begg (1988), Blanchard and Summers (1986) and Lindbeck and Snower (1987a). Furthermore, Lindbeck and Snower (1984, 1987a, 1988) argue that the insiders' wage cannot rise above the sum of the entrants' wage and the relevant labor turnover costs, for otherwise the firm would have an incentive to replace insiders by entrants (i.e., in the context of our analysis, constraint (14) may be binding).
[18] For example, they may all be capable of stimulating employment, and policies (ii) and (iii) both diminish the inequality of market power between insiders and outsiders.

agreement in the wage bargain (e.g. the firing cost in our model), then its labor demand relation will contain a vertical segment. The position of this vertical segment depends solely on the magnitude of the firm's insider workforce, which is historically given and cannot be influenced by current policy measures. By implication, employment is not responsive to policy within a particular wage corridor (whose size is equal to the magnitude of the above labor turnover costs). It is only possible for policy measures to be effective outside this corridor. By implication, the ability of these measures to stimulate employment in an economy with heterogeneous firms would depend on the number of firms operating under the Retention Scenario relative to the number operating under the Hiring and Firing Scenarios.

Second, since a firm faces a different set of costs when it hires entrants than when it fires insiders, it may be expected to respond differently to economic policies under the Hiring and Firing Scenarios. This difference arises not only because the firm's labor demand relation is different under these two scenarios, but also because the firm — being a party to the wage negotiations — exerts a different influence on wage determination when it is hiring than when it is firing.

Third, it is important to emphasize that the distinctive "insider–outsider" features of our analysis are incorporated mainly in the wage setting function. Clearly, the labor supply function is not affected by the exercise of insider power. The labor demand relation differs from the conventional one under imperfect competition in that it explicitly takes into account the labor turnover costs facing the firm (here the marginal revenue product of labor *net of turnover costs under wage agreement* is set equal the nominal wage). However, it is the wage setting function that represents the exercise of insider power in wage bargaining. In the absence of such power, the wage setting function would coincide with the labor supply function, and thus the real wage would fall to its market-clearing level (at the intersection of the labor supply function N^S and the aggregate labor demand relation N^D in Figure 2), and unemployment would disappear.

Thus, to gain an intuitive understanding of how the excercise of insider power influences the effectiveness of government policies, it is useful to compare our policy results with the corresponding ones under market-clearing conditions (as given by the intersection of the labor demand relation and the labor supply curve). Since the salient features of our wage bargaining model are embodied in the position rather than the slope of the wage setting function, it is desirable to abstract from the way in which this slope influences the impact of government policies. We do so by considering only marginal policy changes and assuming that the slope of the labor supply curve at the market-clearing point is equal to the slope of the wage setting function at the insider–outsider equilibrium. In this context, policies which merely shift the aggregate labor demand relation have the same qualitative effects on the real wage and employment in both the insider–outsider and the market-clearing frameworks. By contrast, policies which shift the wage setting function but not the labor supply curve have different qualitative effects in the two frameworks. Here the distinctive insider–outsider features of our analysis have a special role to play in determining the effectiveness of economic policy.

Finally, as we have seen in the preceding section, the aggregate wage-setting curve may be upward or downward sloping, but its slope is always of greater magnitude than that of the aggregate labor demand curve; whereas the slope of the aggregate labor demand curve is unambiguously negative. Thus, for both the Hiring and the Firing Scenarios, policies whose influence is attributable to the distinctive insider–outsider features of our analysis — in the sense that they lead to a shift of the aggregate wage setting function — invariably move the real wage and employment in opposite directions. In particular, an upward shift of the wage setting curve leads to a rise in the real wage and a fall in employment, whereas a downward shift of this curve has the opposite effects.

On the other hand, policies whose effectiveness does not depend on insider power — those which shift the labor demand curve but leave the wage setting curve unchanged — have an ambiguous effect on the real wage, since the slope of the wage setting function is ambiguous. This ambiguity is of no particular concern to us here, since only the policies which operate through insider–outsider channels are the focus of attention in this paper. To fix ideas in the policy analysis below, we will assume that the wage setting function is upward sloping (so that an upward shift of the labor demand curve leads to a rise in the real wage).[19]

Employment-Promoting Policies

In the context of the model above, we examine the effects of three employment-promoting policies: government investment in industrial infrastructure, reductions in payroll taxes (falling proportionately on all employees), and measures to open the economy to foreign competition.[20]

---

[19] Note that, even in the absence of the assumption that the wage setting curve is upward sloping, the employment effects of these policies is unambiguous, since the slope of the wage setting curve is of greater magnitude than that of the labor demand curve. (Thus an upward shift of the labor demand curve invariably leads to a rise in employment, and obversely for a downward shift.)

[20] Since our model is not one of economy-wide general equilibrium, we will ignore how these various policies are financed.

Government infrastructure investment give rise to an increased availability of particular government goods and services to the private production sector, such as roads, railways, harbors, sewage systems, and police services. Let us assume that, in response, the marginal product of all workers rises proportionately. We portray this by a rise in the shift parameter B of the firms' production functions in equation (4).

As a result both the aggregate wage setting curve and the aggregate labor demand curve shift upwards. Consequently the real wage rises,[21] whereas the change in employment is ambiguous.

Note that government infrastructure investment has a more powerful impact on real wages and a weaker impact on employment in our insider–outsider context than under the analogous market-clearing conditions. The reason is that this policy raises the wage setting curve in our model, whereas it leaves the labor supply curve unchanged.

A fall in the payroll tax rate may be portrayed by a fall in the parameter τ. As a result, the aggregate labor demand relation shifts upwards in all three scenarios, since the policy reduces the marginal cost of labor. The wage setting function shifts upwards as well in these scenarios, since the policy raises the firm's profit surplus. By implication, a fall in the payroll tax rate raises the real wage, but the change in aggregate employment is ambiguous.

Thus we can see that a fall in the payroll tax rate provides a stronger stimulus to the real wage and a weaker stimulus to employment under the insider–outsider conditions above than under market-clearing conditions. When the labor market clears, the aggregate labor demand relations shifts upwards along an unchanged labor supply curve, and thus the employment level and the real wage both rise. By contrast, under insider–outsider conditions we have seen that the wage setting function shifts upwards as well as the aggregate labor demand relation, and the rise in the wage setting function boosts the wage and dampens employment.

Measures to open the economy to foreign competition — such as reductions in tariffs and in administrative restrictions on import flows — generally may be expected to raise the price elasticity of product demand. Thus, we depict this policy by a rise in η. As result, the index of monopoly power in the product market, e defined in equation (8), falls.

This decrease in firms' market power leaves the wage setting function unchanged in all three scenarios. However, the policy does shift the aggregate labor demand function upwards (in Figure 2), since the fall in

---

[21] In all our policy exercises we assume that the ratio of consumer to producer prices remains unchanged, and thus — in the absence of a change in the payroll tax — the consumption wage and the production wage in our model always move in the same direction.

monopoly power stimulates employment by raising the marginal value product of labor, as shown in equation (7). Consequently, there is a rise in employment and the real wage. Thus policy measures to open the economy to foreign competition have the same qualitative effects in our insider–outsider framework as in the corresponding market-clearing framework.

Power-Reducing Policies

There is a wide variety of policies which serve to reduce the market power of insiders, ranging from legal restrictions on strikes and picketing to relaxing job-security legislation (e.g. laws to reduce severance pay or to simplify firing procedures). In the context of our model, these policies may be portrayed in terms of (i) a fall in the "a", measuring the relative bargaining strength of the insiders, and (ii) a fall in the real firing cost per insider, $\bar{f}$.

A fall in "a" means that insiders are able to capture a smaller share of the total available economic rent from employment. Thus the wage setting function shifts downwards (*ceteris paribus*) in all three scenarios. The aggregate labor demand relation remains unaffected. Consequently, there is a rise in aggregate employment and a fall in the real wage under the Hiring and Firing Scenarios.[22]

A fall in the real firing cost $\bar{f}$ leads to a downward shift of the segment of the aggregate labor demand relation which pertains to the Firing Scenario (*ceteris paribus*). The reason is that, in this scenario, the real wage is equal to the sum of the real marginal value product of the initial insider workforce and the real firing cost per insider, $\bar{f}$. In addition, the wage setting function in the Firing Scenario shifts downwards (for, the smaller the real firing cost, the greater the firm's profit surplus). By implication, the real wage falls in this scenario, but the change in employment is ambiguous. By contrast, the policy has no effect on the real wage and the level of employment in the Hiring and Retention Scenarios.[23]

It is important to note, however, that the power-reducing policies are not Pareto improving: they generally lead to the employment of outsiders at the expense of reducing the insiders' labor income. Consequently, the implementation of these policies is likely to encounter all the various difficulties, political and social, that are commonly associated with the loss

---

[22] Under the Retention Scenario, clearly, there is only a fall in the real wage.

[23] This last result is an artifact of the static setting of our model. Whenever firms face the possibility that currently hired employees may have to be fired in the future (say, on account of adverse swings in product demand), a fall in firing costs tends to have the same effect on wages and employment as it does in the Firing Scenario; see, for example, Lindbeck and Snower (1989b).

of market power by privileged interest groups and with conflicts over the distribution of income.

This could be a serious obstacle to implementing these policies. Since the insiders stand to lose, they may be expected to resist these policies by engaging in more rent-creating activities — ranging from harassment of workers who seek to gain jobs through underbidding, to the withdrawal of cooperation from such workers in the process to production, to staging strikes and work-to-rule actions, to litigation over firing procedures. In particular, power-reducing policies may give the insiders incentives to engage in rent-seeking activities by making these activities more effective by generating an income effect. For reasons lying outside our particular analytical framework, an expansion of such activities may raise insiders' bargaining strength (a) or the real firing cost $(\bar{f})$, so as to shift the wage setting function upwards.

In short, although policies that reduce the legal protection associated with insiders' jobs may have direct effects that stimulate employment, they may also have indirect effects on rent-creating activities that pull in the opposite direction. This deficiency is not restricted just to power-reducing policies. It is shared by any policy that reduces the insiders' labor income. For example, we have argued that the employment-promoting policy of opening the economy to foreign competition may also reduce the wages received by the insiders and thus are equally prone to stimulate insiders' rent-creating activities.

Enfranchising Policies

The primary purpose of the enfranchising policies is to give the outsiders a better chance of gaining employment and thereby become "enfranchised" in the wage negotiation process. These policies can take many forms. We consider a few prominent examples.

The labor market effects of *vocational training programs* — provided or subsidized by the government — may be usefully compared with those of government infrastructure investment (discussed above). Whereas the infrastructure investment may be expected to raise both the productivity of the current employees and the potential productivity of the outsiders, the vocational training programs are aimed expressly at the latter. Obviously, the impact of such programs depends on the degree to which workers' skills are general, rather than firm specific. The greater the relative importance of general skills, the more outsiders may be enfranchized through the programs.

A formal analysis of these programs requires us to consider a broader class of production functions than that contained in our simple model above — in particular, functions in which the productivities of insiders and entrants can vary independently of one another. For production functions in which output depends on the sum of insiders' and entrants labor in efficiency units, it is straightforward to show — although, for brevity, we do not do so here — that vocational training programs which raise the entrants' marginal product have the same qualitative effects on the real wage and employment as government infrastructure investment that raises the marginal product of labor.

Profit-sharing schemes, whereby employees receive part of their remuneration as a share of profits, are also straightforward to analyze in the context of the model above. In particular, let us assume that each employee's pay is the sum of (i) a time-rate "base" wage and (ii) a "profit-sharing component" which is the product of the firm's profit and a constant profit-sharing coefficient. Furthermore we assume that the profit-sharing coefficient is predetermined in the wage-employment determination process and may be influenced, directly or indirectly, by the government, while the base wage is the outcome of negotiations between each firm and its insiders (along the lines outlined above). Then it can be shown (although, once again, we do not do so here) that the greater the profit-sharing coefficient, the lower the negotiated base wage and the greater the level of employment. In other words, the greater the profit-sharing component of the employees' pay, the lower the marginal cost of labor (given by the base wage), and the greater the number of outsiders that firms are induced to hire. Once these outsiders become insiders, they gain power in future wage negotiations and use this power to retain their jobs by agreeing to comparatively low base wages. In this sense, our analysis supports Weitzman's (1987) contention that profit-sharing schemes promote employment and reduce unemployment.

These schemes may, however, encounter the same problems as the power-reducing policies: unless the profit-sharing component of labor remuneration is sufficiently large, the schemes will not be Pareto-improving and consequently they may promote rent-creating activity by the insiders. Yet that is not all. If the profit-sharing component is large enough to avoid this outcome, the scheme may cease to be profitable to the firms. Of course, firms may attempt to avoid this possibility through wage contracts which give the new entrants a permanently lower profit-sharing component than the current insiders. However, such two-tier wage systems may be unacceptable to the current insiders since they tend to be time inconsistent: the firms will generally have an incentive to replace the senior workers by junior workers once the latter have acquired the requisite skills.

Furthermore, profit-sharing schemes are costly to implement. They may give workers the incentive to bear the costs of monitoring managers' profit accounting practices. Managers, for their part, may well wish to avoid a remuneration system that subjects them such monitoring. In addition, the profit-sharing schemes impose risk on employees, since the receipt of profit is uncertain and insurance against profit fluctuations is unavailable. To compensate workers for the cost of such risk, firms may have to hand over a substantial share of their profit. All these problems, however, should not obscure the genuine possibility that the above-mentioned benefits of these schemes may in fact outweigh all the relevant costs.

Government policies to reduce barriers to the entry of new firms may be an effective way to enfranchise outsiders, because new firms generally start out without insiders and therefore may be in a good position to create new jobs. These policies may consist of the dismantling of government regulations concerning the creation of new firms, increasing competition among financial institutions with a view to reducing credit restrictions on new firms, changing the tax system (e.g. profit, income, capital gain, and wealth taxes) to put new firms at less of a disadvantage *vis-à-vis* established firms, and instituting measures to reduce the occupational, industrial, and geographic coverage of union wage agreements.

These policies have two reinforcing effects on employment in the context of our model: (a) the direct effect of a rise in the number of firms in the economy is to shift the aggregate labor demand relation rightwards, thereby generating more employment at any real wage and (b) an indirect effect may reduce firms' market power in the product market (represented by the coefficient e), thereby shifting the aggregate labor demand curve even further to the right under the Hiring and Firing Scenarios and shifting the wage-setting function downwards.

Finally, *job sharing schemes* deserve mention as an enfranchising policy. The aim of these schemes is to give insider status to a larger number of workers. These workers may then be expected to negotiate their future wages with a view to protecting their job security. In other words, the workers who gain employment through these schemes may have an incentive to keep wages sufficiently low to maintain that employment. Thus, whereas the initial institution of job sharing may require legislative coercion, this arrangement may be perpetuated by decentralized wage bargaining. For brevity, we will not analyze these schemes formally here. Suffice it to say that job sharing schemes have a chance of being effective only if they do not substantially increase firms' hourly labor costs and only if they do not induce incumbents to engage in significant rent-creating activity.

In sum, supply-side policies may stimulate employment by making all workers more productive, by reducing the market power of insiders, and by enfranchising the outsiders. However, some of these policies reduce the labor income of the current insiders and may therefore induce insider resistance in the form of rent-creating activities, which limit the overall employment gains. This specific problem is generally not shared by demand-side policies which improve the employment prospects of the outsiders without making the current insiders worse off. However, the demand-side policies — as noted below — are associated with other difficulties.

VI. Demand-side Policies

Demand management policies which are designed to influence employment may be divided into two broad groups: (i) variations in government employment and (ii) government policies that affect aggregate spending in the product maket.

The first type of policy is of substantial practical importance, but it does not need much attention here, since its effects are quite straightforward in the context of our model. A rise in government employment shifts the aggregate labor demand relation outwards, and thereby leads to a rise in employment and the real wage. Note that this policy does not affect the position of the wage setting curve and thus the impact on the real wage and employment are the same under market-clearing and insider–outsider conditions.

The second type of policy is concerned exclusively with the transmission of policy impulses from the product to the labor market. In the Keynesian literature, this transmission depends on the assumption of either sluggish nominal wages, or sluggish prices, or both.

We do not dispute that the Keynesian channels of policy transmission from the product to the labor market may operate under the various circumstances under which wages and prices may be expected to be sluggish (e.g. infrequent price changes or long-term wage contracting). Yet it is nevertheless worth asking if there are transmission mechanisms whereby variations in aggregate product demand affect employment even when wages and prices are set flexibly under conditions of imperfect competition. The model above is designed to handle this question, since it contains imperfectly competitive price and wage setters and since prices and wages are assumed to respond immediately to government policies.

The demand management policies in the product market may be represented quite generally by the parameter A in the aggregate product demand function (1). (The parameter may, for example, stand for government expenditures, transfers, or taxes.) To fix ideas, suppose that this parameter rises, while the market power parameter e, the payroll tax rate τ, and the parameters of the production function (B and α) remain unchanged. Clearly, a rise in parameter A can influence the equilibrium real wage and employment level in our model only if it shifts either the aggregate labor demand function or the wage setting function, or both.

To see whether the rise in A shifts the labor demand function (in real wage — employment space), we inquire whether it affects the firm's profit-maximizing level of employment *at any given real wage*. In other words, we ask whether a rise in A alters the profit-maximizing employment level when the nominal wage (W, which is exogenous to the firm's decision making) rises proportionately to the price level (P, which is set by the firm). For this purpose, let us return to the firm's marginal conditions, in equations (7) and (10), according to which the profit-maximizing employment level brings the marginal revenue product of labor (plus the firing cost, in the Firing Scenario) into equality with the nominal wage (inclusive of the payroll tax). In this context, it is clear that an increase in A raises the demand price P (at any given level of output) and thereby raises the marginal revenue product of labor. If the nominal wage (W) rises proportionately to P, then the marginal cost of labor rises proportionately to the marginal revenue product of labor (as equations (7) and (10) show). By implication, the aggregate labor demand relation is not affected by the rise in A, provided that e, τ, B, and α all remain unchanged. This can be seen at a glance by observing that the parameter A does not appear in the aggregate labor demand relation, as given by (19a)–(19c).

Nor does the parameter A appear in the wage setting functions (18a) and (18b). In other words, demand management policies which shift the parameter A — without affecting the relative bargaining strength of the insiders *vis-à-vis* their firm (a), the threat-point wage (w_0), and the production function parameters (B and α) — have no effect on the wage setting function in real wage-employment space. The reason is that a proportional change in P and W leads to a proportional change in the bargaining objectives of the firms and their insiders and no change in the relative profitability constraint. Thus it leaves the real wage that emerges from the bargaining process is unchanged as well.

We may conclude that a demand-side policy whose only impact effect is to change the demand parameter A — without simultaneously affecting the price elasticity of product demand, the number of firms in the economy, the marginal product of labor, the relative bargaining strength of the insiders *vis-à-vis* their firms, and the threat-point wage — has no effect on employment and the real wage in the context of our model.

This negative conclusion also have a positive side, namely, that demand management policies in the product market *can* influence the labor market in various ways, the following of which strike us as particularly important:

(i) *Entry of firms*: If a rise in government product demand creates incentives for the entry of new firms, then the aggregate labor demand relation shifts upwards (as we have discussed in connection with government policies to reduce barriers to the entry of new firms). If new, entering firms compete with the old ones in the product market, each firm's monopoly power in that market may fall, thereby leading to a further rightward shift of the labor demand relation. Moreover, a rise in the number of firms leads to an upward shift of the wage setting function.[24] Consequently, the real wage rises by more than it does under market-clearing conditions, whereas employment rises by less — and possibly even falls.

To see how a rise in product demand could lead to the entry of new firms, suppose that the nominal wage does not respond promptly to the policy whereas prices do (or, more generally, that nominal wages are more sluggish than prices). Then the policy leads to a rise in the product price and a fall in the real wage, and thereby raises the profit to be earned by each firm. This encourages the entry of new firms. Then, even if the real wage returns to its initial level, the aggregate demand for labor remains above its initial level (because the number of firms, M, has increased and their market power, e, has fallen). For this reason the aggregate labor demand relation shifts to the right.[25] As noted above, however, the resulting stimulus to employment is at least partially offset by the upward shift of the wage setting curve.

(ii) *The marginal product of labor, B*: As we have seen, a rise in the shift parameter, B, of the production function shifts both the wage setting curve and the aggregate labor demand curve upwards, by equations (20a–c). Consequently a demand-management policy operating through this channel of transmission has a stronger effect on the real wage and a weaker effect on employment under insider–outsider conditions than under market-clearing conditions.

There are two main ways in which expansionary demand management policy could raise the marginal product of labor. First (as noted in Section V), it could do so directly, through government spending that increases the economy's industrial infrastructure. Second, the policy could have an indirect effect on the marginal product of labor by stimulating the use of factors which a complementary to labor (or discouraging the use of factors which are substitutes for labor).

The latter channel may have a particularly important practical role to play when the policy raises firms' rates of capital utilization under conditions of excess capital capacity. This is likely to happen when the economy is recovering from a recession and workers are recalled to man

---

[24] For common specifications of the product demand function, a rise in the number of firms is associated with a fall in employment (n) by the representative firm. By the microeconomic wage setting functions (18a) and (18b) a fall in the firm's employment level is associated with a rise in the real wage.

[25] For a detailed analysis of this transition mechanisms, see Lindbeck and Snower (1987b).

vacant machines and bring established assembly lines back into operation. The capital equipment that comes into use under these circumstances is generally complementary to labor. Once the capital utilization rate is sufficiently high, firms may have an incentive to engage in net investment. The resulting rise in the capital stock may further raise the marginal product of labor. (A formal analysis of this policy effect is given in Lindbeck and Snower (1987b) and lies beyond the scope of our model.)

Our discussion above suggests three potentially important channels of transmission, each of which has noteworthy policy implications and each of which has a weaker impact on employment under insider–outsider conditions than under market-clearing conditions:

— There is a *short-run* channel, whereby changes in product demand affect the level of capital utilization which, in turn, affects the marginal product of labor. This channel is open whenever excess capital capacity exists; it does not depend on the level of unemployment. By implication, an increase in government product demand may lead to an increase in employment at constant or rising real wages when there is excess capital capacity, but not once full capacity utilization has been reached.

— In the *medium run*, there is a channel involving the entry (and exit) of firms). In order for this channel to be operative, it is important that the demand-side policy be supported by the relevant supply-side policy, viz. the removal of barriers to the entry of firms. There is also a medium-run channel whereby a rise in product demand stimulates net investment, and this channel is operative only when the rate of capital utilization is sufficiently high.

— The *long-run* channel involves the buildup or rundown of industrial infrastructure. Here, the policy operates simultaneously on the demand side (via changes in government spending) and the supply side (via changes in the economy's production possibility frontier). Our analysis implies that demand-side policies with such supply-side effects may have a much larger impact on employment than policies (such as changes in transfer payments or government consumption) which do not affect labor productivity.

VII. Concluding Remarks

It is important to emphasize that our results have been derived within a static context. Although a dynamic analysis lies beyond the scope of this paper, the dynamic effects of the policies above may be just as important as the static ones. The main source of dynamics implicit in our model is that the initial insider workforce depends on past employment: the greater the number of entrants hired in the past, the greater the number of insiders

174 A. Lindbeck and D. Snower

firms inherit at present. This means that a supply- or demand-side policy which leads to a rise in current employment will raise the future insider workforce. Thus the aggregate labor demand relation shifts rightwards through time, thereby generating a rise in future employment.

Elsewhere, it has been shown that these persistent effects of policies may be "symmetric" and/or "asymmetric". Under symmetric persistence, the future employment rise from a current expansionary policy is just as large as the future employment fall from a contractionary policy of equal magnitude; whereas under asymmetric persistence, contractionary policies have a stronger effect on future employment than expansionary policies do; see, for example, Lindbeck and Snower (1987a, 1989a). In countries with high unemployment and significant symmetric persistence, a particularly strong case could be made for expansionary demand-side policies and employment-promoting supply-side policies, since current policy shocks — even if they are transient — will raise employment in the future. Yet in countries with significant asymmetric persistence, such policies may not be very effective: whereas contractionary policies may reduce employment, the expansionary ones may do little to stimulate it. Under these circumstances, the power-reducing and enfranchising supply-side policies may be called for, in order to create greater equality of opportunity in the labor market and thereby make the other policies above effective. The study of these policy issues appears to be a promising area for future research.

References

Begg, D.: Inside-out: Counterintuitive properties of a dynamic game in an insider–outsider framework. Mimeo, 1988.
Bentolila, S. & Bertola, G.: Firing costs and labor demand: How bad is Eurosclerosis? Mimeo, June 1988.
Bertola, G.: Job security, employment and wages. Mimeo, 1989.
Blanchard, O. & Summers, L.: Hysteresis and the European unemployment problem. *NBER Macroeconomics Annual*, Vol. 1, MIT Press, Cambridge, MA, 15–71, 1986.
Gottfries, N. & Horn, H.: Wage formation and the persistence of unemployment. *Economic Journal 97*, 877–84, 1987.
Lindbeck, A. & Snower, D. J.: Involuntary unemployment as an insider–outsider dilemma. Seminar Paper No. 282, Institute for International Economic Studies, University of Stockholm (1984). Revised version in W. Beckerman (ed.), *Wage Rigidity and Unemployment*, Duckworth and Johns Hopkins Press, 97–125, 1986.
Lindbeck, A. & Snower, D. J.: Union activity, unemployment persistence, and wage-employment ratchets. *European Economic Review, Proceedings 31*, 157–67, Feb. 1987a.
Lindbeck, A. & Snower, D. J.: Transmission mechanisms from the product to the labor market. Seminar Paper No. 403, Institute for International Economic Studies, University of Stockholm, 1987b.

Lindbeck, A. & Snower, D. J.: Cooperation, harassment, and involuntary unemployment. *American Economic Review* 78 (1), 167–88, March 1988.
Lindbeck, A. & Snower, D. J.: *The Insider–Outsider Theory of Employment and Unemployment*. MIT Press, Cambridge, MA, 1989a.
Lindbeck, A. & Snower, D. J.: Macroeconomic policy and insider power. *American Economic Review, Proceedings*, May 1989b.
Weitzman, M. L.: Steady state unemployment under profit sharing. *Economic Journal 97*, 385, 86–105, 1987.

Comment on A. Lindbeck and D. Snower, "Demand- and Supply-side Policies and Unemployment: Policy Implications of the Insider–Outsider Approach"

Bengt-Christer Ysander

University of Uppsala, Sweden

The specific purpose of this paper is to analyze the policy implications of the insider–outsider analysis of unemployment. In particular, the authors present new insights concerning the possibility of modifying the wage-bargaining process by way of public policy. The analysis hinges on their perception of how wage-setting is carried out.

The authors model wage-setting as the outcome of a Nash bargain. The objectives of the bargaining parties can be represented mainly as profit and wage, with the relative bargaining power taken as given. Interest is focused on the "excess wage" — compared to a market-clearing wage — which the negotiating employees can extract by establishing and exploiting the bargaining power due to their "insider" position. I have three comments or questions concerning this analysis.

(1) How much of the "excess wage" is necessarily due to the insiders' bargaining power? Even in the absence of any bargaining — when employers set the wage — insiders could expect a higher wage offer than outsiders would claim, for efficiency reasons and to keep down quitting with its concomitant costs of hiring and training. Before we know the extent to which the excess wage is due to rent-seeking activities underpinning the bargaining power of the insiders, it is impossible to judge the cost effectiveness of public policies aimed at diminishing this bargaining power and/or the scope for bargaining.

(2) It is undoubtedly true that the bargaining power of the insiders — and thereby their wage — can be increased by various rent-seeking activities or threats about such activities. The authors seem to view the possibility of organized rent-seeking behavior and the sheltered employment position of the negotiators as important props for the bargaining power of labor. Unfortunately, they do not explicitly discuss the determinants of this bargaining power, although various

hints are given implicitly in the discussion. A great deal of the policy conclusion, however, would seem to depend critically on an empirical question: how much of the scope and power of labor negotiations depends on job security legislation and organized rent-making behavior, and on labor-market conditions and the relative position of the industry in terms of profit and wage levels, respectively?

(3) The authors use the established definition of an insider as an incumbent worker. There is, however, another kind of "insider–outsider" division which cuts right across the established classification. According to this latter division, "insiders" are young, well-trained people at the height of their productive ability. "Outsiders" are older, less well-trained workers and the disabled. Together they make up a considerable share of the workforce and tend to dominate long-term unemployment, regardless of whether it is open or disguised as chronic illness and early retirement. The "insider–outsider" problem in this case is that neither employers nor labor unions may have enough incentive to substitute retraining and adjustment of work organization for higher wage, especially if the "outsiders" are considered to be a responsibility in the public domain. This latter "insider–outsider" problem could even become a more serious threat to full employment in the future than the one usually discussed. The two problems are intertwined, however. At any one time there are "outsiders" among the incumbent insiders who are not helped by any seniority rules in the long run and the threatened more than helped by rent-seeking activities. On the other hand, there are "insiders" among the nonincumbent outsiders who will gain in time by the full exploitation of employment rent. In order to solve both kinds of insider–outsider problems, we would need other policies than those discussed in the paper.

The Real Effects of Tax-based Incomes Policies

Richard Jackman and Richard Layard

London School of Economics, London, England

Abstract

We show how (in the context of a steady inflation rate) TIP reduces the NAIRU. This is so in a one-sector world of involuntary unemployment, based on efficiency wages or decentralized union bargaining. It also holds in a two-sector world in which there is a secondary market-clearing sector; here the proportional effect on unemployment will be larger than in a one-sector world, provided the labour supply elasticity to the secondary sector is sufficiently high. The most obvious problem with TIP is its effect on worker effort. We show, however, that even allowing for this, TIP will raise social welfare provided the elasticity of effort with respect to wages is sufficiently low.

I. Introduction and Summary

In most countries the citizens desire lower unemployment. They also understand that this raises a problem of inflation and are consequently sympathetic to incomes policy. However, most actual incomes policies have collapsed — often after a period of success.

There are three main reasons why mandatory attempts to impose wage norms fail. First, of necessity they involve interferences with (or even suspension of) free collective bargaining between individual employers and their workers. Neither individual firms nor local union leaders like this. Second, they rigidify the wage structure, which can lead to labour shortages that are undesirable and generate huge pressures on wages. Third, the policies are typically too crude to contain earnings drift, through regrading of staff, bonuses and other evasive tactics.

In order to deal with these problems, some economists, beginning with Wallich and Weintraub (1971), have suggested replacing the law (or social sanction) as the mechanism of enforcement by a financial inducement.[1]

---

*We are grateful to the Economic and Social Research Council and the Esmee Fairbairn Charitable Trust for financial support.

[1] For more recent discussions, including by ourselves, see Colander (1986).

This would (i) permit free wage bargaining, (ii) permit changes in relative pay and (iii) apply to actual earnings per worker (or worker-hour) rather than to notional wage scales.

In Britain, such a policy was in the election platforms of the Alliance parties in both the last two elections. The idea was also implemented in France in 1975, but not for long enough to permit an analysis of its effects. It is currently being debated in many countries.

In this paper we analyse the economic effects of such a scheme. We concern ourselves with the situation where the inflation rate is fairly steady, as it has been in most advanced countries for some years. The problem is to reduce unemployment without an increase in inflation.

Thus this is a long-run analysis in which inflation is determined by the growth of nominal demand, and the aim of the scheme is simply and solely to lower the NAIRU.[2] For simplicity we use a one-sector model of identical firms, in which the labour market fails to clear.[3] This failure may arise from one of two sources, which we model in turn. The first is efficiency wages set by employers, and the second is collective bargaining.

In the proposed scheme there is a norm (n) for the proportional growth of money earnings per worker (or worker-hour). If a firm pays more than the norm, it pays a tax equal to t times the excess wage-bill (and this tax can be negative). As a result, a 1 per cent increase in the earnings (W) received by the worker involves a $(1 + t)$ per cent increase in the firm's labour cost per worker (C). This reduces the firm's willingness to pay high wages in order to satisfy its workers.

As we shall see, the key requirement is not simply a wedge between labour cost and earnings but a wedge that increases faster than either. Thus a progressive tax on the *level* rather than the *growth* of wages will also bring about the desired effect. Since a tax on the wage level is simpler to explain, we begin (in Section II) with this case, using the efficiency wage model. We show that on the (slender) available evidence, the tax will have a significant effect on unemployment. We then show the equivalence of TIP, using the same model.

We next (in Section III) turn to the case where wages are set by collective bargaining. Again we find significant reductions in unemployment. However the evaluation of these effects becomes more complicated once we allow for possible adjustments in effort. When we analyse this case, we find that TIP will lead to lower effort, but using reasonable parameter estimates social welfare will improve.

---

[2] In cases where the aim is to alter the inflation rate, additional issues arise about the effect of TIP on the length of the lags in wage and price dynamics.

[3] In Section IV we add on a second market-clearing sector and show that our results still hold.

In Section IV we expand the model to include a secondary market-clearing sector of the labour market. The effects of TIP upon unemployment now vary labour supply, the unemployment effect of TIP is greater than in a one-sector model. With completely inelastic labour supply it is less.

Many people, while conceding the economic case for TIP, have dismissed the idea of the ground that it would be an administrative nightmare; cf. Dornbusch and Fischer (1987, p. 530). But as we have shown elsewhere, in Colander (1986, Ch. 9), it can in fact be relatively simple to administer. It should be judged on the economic case.

The tax should be based on average *hourly* wages at the level of the firm and would thus be free of one of the most serious objections to the taxation of weekly earnings. There would of course be *some* distortions, which we discuss in the Colander volume, but the main one is discussed in Section III below. Taking everything into account, our judgement is that the benefits outweigh the costs.

II. TIP under Efficiency Wages

Suppose each firm pays a net real tax per worker of $tW - S$, where W is real earnings per worker, t the tax rate and S a positive per worker subsidy. Hence labour cost is

$$C = W(1 + t) - S$$

and

$$\frac{dC}{dW} \cdot \frac{W}{C} = (1 + t)\frac{W}{C} > 1.$$

We assume that the scheme is self-financing, so that in the *ex post* general equilibrium $tW = S$ or $C = W$. Thus at general equilibrium values of W and C

$$\frac{dC}{dW} \cdot \frac{W}{C} = 1 + t.$$

To see how this affects equilibrium unemployment, we begin with the case where wages are set by firms, as efficiency wages. Efficiency (e) is increased by higher relative take-home pay $(W/\overline{W})$ and by unemployment (u):

$$e = e\left(\frac{W}{\overline{W}}, u\right) \qquad e_1, e_2 > 0.$$

This is a convenient general formulation which captures the implications of most efficiency wage models based on gift exchange, shirking, adverse selection, turnover, etc.; cf. Jackman *et al.* (1988).

The firm chooses W and N to maximize its profit:

$$\pi = R(eN) - CN$$

$$= R(eN) - \frac{C}{e} eN$$

where the revenue function $R(\ )$ includes the labour input as one variable and N is employment. The problem can be solved sequentially for W and N. W is chosen to minimize C/e — or maximize e/C. This requires

$$\frac{Ce_1}{W} - e\frac{dC}{dW} = 0$$

or

$$e_1 = e\frac{dC}{dW} \cdot \frac{W}{C}.$$

Hence in general equilibrium (with $W/\bar{W} = 1$)

$$e_1(1, u) = e(1, u)(1 + t).$$

While each firm sets wages taking the unemployment rate and wages in other firms as given, the equilibrium unemployment rate must be such that all firms choose to set the same wage. The equilibrium unemployment rate then determines employment in equilibrium (the labour force being taken as given) and employment together with labour productivity and product market competition determines the *ex post* equilibrium real wage.

Returning to the effects of the tax, as t is increased, unemployment changes according to

$$\frac{du}{dt} = \frac{e}{e_{12} - e_2(1 + t)}.$$

This expression is negative if the efficiency wage function is in terms of expected incomes:

$$e = e\left(\frac{W}{\bar{W}(1 - u)}\right) \qquad e'' < 0.$$

Or some readers may prefer a function in which it is assumed that $e_{12} < 0$

due to the reduced relevance of relative wages ($W/\bar{W}$) in the presence of high unemployment. Either way the tax reduces unemployment.

In fact, empirical estimates by Wadhwani and Wall (1988), which assume that wages are based on efficiency wage considerations, give

$$\frac{e_{12}}{e} = -\frac{0.08}{u} \; ; \; \frac{e_2}{e} = \frac{0.26}{u} \; .$$

This implies approximately (with $t \doteq 1/2$)

$$-\frac{du}{dt} = 2u.$$

Clearly the effect of the tax is the same whether it is levied on firms or workers, as can be seen by using instead the expression $W = C(1 - t) + S$. All that matters is the degree of progressivity.

However, wage level taxes of this kind may raise political problems, in a world of heterogeneous labour, and they may also distort work effect. Since the objective is to attack the leap-frogging of wages, it may be more politically acceptable to have a tax on wage-growth rather than on the level of wages. It may even be more effective, since human responses are affected in part by perceptions and not simply by what economic calculus would dictate, given fully accurate perceptions.

Tax-based Incomes Policy

This leads to the proposal for a tax-based incomes policy. The original proposal, by Wallich and Weintraub (1971), envisaged a variable rate of profits tax depending on whether a firm was sticking to the wage norm or not. However, in many countries, many firms avoid profits tax. Wallich and Weintraub's purpose in using the profits tax was to stop firms passing on the tax in prices. But the latter can easily be prevented at the aggregate level through a wage tax whose proceeds are distributed as a uniform per worker subsidy. This is the scheme we propose.

Thus the real tax per worker is $T(W - W_{-1}(1 + n)) - S$, where T is the tax rate, and n is the norm for the growth rate of real earnings. The tax is of course expressed in nominal terms, but from the firm's point of view the general rate of inflation is exogenous. Thus the real norm (n) is the nominal norm minus expected price inflation. (One obvious possibility is to fix the nominal norm equal to expected price inflation, in which case $n = 0$).

Let us analyse such a system. If differs from the simple tax on the wage level in that if a firm raises its wages now (and expects the tax to continue), its wage growth next year will, other things equal, be *lower*. Hence it will save on future taxes, even though it pays more taxes now. In fact the tax will only work because of discounting, and we shall discover that, if the tax rate on wage growth is T,

$$\frac{\mathrm{d}u}{\mathrm{d}T} = \frac{\mathrm{d}u}{\mathrm{d}t}(r-n)$$

where r is the real discount rate, n the real norm and $\mathrm{d}u/\mathrm{d}t$ is the effect of a wage *level* tax.

The firm wishes to maximize its present value. If $R(\ )$ is real revenue, the present value of real profit is

$$PV = \sum_j (1-r)^j \left\{ R_j \left[e\left(\frac{W_j}{\bar{W}_j}, u_j\right) N_j \right] - N_j[W_j(1+T) - TW_{j-1}(1+n) - S] \right\}$$

which is maximized with respect to W_j and N_j. Hence

$$\frac{\partial PV}{\partial W_j} = (1-r)^j \left(R'_j \frac{e_1}{\bar{W}_j} N_j - N_j(1+T) \right) + (1-r)^{j+1} N_{j+1} T(1+n) = 0.$$

$$\frac{\partial PV}{\partial N_j} = (1-r)^j [R'_j e - W_j(1+T) + TW_{j-1}(1+n) + S] = 0.$$

Thus a steady-state employment we have (in general equilibrium with $W/\bar{W} = 1$) a wage equation

$$R'e_1(1, u) = W(1 + (r-n)T)$$

and a price/employment equation

$$R'e(1, u) = W$$

(since $T(W_j - W_{j-1}(1+n)) = S$). Combining the wage and price equations gives

$$e_1(1, u) = e(1, u)(1 + (r-n)T).$$

Hence a wage growth tax at rate T has an effect $(r-n)$ times the effect of a wage level tax at the same rate. This makes it clear that a tax on wage growth must be very high (e.g. 100 per cent) and the nominal norm must be set at or below the rate of price inflation (thus making $n \leqslant 0$). Needless to say a given tax on wage growth would be much more effective if it were not expected to last. But it is not desirable to design such taxes on a temporary basis — it is precisely the on/off nature of previous incomes policies that we are trying to get away from.

III. TIP under Wage Bargaining

We now assume that wages are set by a bargain between the employer and a union representing all those currently employed in each firm. For simplicity we assume that each union is specific to a firm, that there are no employers' federations and that each firm is sufficiently small to be treated atomistically (i.e., it ignores the impact of its decisions on the rest of the economy). Throughout we assume the union is concerned about wages (and effort where this is endogenous). We ignore any concern the union may have over employment. There are many reasons why under certainty a union would not at the bargaining margin care about employment: natural wastage provides existing workers with wide safety margins, and seniority rules further protect the median voter; see Jackman *et al.* (1988) and Oswald (1987).

The unions do not bargain over employment, cf. Oswald (1987), which is determined by firms. Initially we assume the bargain is only over wages, with workers' productivity exogenous. Later we modify this. We confine ourselves to the case of a tax on the wage level, which again can be shown to be equivalent to a tax on wage growth.

The outcome of the bargain is the wage which maximizes the Nash expression

$$\Omega = (W - \bar{Z})^{\beta\pi}$$

where β measures the relative discount rate of firm and union, π measures *operating* profits (so that the firm's fall-back is zero) and $\bar{Z}$ is the union fall-back. We assume that $\bar{Z}$ is a weighted average of wages paid in other jobs ($\bar{W}$) and unemployment benefits payable to strikers (B), the weights depending on unemployment:

$$\bar{Z} = (1 - \varphi(u))\,\bar{W} + \varphi(u)\,B. \qquad (\varphi' > 0)$$

The optimal wage is given by

$$\frac{\mathrm{d}\log\Omega}{\mathrm{d}W} = \frac{\beta}{W - \bar{Z}} + \frac{1}{\pi} \cdot \frac{\mathrm{d}\pi}{\mathrm{d}C} \cdot \frac{\mathrm{d}C}{\mathrm{d}W}$$

$$= \frac{\beta}{W - \bar{Z}} - \frac{NC}{\pi}\left(\frac{\mathrm{d}C}{\mathrm{d}W} \cdot \frac{W}{C}\right)\frac{1}{W} = 0.$$

Hence in general equilibrium (with $W = \bar{W}$)

$$\frac{W - \bar{Z}}{W} = \frac{\beta\gamma}{1 + t}$$

where $\gamma = \pi/NC$, which is constant in a Cobb-Douglas world with monopolistic competition and constant demand elasticities. Thus

$$\varphi(u) = \frac{\beta\gamma}{(1+t)(1-\rho)}$$

where $\rho = B/W$, taken as exogenous. Again the system solves for the equilibrium unemployment rate, which then determines employment and real wages in equilibrium. And, once again, the tax reduces equilibrium unemployment.[4]

To get an idea of magnitudes, note that if $\varphi(u)$ is a proportional function

$$-\frac{du}{dt} = \frac{u}{1+t}.$$

Effort Endogenous

However, many commentators have criticized TIP on the grounds that it might discourage productivity bargains. This in turn has led to the view that productivity bargains would have to be exempt — and, since that is administratively impossible, that TIP is a nonstarter. To find how TIP affects productivity bargaining, we now assume that effort (e) is observable (e.g. it varies inversely with manning ratios) and is bargained over.[5] Individual workers dislike effort and their utility is given by

$$Z = Wg(e) \qquad g' < 0$$

---

[4] If we consider a tax on annual wage growth we choose W_0 to maximize

$$\Omega_0 = (W_0 - \bar{Z}_0)^\beta \pi_0$$

where subscripts reflect time-periods and we include in $d\pi_0/dW_0$ the discounted effect of W_0 on profits in period 1. Thus

$$\frac{d \log \Omega}{d W_0} = \frac{\beta}{W_0 - \bar{Z}_0} + \frac{1}{\pi_0}\left[-N_0 \frac{dC_0}{dW_0} - \left(N_1 \frac{dC_1}{dW_0}\right)(1-r)(1+n) \right]$$

$$= \frac{\beta}{W_0 - \bar{Z}_0} + \frac{1}{\pi_0}[-N_0(1+T) + (1-r)N_1 T(1+n)] = 0.$$

Hence in a steady state

$$\frac{W_0 - \bar{Z}_0}{W_0} = \beta \frac{\pi_0}{N_0 W_0} \frac{1}{1+(r-n)T}.$$

[5] Efficiency wage theory is, of course, concerned with those dimensions of effort which are unobservable.

(This gives a vertical labour supply curve, which is realistic). Hence the Nash maximand is

$$\Omega = (Wg(e) - \bar{Z})^{\beta\pi}$$

where

$$\bar{Z} = (1 - \varphi(u)) \, \bar{W}g(\bar{e}) + \varphi(u) \, B$$

where B denotes the utility of unemployment. Since both wages (W) and effort (e) are bargained over, Ω has to be maximized with respect to each, subject to the firm's demand for labour. The optimal wage is given by

$$\frac{\partial \log \Omega}{\partial W} = \frac{\beta g(e)}{Wg(e) - \bar{Z}} + \frac{1}{\pi}\frac{d\pi}{dC} \cdot \frac{dC}{dW} = 0.$$

Hence, after performing the usual manipulations, we get the usual answer:

$$\varphi(u) = \frac{\beta\gamma}{(1+t)(1-\rho)} \tag{1}$$

where ρ is now the replacement ratio in utility terms. Thus, as before, TIP reduces unemployment.

But what dreadful things does it do to effort? The optimal effort is given by

$$\frac{\partial \log \Omega}{\partial e} = \frac{\beta \, Wg'}{Wg(e) - \bar{Z}} + \frac{1}{\pi}\frac{\partial \pi}{\partial e} = 0.$$

But[6] $\partial \pi / \partial e = CN/e$, so that

$$\frac{Wg(e) - \bar{Z}}{Wg(e)} = -\beta\gamma \frac{g'e}{g} \, .$$

Thus

$$\varphi(u)(1 - \rho) = -\beta\gamma \frac{g'e}{g} \tag{2}$$

---

[6] $\pi = R(eN) - CN$, so

$$\frac{\partial \pi}{\partial e} = R'N + (R'e - C)\frac{\partial N}{\partial e} = R'N = \frac{CN}{e}.$$

and hence, using (1),

$$-\frac{g'e}{g}=\frac{1}{1+t}.$$

This conclusion would also follow if effort were set unilaterally by the employer.[7] It implies that the tax reduces effort.

Going on, it is helpful to set

$$-\frac{g'(e)e}{g(e)}=h(e)=\frac{1}{1+t} \qquad h'>0.$$

so that

$$\frac{de}{dt}\frac{1}{e}=-\frac{1}{(1+t)^2 h'(e)e}.$$

We know of no estimates of the value which workers place on effort but an indication may be provided by the value which they place on leisure. We might, for example, assume that workers dislike a 10 per cent increase in effort about as much as they dislike a 10 per cent increase in hours. If e

---

[7] The employer will choose effort knowing that this will affect the wage outcome in the bargain. Hence the employer chooses effort to maximize

$$\pi = R(eN)-(W(1+t)-S)N$$

subject to

$$\frac{\partial \log \Omega}{\partial W}=\frac{\beta g(e)}{Wg(e)-\bar{Z}}+\frac{1}{\pi}\frac{d\pi}{dC}\cdot\frac{dC}{dW}=0$$

that is

$$W=\frac{\bar{Z}(1+t)}{(1+t-\beta\gamma)g(e)}.$$

Thus

$$\frac{\partial \pi}{\partial e}=N\left[R'+\frac{(1+t)g'(e)}{g(e)}\cdot W\right]=0$$

and, since when N is optimal $R'=C/e$,

$$-\frac{eg'(e)}{g(e)}=\frac{1}{1+t}.$$

were hours, the compensated labour supply elasticity would be $1/h'(e)e$.[8] The most relevant estimates of this relate to male workers, since for female workers the whole choice of participation is involved and the spread of hours much wider. Typical estimates of the male compensated elasticity are around 0.1; see Pencavel (1986). Then

$$\frac{de}{dt}\frac{1}{e} = -\frac{0.1}{(1+t)^2}.$$

We can now look, first, at the effects of the tax upon national output and then upon welfare. For simplicity we assume output (Y) proportional to labour input eN. Then

$$\frac{d\log Y}{dt} = \frac{d\log e}{dt} - \frac{du}{dt}$$

$$= \frac{-0.1}{(1+t)^2} + \frac{u}{1+t}.$$

On this basis the tax would increase GDP provided initial unemployment was higher than say 7 per cent.

---

[8] If w is the net reward per unit of effort, the individual maximizes

$(we + Y)g(e)$

where Y is nonemployment income. This gives a supply curve

$$\frac{w}{we+Y} + \frac{g'(e)}{g} = 0$$

or

$$-\frac{g'(e)e}{g} = \frac{1}{1+Y/we} = h(e).$$

We now vary w and Y simultaneously, with $dY = -e\,dw$. Since we assume Y approximately zero, it follows that

$$-\frac{dY}{we} = \frac{dw}{w} = h'(e)\,de$$

and

$$-\frac{1}{h'(e)e} = -\frac{de}{e}\Big/\frac{dw}{w}.$$

But on top of this we should allow for the fact that workers dislike effort and are glad to be making less of it.[9] The proportional change in welfare due to this source is

$$\frac{g'e}{g}\frac{de}{dt}\frac{1}{e}S_L$$

$$=\frac{0.1\,S_L}{(1+t)^3}$$

where S_L is the share of labour. Thus the overall change in welfare is

$$\frac{1}{1+t}\left[u-\frac{0.1(1+t-S_L)}{(1+t)^2}\right].$$

For a 50 per cent tax rate and $S_L = 0.75$ this is positive for any unemployment above around 3 per cent.[10]

IV. Adding a Market-Clearing Sector

All the estimates arrived at so far relate to a world in which there is a single nonmarket-clearing sector. We now ask whether in the more realistic case where there is also a secondary market-clearing sector TIP has a larger or smaller proportional effect upon unemployment.

We shall show that the proportional effect of the tax on unemployment may be higher or lower than we have so far suggested. If the supply to the secondary sector is infinitely elastic, the cut in unemployment is higher, and if supply is completely inelastic the cut in unemployment is lower.

To understand why this is so consider the case of highly elastic supply. The tax cuts the primary sector wage. This increases employment in the primary sector and reduces the pool of workers available for the secondary sector. This tends to raise the wage in the secondary sector and increases the proportion of people outside the primary sector who are willing to work in the nonunion sector. Thus employment falls proportionately more than the fall in the number of people outside the primary sector. If by contrast the supply is inelastic, this bonus is lacking. To sharpen the argument we shall concentrate on the two extreme cases.

---

[9] We are assuming that when an unemployed worker becomes employed, social welfare rises by his output.

[10] The cost of lower effort and lower wages could be much less if we allowed for jealousy over wages in the utility function; cf. Boskin and Sheshinski (1978) and Layard (1980). The fall in the wages of others would then raise individual utility.

Infinitely Elastic Supply

First, we assume that the supply to the secondary sector is infinitely elastic at a wage *B*. The unemployed are all those who have no primary jobs *minus* demand in the secondary sector (see Figure 1).

Union bargaining or efficiency wages determine the mark-up of the primary wage over *B*. From now on we talk of the union wage and use the union as the model of the primary sector. But the analysis could apply equally well for the efficiency wage case in the primary sector.[11]

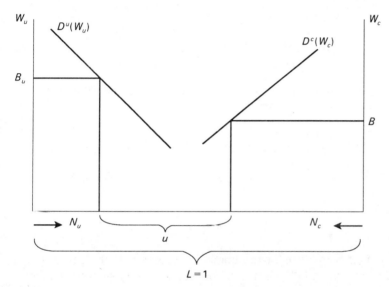

Fig. 1. A primary sector (subscript *u*) and a secondary sector (subscript *c*).

---

[11] Under efficiency wages we can obtain a neat formula for the mark-up if one assumes, with Summers (1987), that

$$e = (W - A)^\alpha$$

where *A* is the expected outside income. In this case a firm maximizing e/C with respect to *W* sets

$$\frac{\alpha}{W - A} - \frac{1}{C}\frac{dC}{dW} = 0$$

so that in general equilibrium with $C = W$

$$\frac{W - A}{W} = \frac{\alpha}{1 + t}.$$

We continue to assume that the tax is self-financing and that it is self-financing *within* each sector (as it would be if it were in the form of a tax on wage growth). Hence, using t to mean the effective tax rate, $(r-n)\,T$, the union wage $(W_u = C_u)$ is given by

$$\frac{W_u - \bar{Z}}{W_u} = \frac{\beta\gamma}{1+t}.$$

In the present case, normalizing on a labour force of unity,

$$\bar{Z} = (1 - \varphi(1 - N_u))\,W_u + \varphi(1 - N_u)\,B.$$

Hence

$$\varphi(1 - N_u)(1 - B/W_u) = \frac{\beta\gamma}{1+t}.$$

Thus if B/W_u is independent of t (as we shall show) then the change in union employment when t rises is

$$\frac{dN_u}{dt} = \frac{1 - N_u}{1+t}.$$

The change in total employment (fall in total unemployment) is

$$-\frac{du}{dt} = \frac{dN_u}{dt} + \frac{dN_c}{dt}$$

where N_c is employment in the competitive sector. If the proportional change in employment is the same in both sectors (as we shall show), then

$$-\frac{du}{dt} = \frac{dN_u}{dt} + \frac{dN_c}{dt} = \frac{1 - N_u}{1+t}\left(\frac{N_u + N_c}{N_u}\right) > \frac{u}{1+t}.$$

This greatly exceeds the findings of the one-sector model.

It can now be shown why, if B is constant for given productivity, B/W_u and N_u/N_c are invariant when t changes — using some rather specific assumptions. We assume monopolistic competition *à la* Dixit-Stiglitz, with each worker producing one unit of output. All firms are identical and face demand curves with elasticity η. It follows that in each firm i the relative price will be proportional to the real wage W_i:

$$P_i = W_i(1 - 1/\eta)^{-1}.$$

Hence the firm's demand for labour is given by

$$N_i = W_i^{-\eta}\,\bar{Y}(1 - 1/\eta)^{-\eta}$$

where $\bar{Y}$ is aggregate demand per firm. Hence the demand for labour in union firms (N_u) relative to competitive firms (N_c) is

$$\frac{N_u}{N_c} = \left(\frac{W_u}{W_c}\right)^{-\eta} \frac{n_u}{n_c} \tag{1}$$

where n_u, n_c are the relevant number of firms in the two sectors.

In addition pricing behaviour is such that

$$\bar{P} = 1 = \left(\frac{N_u}{N_u + N_c} W_u + \frac{N_c}{N_u + N_c} W_c\right)(1 - 1/\eta)^{-1}$$

or

$$1 - 1/\eta = \frac{N_u}{N_u + N_c} W_u + \frac{N_c}{N_u + N_c} W_c. \tag{2}$$

For given $W_c = B$, equations (1) and (2) determine W_u and N_u/N_c.

Thus, when the tax is imposed, real wages in each sector are unchanged. But wage pressure in the union sector is reduced so that unemployment can be reduced. This happens through an equiproportional rise in union and nonunion employment.

Infinitely Inelastic Supply

We now consider the case of inelastic labour supply to the competitive sector. In this case there is a fixed proportion (S) of nonunion personnel who are willing to work in the nonunion sector.

The union mark-up is given by

$$\frac{W_u - \bar{Z}}{W_u} = \frac{\beta\gamma}{1 + t}$$

where $\bar{Z}$ now is

$$\bar{Z} = [1 - \varphi(1 - N_u)] W_u + \varphi(1 - N_u)[SW_c + (1 - S)B].$$

Hence

$$\varphi(1 - N_u)\left(1 - S\frac{W_c}{W_u} - (1 - S)\frac{B}{W_u}\right) = \frac{\beta\gamma}{1 + t}.$$

When t rises W_c/W_u now rises, as does B/W_u (taking B as invariant, like

194   *R. Jackman and R. Layard*

$\bar{W}$). Hence the fall in $(1 - N_u)$ is partially offset and

$$-\frac{d(1 - N_u)}{dt} \frac{1}{1 - N_u} < \frac{1}{1 + t}.$$

In addition since $u = 1 - N_u - N_c = (1 - N_u)(1 - S)$

$$-\frac{du}{dt} \frac{1}{u} = -\frac{d(1 - N_u)}{dt} \frac{1}{1 - N_u}.$$

Hence

$$-\frac{du}{dt} = -\frac{-d(1 - N_u)}{dt} \frac{u}{1 - N_u} < \frac{u}{1 + t}.$$

This is less than the findings of the one-sector model. For some supply elasticity between zero and infinity, the one-sector and two-sector models would show the same effect of a TIP.

References

Boskin, M. J. & Sheshinski, E.: Optimal redistributive taxation when individual welfare depends upon relative income. *Quarterly Journal of Economics 92* (4), Nov. 1978.
Colander, D. (ed.): *Incentive-based Incomes Policies.* Ballinger, Cambridge, MA, 1986.
Dornbusch, R. & Fischer, S.: *Macroeconomics.* 4th edition, 1987.
Jackman, R., Layard, R. & Nickell, S.: *Unemployment.* Mimeo, 1988.
Layard, R.: Human satisfactions and public policy. *Economic Journal 90,* 737–50, Dec. 1980.
Oswald, A.: Efficient contracts are on the labour demand curve, theory and facts. DP No. 284, London School of Economics, Centre for Labour Economics, 1987.
Pencavel, J.: Labor supply of men: A survey. In O. Ashenfelter & R. Layard, *Handbook of Labor Economics,* Vol. I, North-Holland, Amsterdam, 1986.
Summers, L.: *Relative Wages, Efficiency Wages and Keynesian Unemployment.* Mimeo, 1987.
Wadhwani, S. & Wall, M.: A direct test of the efficiency wage model using U.K. micro-data. DP No. 313, London School of Economics, Centre for Labour Economics, 1988.
Wallich, H. & Weintraub, S.: A tax-based incomes policy. *Journal of Economic Issues,* No. 5, 1–19, June 1971.

Comment on R. Jackman and R. Layard, "The Real Effects of Tax-based Incomes Policies"

Peter Diamond

MIT, Cambridge, MA, USA

This paper analyzes two real models of the allocation process and then draws conclusions from these models for the possible virtues of a tax based income policy. The first model assumes efficiency wages and wage setting by firms. As is well known from the efficiency wage literature, the equilibrium that comes from this combination of assumptions is not a welfare maximum. The analysis does not consider the welfare evaluation of equilibrium but merely asks the question whether a tax on wage income will lower unemployment. No public finance economist would be surprised that taxes can alter the quantity of unemployment in a model like this. Taxes also can improve the level of social welfare.

The second model analyzed is also a real model which assumes that wages are set as the Nash bargaining solution between firms that want to maximize profit and unions that want to maximize wages ignoring employment. Again, the wage tax can affect the level of unemployment. Moreover, since the union is not interested in the welfare of the workers, a wage tax can raise social welfare.

Situations where there is no mobility of labor are analyzed in Sections II and III. A competitive sector with labor mobility is added in Section IV, which continues to analyze the effect of the wage tax on unemployment.

Rather than discussing the details of the formal modeling or the use of available empirical work to produce estimates of the size of the effect of the tax on the unemployment rate, I want to ask about the relevance of such an exercise for the policy question of whether a tax based income policy, or more specifically, an increase in wage income taxes, will improve the inflation unemployment tradeoff. Frankly, I see little relevance.

There are two very different ways of thinking about tax based income policies. One way has TIP as a permanent feature of the tax structure, much as economists would have pollution taxes as a permanent feature of the tax structure. Alternatively one can think of TIP as part of the temporary policy package designed for an economy that currently has a high level of inflation. Let me start with consideration of a permanent TIP.

If the underlying models of the labor allocation process are correct, then one would favor a TIP as a welfare improving measure on a micro economic basis. The case for the relevance of such a tax would not come, as with much of the discussion of TIP, as a way of holding down the inflation rate, but rather would come in a fashion similar to analysis of the magnitude of externalities generated by pollution. This would follow a detailed analysis of real wage setting, worker behavior, and firm behavior. Analysis of the distortions by a wage tax would be a necessary part of determining an optimal tax. This would require a model with heterogenous labor since the tradeoff between expensive and inexpensive labor is being distorted. Macro economists frequently criticize micro theorists for the lack of connection with empirical work. When it comes to detailed policy analysis I think the shoe is on the other foot. Micro economists proposing pollution and congestion corrective taxes regularly do very detailed analyses of the cost generated by externalities as a basis for choosing the magnitude for corrective taxes. While I am not widely read in the TIP literature (in fact I had read nothing before it became my lot to discuss this paper), I have the impression that the degree of empirical work is causal. There clearly is something in the efficiency wage idea. Yet having macro economists takes it from there to aggregate data is no basis for choosing a tax to correct this externality.

But what if the empirical work appropriate for this kind of model were undertaken and it supported the findings of this model. Then, of course, one would favor such a tax just as one favors subsidized worker retraining programs that are seen to have adequate empirical justification. It seems appropriate in this setting, however, to ask the sense in which one can be said to have improved the inflation unemployment tradeoff. One sense is clear. Provided that this tax does not alter the responsiveness of the economy to the causes of the business cycle, we would expect an improvement in unemployment inflation outcomes. Perhaps this is best thought of as a parallel shift in the short-run Phillips Curve and a similar parallel shift in the long-run Phillips Curve. However, there is no argument made that a wage tax will not worsen the business cycle. Moreover, for a central bank trying to decide on policy in the aftermath of shocks which were responded to in a way that allowed high inflation, it is not clear that the dilemma of the unemployment inflation tradeoff is noticeably changed. To address that question, one would want a model that has in it inflation-unemployment tradeoffs, coming no doubt from limitations on the short-run adjustment of the economy to all sorts of events.

If one were to consider the TIP as part of the temporary stabilization effort designed to lower the current inflation rate while holding down the cost in unemployment of doing it, there may indeed be a case that the TIP would be superior to temporary wage and price controls. For analysis of such a possibility, one would want a model that was focused on short-run adjustments, inflation expectations, and price and wage setting incentives. A real model like the ones in this paper does not seem to me to be terribly relevant.

I want to conclude with a few comments on TIP, stimulated in part by the paper. First, I was interested to see the discussion in the paper of the contrast between the wage level tax and a wage growth tax. In the context of the model they are interchangeable. In a world with lots of reasons for changes in relevant wages, either part of a steady shift (as with age and experience) or in resonse to temporary imbalances, there is no apparent reason why, from an allocation point of view, the wage growth tax is as good as a wage level tax if the tax is linear. If the tax is nonlinear then it may well be the case that a uniform origin for a simple progressive tax will be inferior to individual specific origins that are historically set, provided that temporary use of TIPs is a rare event. Then use of a wage growth tax will probably not have so much in the way of adverse medium or long-term response.

If the focus of TIP is on inflation, then it seems more natural to think about a policy directly focused on inflation rates. Consider a country with a national sales tax. Assume that enforcement difficulties do not arise if the sales tax is set at a subsidy level. Then, in the short run, one can cut the magnitude of the sales tax as a way of reducing inflation, making up the revenue from some other tax increase which our theory suggests is not so tightly linked to the current inflation rate. We can even think of this as a permanent policy. Each month the sales subsidy is adjusted so that the rise in the consumer price index from the previous month to the month before is exactly offset. While this would not give a perfectly constant consumer price index, it will not be far off. If one believed that this subsidy plus the taxes needed to finance it did not particularly impact on the unemployment rate, we have dramatically altered the inflation unemployment tradeoff. Recognizing the link between unemployment and aggregate activities shocks and the impact on price setting of aggregate demand policies designed to offset those shocks; it becomes unclear that this is either a stable or a good policy. My guess is that once one found out what was wrong with such a proposal the same thing would be wrong with a permanent TIP and whatever is right about a TIP would work even better for a final sales subsidy.

If TIP is a powerful tool for lowering unemployment, then perhaps one can learn about it by observing occasions when payroll taxes have risen, a very common event in the history of many economies. Even if one wanted a tax structure where earnings are taxed and the revenue is returned in a lump sum fashion, one sees approximations of that tax change in U.S. payroll tax increases used to finance increases in planned retirement

194 P. Diamond

benefits, since the progressivity of the retirement benefit formula implies a significant tax cost to the wage increase above the value of increased future benefits from higher wages. I have not looked to see whether there is any sign of improved inflation-unemployment tradeoffs. Any improvements were not large enough to have caught the eye of people who have been doing empirical work. If one favors a permanent TIP rather than a single episode of use then such empirical work seems to me to be a necessary part of making the case.

Comment on R. Jackman and R. Layard, "The Real Effects of Tax-based Incomes Policies"

Karl Ove Moene

University of Oslo, Norway

In the paper the implications of the proposed reform are derived under varying assumptions about why there is unemployment in the first place. I sympathize with this approach and with the view that partial losses in efficiency should be tolerated as long as long-run unemployment is reduced. There are, however, possible effects of the proposed reform not discussed in the paper, which may turn out to be harmful to long-run employment. As indicated below, TIP can (i) favour declining industries at the expense of expanding ones and (ii) reduce investment incentives.

The proposed reform taxes wage increases above a constant norm. The tax is compensated by a subsidy S per worker which is set independently of the wage costs in the individual firms. A situation can then easily arise where employment is subsidized in low-productive firms, while more productive firms that pay higher wages are heavily taxed. This may delay necessary structural change and reduce long-run growth and employment opportunities.

The paper is similar to Weitzman's work on profit sharing in several ways. First, like Weitzman, Jackman and Layard discuss the problem of inflation in nonmonetary models where nominal wage increases are irrelevant.

Second, the main goal of both reforms is to reduce the marginal cost of labor power with a self-financing scheme. Profit sharing is identical to an employment subsidy financed by a profit tax, while the present version of TIP subsidizes employment financed by a tax on wage increases (or simply wages).

On the other hand, the TIP scheme differs from profit sharing in that TIP increases employment by reducing the real wage, while employment under profit sharing can be increased with the same (or a higher) real pay.

In fact, under TIP, both firms and workers may gain by agreeing on higher wages paid as employee shares. By so doing taxes can be reduced. Thus TIP can be seen as an inducement mechanism for profit sharing in the form of employee-owned shares. Britain has tried to induce profit sharing arrangements by subsidizing firms which introduce such compensation schemes. A tax on wage increases may have the same effect.

Finally, like profit sharing, TIP can reduce incentives to invest. To see why TIP may have this effect, consider the case with wage bargaining where capital investment K is decided before and employment after the wage bargaining takes place. The outcome of the wage negotiations is denoted by

$$W = W(K, t) \tag{1}$$

where $W_K > 0$ (due to higher labor productivity) and $W_t < 0$ (as shown in the paper). The indirect profit function of the firm (with the optimal employment level) can then be written as

$$P = P(W(K, t)(1 + t) - S, K). \tag{2}$$

The optimal level of K must satisfy the first-order condition

$$P_1 W_K(1 + t) + P_2 = 0 \tag{3}$$

where $P_1 < 0$. An efficient level of investments requires that $P_2 = 0$. Because wages go up with investment, employers will underinvest. This well-known effect of wage bargaining is captured by the first term of (3). As can be seen, this effect is enhanced by the factor $(1 + t)$ under TIP which induces an even lower level of investment. In fact, TIP can be considered an indirect tax on investments that will be particularily harmful to growing industries. As a consequence, long-run employment may go down.

The Macroeconomic Tradeoffs of Price and Income Policies

Edmond Malinvaud

Collège de France, Paris, France

Abstract

Under some conditions price and income policies may succeed in reaching the objectives they pursue. But in all cases, tradeoffs place limits on what they can achieve. These tradeoffs are discussed for three kinds of objectives: reducing inequalities, solving the inflation-unemployment dilemma and restoring business profitability. The uncertainties, particularly the relationship between wages and employment, are emphasized.

I. Introduction

When economic evolution appears unsatisfactory from some point of view, it is often a rather natural idea to think of interferring with the spontaneous determination of prices and remuneration rates, in the hope of reaching better results.

Many times, efforts to implement this idea turned out to be deceptive. Sometimes governments simply did not succeed in controlling the formation of incomes and prices. When they did succeed, their policy often had perverse effects, which economists, however, tended to over-emphasize; in any case, there turned out to be a tradeoff between the objectives of the price and income policy and other economic objectives.

My role in this conference is to open the discussion on precisely what these tradeoffs may be, in the light of what has now become long experience. Emphasis should then be placed on the analysis of the likely effects of exogenous shocks on wages or prices and how these effects may depend on the reference situation. But any examination of this topic should first pay attention to the effectiveness of price and income policies. Moreover, in order to focus the discussion, I intend to select and consider successively three main objectives among those assigned to such policies: reducing inequalities, curbing the inflation-unemployment tradeoff and restoring business profitability. I insist more particularly here on this last objective, which has played an especially important role in some European countries during recent years.[1]

II. When can Price and Income Policies be Effective?

The often heard presumption that governments cannot act on prices and remuneration rates is certainly too negative. Decisions on particular prices have often been implemented. This was the case not only for prices of public utilities but also for instances when and where rent control was introduced; the laws or regulations that were passed in this respect were applied as accurately as many other public decisions. Similarly, outside of the black economy, legal minimum wages are enforced. Taxes and subsidies also react on prices and/or incomes.

What is in question is rather the ability of governments to so act on the general levels of prices or wages. In market economies, few instruments are available for achieving this goal through price and income policies. Movements in the overall rate of indirect taxes or subsidies have to be motivated by other considerations of public finance, even though attempts occurred to use their exact timing so as to best achieve some result for the price level (maximum impact in the case of a reduction in tax rates, minimum impact in the case of a rise). Administrative controls on the evolution of prices require a qualified staff that does not exist except in countries that have a long tradition of price control; where it existed, as in France, designing and revising rules to be applied for price changes turned out to be a very delicate task and there is room for doubting whether much was so achieved, except to make business operations more cumbersome.[2]

On the other hand, it is a fact that wages and many prices are not determined by direct operation of the textbook law of supply and demand. It is then conceivable that governments interfere with the actual, more or less organized, bargaining processes. The question lies in knowing whether such action can be successful.

The literature that followed the new interest devoted to corporatism is interesting in this respect. It focused attention on the somewhat different question of knowing whether centralized wage bargaining leads to superior economic performances; see in particular Calmfors and Drifill (1988) and Pohjola (1988). Thus far the results concerning such a broad question are

---

[1] In the debate during the conference, Calmfors pointed to one reason for the frequent lack of conclusiveness of discussions about price and income policies: these discussions consider too many questions at the same time. I fully agree and I recognize that the criticism somewhat applies to this article, which aims at surveying a wide field.

[2] Axell (1985) argues along these lines, even claiming that price controls are likely to increase inflation rather than reduce it.

too weak and unstable with respect to specification of the tests to be really convincing. But discussion of the issues supported the intuition according to which government policy can be more or less effective, depending on how wage bargaining proceeds.

Another intuitive idea also seems to be supported, i.e., that the degree of consensus on broader issues among the various parties plays an important role. Depending on what it is, parties will end up with either a cooperative or an inferior noncooperative solution. In particular, the efficiency of government intervention depends on whether it succeeds in being recognized as favorable to the common good. Such an outcome may be made easier with a centralized wage bargaining system, but this is neither a necessary nor a sufficient condition. Whatever the exact bargaining institutions, the reactions of public opinion matter. If government interventions are understood, they have a better chance of being effective than would otherwise be the case. This is why public authorities can act in a more subtle way than issuing regulations, or even simply giving norms or guidelines; they may achieve some results by promoting ideas as to what the current situation of the country requires.

This is all the more so as the problem with price and incomes policy is often more its fate in the medium run than its immediate effectiveness. A price and/or wage freeze in particular has often succeeded in slowing down inflation for a time, but frequently at the cost of an acceleration later on, when the freeze has come to an end. The exact pattern of the policy has to be chosen with due concern for such backlash effects; public support will also be helpful in order to minimize them.

A kind of test of the effectiveness of explicit and well-defined price and incomes policy measures comes from the econometric fits of price and wage equations: do variables representing these measures appear as significant with the correct sign? The answer has often turned out to be positive, but the impact has typically been found to be smaller and more temporary than was intended. I may add to the existing econometric literature available in English by quoting some results for France. They are due mainly to Feroldi and Meunier (1984), Ralle (1987) and J.-M. Jeanneney and associates (1989).

It appears that in France, as elsewhere, government decisions seem to play a larger role in the wage equation than in the price equation. Over the last two decades the variable that best catches the role of wage policy concerns the legal minimum wage, or more precisely its discretionary increase beyond price indexation as stipulated by law; other instruments such as those concerning wages and salaries in the public sector do not seem to add anything significant, but of course they are correlated with the minimum wage variable. In regressions that include no variable representing government wage decisions, important residuals appear, precisely at the time of active policies, regardless of whether they pushed up wages (in 1968 and during the first year in office of President Giscard d'Estaing and again of President Mitterrand) or put restraint on them, as in the last six years.

The rigorous policy led by Mr. Delors is particularly interesting because its aim was to change the process of wage determination in France, in particular with respect to indexation on the cost of living. The initial wage and price freeze in the summer of 1982 was quite significant, but most of its impact was counterbalanced at the end of the freeze in the winter of 1983. The lags in the effect of price changes on wages increased significantly after 1982, by roughly one quarter. The extent of long-term indexation seems to have decreased slightly, with a Student statistic that is significant at the 10 per cent but not at the 5 per cent level.

The general conclusion then is that, in our countries, price and income policies may have some limited power, but only under some conditions. This unenthusiastic assessment should, however, be judged against what can be said about other tools of macroeconomic policy. We have learned that aggregate demand management is more constrained and less effective than we used to think. Within this broad context, price and income policies will remain as an instrument to be used with care and moderation.

III. Reducing Inequalities

In Western Europe reducing economic and social inequalities among people has been one of the great public aspirations of this century. Recently, however, concern seems to have weakened, even in countries such as France where inequalities remain quite substantial and definitely greater than for instance in Sweden. I do not intend to speculate much on the origin of this evolution, but it may be explained in part by the general realization that rules and institutions that were set up in order to promote equality were not as successful as expected: their direct effects had been overestimated; they had unfavorable side effects, which moreover were often detrimental to the poor. Today the tradeoffs facing the various kinds of equalizing reforms or public decisions are regarded by informed opinion as more troublesome than they appeared in the past.

In order to survey what we now believe to be known about these tradeoffs, I begin with those concerning price and incomes policies *stricto sensu*. I also deal briefly with the taxation system, which affects prices and incomes, is often motivated by equality considerations and results from policy decisions. But I do not approach further remote questions, such as those concerning the organization and financing of the education system.

Minimum wage laws were certainly motivated by the wish to provide low-paid workers with a better income than they would otherwise have received. But the floor thus imposed on the cost of the least qualified labor was also likely to lower the demand for this labor, hence to increase unemployment of those supplying it. There was a tradeoff between two social objectives: an egalitarian society and full employment.

The nature of this tradeoff was studied and discussed a great deal in the United States. So far as I know, work in other countries led to similar conclusions. The results were recently surveyed by Brown (1988) who showed that both the benefits and costs were smaller than anticipated.

Where the minimum wage is relatively high, as in the U.S. or France, it does play a role in reducing the size of the lower tail of the wage distribution — a spike appearing at the level of the minimum wage. But this effect is to a large extent erased when considering households' income distribution rather than individual wage distribution; incomes from workers paid the minimum wage make up only a fraction of the incomes of poor families and go mainly to households in intermediate income brackets.

Similarly the negative impact on employment is not found in econometric studies, except for young workers. Even for teenagers, where it clearly appears, it is not very large, since a 10 per cent increase in the minimum wage is estimated to reduce employment in this age group by between 1 and 2 per cent, with the possibility that employment of older workers will even be improved somewhat.

Probably because of a lack of familiarity with the relevant literature, I do not know of any good study of the tradeoffs facing a policy of selective price controls motivated by distributional concerns. But I am well acquainted with some of the problems raised by rent controls, because France has lived with them almost permanently since 1914. Keeping rents down, of course, benefits tenants who on average are less wealthy than owners. But, if the transfer is to be durable and significant, and it has been at various times in France, inefficiencies in the use of rented dwellings develop (e.g. old people living part-time in large apartments) and the supply of dwellings for rent declines. Young people can only find quite inconvenient lodgings, or exceedingly costly ones if a free section remains on the market (such as for furnished or newly built dwellings). As time goes on, even the equalizing effects of the control is eroded; but removing the control would significantly change the welfare of many people and public authorities are faced with a political dilemma. This is a case in which the tradeoff has an important time dimension; the initial social benefit should be weighted against the subsequent inefficiencies, inequalities and problems.

Recent events in a number of countries show that food price controls raise similar issues, if they are admitted to be initially beneficial. But this hypothesis may even be questioned in this case, when the welfare of farmers has to be compared with that of the urban population.

In the mixed economies of Western Europe, policies aimed at equalization rely more on public transfers than on controls: taxes and social security contributions are used to finance subsidies and social benefits. This is mainly how the welfare state operates. There is now a rich literature that could be relevant for this purpose, so rich that is out of question to attempt to survey it here. Suffice it to say that it leaves many questions unanswered and that even qualitative conclusions are hard to draw from it.[3]

On the one hand, empirical studies have evaluated the direct impact of public transfers in many countries. They show in particular that indirect taxation in Western countries does not reduce inequality in real incomes to any large extent, notwithstanding the use of different rates on different goods and services, with higher rates on supposed "luxuries" than on supposed "necessities". While direct taxation and social benefits do redistribute incomes, they are found to be less effective for doing so than one might have thought.

But such calculations rest on somewhat unrealistic assumptions about the incidence of taxes and transfers, since they do not recognize that taxes may be fully or partially shifted. Attempts at using more sophisticated assumptions have shown high sensitivity of the results with respect to the specification chosen. Moreover, the calculations do not say by how much aggregate income may be affected by the presence of a system of public transfers intended to redistribute it. Since incentives are likely to be reduced and distortions likely to appear in resource allocation, a negative impact of redistribution on aggregate income is usually expected. In other words, there should be a tradeoff between the two objectives of efficiency and equalization.

On the other hand, many theoretical analyses have dealt with the various disincentives and sources of inefficiency. Some of them even went so far as to study particular tradeoffs and to derive rules for optimal taxation, often paying attention to other kinds of tradeoffs than those which concern us here. It was learned from this theoretical work that precise knowledge of many elasticities would be required in order to derive results to be applied in the real world. To take just one example of the questions I have in mind, let me consider the disincentive effect of taxation of labor incomes: do we know by how much highly qualified personnel reduces its work effort and increases its leisure when its rate of taxation increases? Can we discard in this country the idea that the welfare state has increased workers' morale and that the phenomenon should be taken into account in any assessment of the tradeoff?

---

[3] If I must give a reference, it would be to the book by Atkinson and Stiglitz (1980).

A fair amount of econometric work has been carried out in order to evaluate some elasticities, such as those concerning the effect of social security on saving or that of unemployment compensation on participation rates and intensity of job search. But even for these cases, agreement on approximate estimates does not seem to have been reached.

IV. Curbing the Inflation-Unemployment Tradeoff

Price and incomes policies have often been contemplated in the wish to escape the unpleasant dilemma faced by demand management, i.e., to have to accept either unemployment or inflation. Can they be helpful in this respect? If so, under what conditions?

These questions cannot be discussed without relying on a model that exhibits the true nature of the dilemma. It is now common to refer to the augmented Phillips Curve, while assuming unemployment to be a decreasing function of aggregate demand, possibly involving some lags, the price level being a function of the nominal wage and of some exogenous variables such as the price of imports and the rate of indirect taxation. Actually this model may be too simple because supply may not be independent of prices, incomes and unemployment. I take supply aspects into consideration in the next section, but neglect them in this one.

The objective assigned to price and incomes policies, if they are to be used in this context, is to create a shock that will lead agents to revise downward their expectations about the pace of inflation. Whether public authorities are able to produce such a shock has to be assessed in each particular case; this is precisely the main question raised in Section II of this paper, since many cases of failure to succeed can be found; when and where a credible shock was initiated, the size and effectiveness of its impact on expectations often turned out to be smaller than intended, as private agents sometimes took the dent in price and wage inflation to be purely temporary. But here let us assume a favorable situation in which curbing expectations is feasible to some extent.

After the shock, the position of the short-term Phillips Curve in the unemployment-wage inflation plane will be lower. One may wonder how to best take advantage of this move, i.e., how to reach the preferred point on the curve and keep the curve low for as long as possible. These two objectives will be considered in turn.

In order to achieve the first objective, proper account must be taken of the effect of the price and incomes policy on aggregate demand. If the shock concerns prices first, as it does for instance when the rate of indirect taxation is decreased, the purchasing power of private incomes and wealth will increase; demand will then also increase, other things assumed equal. But a shock that concerns wages first has a depressing impact on demand (see the next section). These side effects cannot be neglected. They are sometimes viewed as usefully reinforcing the intended policy, for instance when the latter slows down wages and when fighting inflation has become the priority. But it might often be desirable to avoid significant movements along the Phillips Curve, so that a compensating action on demand will appear advisable: this was indeed recommended as a complement to wage austerity, when its main objective was to restore profitability; see Meade (1982) and Malinvaud (1982).

How long will the effect of the shock last after the end of the action that produced it? Some time ago conventional wisdom would have said that it cannot last very long: with adaptive expectations and the notion of an exogenously given NAIRU, inflation will soon return to what the monetary policy permits and the unemployment rate to its "natural" level. Are we still sure that this is the correct answer, now that the NAIRU is recognized as being subject to strong hysteresis, for whatever reason? Is not the growth of the money supply itself somewhat dependent on past inflation? I raise these questions without claiming to find answers to them in a well-founded macroeconomic theory; rather they are intended to suggest that our understanding of the phenomena involved is still uncertain.

But I believe we can say one thing about the durability of the supposed beneficial effect of a shock coming from a price and incomes policy. It will depend both on the broader policy package, including in particular demand management, and on the characteristics of the situation to which it applies. I particularly have in mind the nonlinearity of the Phillips Curve and more generally all the nonlinearities that disequilibrium macro-economics has led us to recognize. For instance, if the shock occurs at a time when the pressure of demand is high and if the policy package does not depress demand, the initial effect will soon be wiped out by the underlying inflationary forces that will immediately jeopardize the credibility of the policy.[4] On the contrary, when inflation coexists with gen-eralized excess supply, it is hardly sensitive to aggregate demand and much more depends on hysteresis in expectations; success in breaking expecta-tions has a better chance of durability.

V. Restoring Business Profitability

In the 1980s the objective given to price and incomes policy in Western Europe was not only to slow down inflation but also, and in some countries still more, to restore business profitability, which was seriously damaged. This new emphasis raised analytical questions that had not been

---

[4] I had an opportunity to describe a case of this type elsewhere; see Malinvaud (1978).

previously considered in recent times, such as how to find out what the appropriate real wage should be. As long as theoreticians do not have a clear conception on such issues and econometricians do not dispose of adequate tools and methodology to implement it, policymakers will act in the fog. This is why we have to devote attention to this now important aspect of our topic.

The Commission of the European Communities (1988) has computed an aggregate profitability index for the 12 countries of the Common Market from 1970 to 1988 (1961–1973 = 100). The index shows a small decline in the early 1970s, a drop to roughly 60 in 1975 and, after a slight improvement, to 59 in 1982. Although profitability recovered from this dramatic fall, the index for 1988 is still only at 82.

The definition of this index could be disputed[5] and it should be said more generally that problems and queries remain regarding the proper numerical characterization of the relevant features of the system of relative prices, costs and profit margins. The discussions and proposals concerning measurement of the "wage gap" in particular were recently surveyed by Helliwell (1988) in a very useful and thoughtful article that is interesting for our present purpose. The article shows that any well-founded measure of the wage gap has to rely on an explicit representation of the supply decisions taken by enterprises and that, at the present stage of macro-economics, there are various possibilities for this representation, leading to significantly different results. I may add that I see a basic flaw in the attempts made so far: they all take the capital stock as exogenously given for supply decisions; but the contemplated indicator is intended to serve in the analysis of medium-term evolution — an analysis for which the pace of investment is a crucial endogenous variable.

In order to consider indicators more directly relevant than the wage gap, we may concentrate on the profit rate and the real interest rate, since they play a major role when enterprises have to decide whether to take the risk of increasing their capacities, of creating or entering a market, sometimes even of remaining on a market.[6] But the definition of the profit rate should be properly corrected for inflation, which again raises conceptual and practical problems. Notwithstanding the difficulty of proper measurement, the trends were strong enough for us to know that profitability seriously deteriorated in Western Europe in the early 1980s and that, considering in particular the high level of real interest rates, it is still significantly less favorable than it was in the 1960s.

---

[5] So far as I understand, the index refers to the nonagricultural business sector (excluding housing) and profitability is defined as the ratio of the net operating surplus (as measured in national accounts) to a measure of the capital stock.

[6] Actually my work in Malinvaud (1987) leads me to prefer, instead of the profit rate, a chain index whose variation measures the impact of price and cost changes on this rate.

By the way, this historical case shows that there is more autonomy in the structure of relative prices and remuneration rates than neoclassical teaching would suggest. The notion of a factor price frontier now appears misleading when medium-term macroeconomic problems are discussed. I wonder whether this has been well realized in the profession.

Be that as it may, the case was clear five to seven years ago: business profitability had to be restored and incomes policy had to contribute to it to the extent that this was feasible. But in order to know what should be done now when the situation is less clear-cut, we need problematics that seem to be lacking. It is on the definition of these problematics that we now focus our attention.

It is convenient for the analysis to assume that government can control real unit costs, of labor, of capital, of imports and so on. Even in cases where price and incomes policy has some useful margin for action, real unit costs are intermediate objectives rather than instruments. Thus, the assumption is severe and I understand that it was criticized when I previously used it, in Malinvaud (1982). But I maintain that a good understanding of what government should do if it did control real costs is a prerequisite for being able to work out good advice to be given in practice.

Intuition tells us that at a given time, when the objective is employment at a 5 to 10 years' horizon, there is an appropriate level for the real wage and that this level depends on other real costs. Both a too low and a too high real wage would lead to less employment than this appropriate

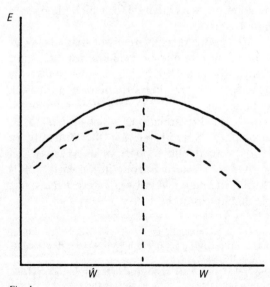

Fig. 1.

optimal wage does. Figure 1 illustrates the intuition without claiming to be more than suggestive (the lower curve refers to a situation in which the expected nonlabor real costs are less favorable than in the situation corresponding to the upper curve). This intuition is not new, as can be realized by reading, for instance, Robertson (1954).

To the extent that the intuition is valid, a tradeoff between employment and the purchasing power of those employed appears when starting from a situation where the real wage exceeds the level $\hat{w}$ that would be optimal for employment. As shown in Figure 1, this is also a tradeoff between full employment and income equalization, as lower wages mean higher profits, a tradeoff in which our fellow citizens now seem to believe since they do not object to the sharp restoration of profits.

Macroeconomists then have to elucidate whether the intuition is correct and, if so, how the relationship between the real wage rate and employment can be precisely defined and determined. This relationship involves three main routes, passing through the choice of capital intensity, the choice of productive capacity and the formation of aggregate demand, respectively. Let us consider them in turn.[7]

Capital intensity plays an unambiguous role. A rise in the real cost of labor induces, other things equal, a substitution of capital for labor. It thus depresses the demand for labor at a given level of the demand for goods. The causation chain involves long lags, since the substitution occurs mainly when capital is replaced or grows and since the crucial variable is not the current value of the real wage, but the expected value over the useful lifetime of the new equipment, an expected value that is likely to react slowly. Thus, capital-labor substitutability alone would make employment a decreasing function of the real wage, but a slowly decreasing function unless the horizon is quite long. Among the other variables that determine the speed of the substitution, the main one is the real cost of capital.

The role of productive capacity is more difficult to determine precisely. On the one hand, higher capacity means a higher demand for labor. This is particularly true in an open economy where competition from abroad disputes market shares with domestic producers. But the phenomenon occurs even in a closed economy: high or quickly growing productive capacity stimulates a rich supply of goods, hence a higher fulfilled demand for goods and a higher demand for labor.

On the other hand, the link between the real wage rate and productive capacity is somewhat ambiguous. I argue below that the demand for goods is an increasing function of the real wage. A higher wage therefore stimulates the growth of capacity through the formation of aggregate

---

[7] The argument is spelled out more fully in Malinvaud (1988).

demand. But it also depresses it through its effect on profitability. Indeed, higher costs mean a lower profit rate and the expectation of lower profits makes it less easy for entrepreneurs to take the risk of creating new productive capacities.

Of this positive effect through aggregate demand and negative effect through profitability, which one dominates? A precise answer cannot be given today because our econometric knowledge is too limited. This answer is likely to depend on the reference situation. In particular, my work in Malinvaud (1987) led me to conclude that profitability had a weak effect on capacity when starting from a situation of good profitability, but a strong effect in the opposite case. Thus, consideration of productive capacity building alone would make employment an increasing function of the real wage at low levels of this wage, but a decreasing function at high wages.

The relationship between real wage and employment through productive capacity moreover implies a number of other variables. I will not list them here, but only mention the real costs of capital and imported inputs. Increases in these costs deteriorate profitability, hence the demand for labor on this account.

The view according to which an increase in the real wage rate stimulates the demand for goods, thereby also the demand for labor, has long been held by some economists, but does not yet seem to be generally accepted. The crucial question is to know whether a shift in income distribution in favor of wages decreases national saving. In Malinvaud (1986) I gave my reasons for believing in truth of the property. But I noted, on that occasion in particular, that my conclusion was not shared by everybody. I later noticed that Marglin (1984) devoted a good deal of attention to the issue, with one long and careful chapter on estimations from quarterly U.S. data for the period 1952–79, reaching, however, mitigated conclusions.

In order to have the full impact on aggregate demand, investment also has to be taken into account. An increase in the wage rate accelerates the substitution of capital for labor and this means an increase in investment, which would reinforce the decrease in saving. But an inverse effect will occur if and when capacity expansion slows down as a consequence of wage increase.

It seems clear from the preceding discussion that, in order to know the tradeoff illustrated by Figure 1, an important tradeoff for incomes policy, an appropriate model has to be specified and confronted with all the relevant econometric evidence that can be found. I sketched what I believe to be the main building blocks of this model.

But its full elaboration also requires a decision about its scope, i.e., about the exogeneity assumptions it will accept. These assumptions will then imply how the model can be used when economic policy is considered in practice. For instance, if the model takes budgetary policy as exogenous, as I would recommend, then it will not suffice for the full discussion of price and incomes measures that directly react on government receipt and expenditure. For instance, a decrease in prices through a reduction in indirect tax rates also means an increase in the budget deficit, which has to be financed; this financing may have to be studied outside the model, since it may imply feedback effects on the tradeoff under study. Similarly, when a decision concerning the legal minimum wage is contemplated, it may be necessary to take into account its impact on the expectations of the foreign exchange market, hence on the rate of exchange of the domestic currency; this impact may react in various ways on the phenomena examined here (cost of imported inputs, competitiveness of domestic producers,...).

All this shows the wide extent of the demands that government advisers on economic policy matters may have to address to economic research.

References

Atkinson, A. & Stiglitz, J.: *Lectures on Public Economics.* McGraw-Hill, England, 1980.

Axell, B.: *Can Inflation be Prohibited?* IUI, Stockholm 1985 (in Swedish); summary in English in *IUI Yearbook 1986–87.*

Brown, C.: Minimum wage laws: Are they overrated? *Journal of Economic Perspectives,* Summer 1988.

Calmfors, L. & Driffill, J.: Bargaining structure, corporatism and macroeconomic performance. *Economic Policy,* no. 6, 1988.

Commission of the European Communities: Annual Economic Report, 1988–89, *European Economy,* no. 38, Nov. 1988.

Feroldi, M. & Meunier, F.: La boucle prix-salaires. *Economie et Statistique,* no. 167, 1984.

Helliwell, J.: Comparative macroeconomics of stagflation. *Journal of Economic Literature,* March 1988.

Jeanneney, J.-M. (ed.): *L'économie française depuis 1967.* Le Seuil, Paris, 1989.

Malinvaud, E.: Some problems of prices and incomes policy in France. In R. Stone & W. Peterson (eds.), *Econometric Contributions to Public Policy,* Macmillan, London, 1978.

Malinvaud, E.: Wages and unemployment. *Economic Journal,* March 1982.

Malinvaud, E.: Pure profits as forced saving. *The Scandinavian Journal of Economics* 88 (1), 1986.

Malinvaud, E.: Capital productif, incertitudes et profitabilité. *Annales d'Economie et de Statistique,* mars 1987; presentation in English as Conference Tinbergen in *De Economist,* 1989.

Malinvaud, E.: *Real Wages and Employment: A Decade of Analysis.* The Stamp Memorial Lecture, University of London, 1988.

Marglin, S.: *Growth, Distribution and Prices,* Harvard University Press, Cambridge, MA, 1984.

Meade, J.: Domestic stabilization and the balance of payments. *Lloyds Bank Review,* Jan. 1982.

Pohjola, M.: Corporatism and wage bargaining: A survey. Labour Institute for Economic Research, Helsinki, 1988.

Ralle, P.: Les déterminants macroéconomiques du taux de salaire ont-ils changé depuis 1982? Note INSEE, Paris, 1987.

Robertson, D.: *Wages,* The Stamp Memorial Lecture, University of London, 1954.

Comment on E. Malinvaud, "The Macroeconomic Tradeoffs of Price and Income Policies"

Seppo Honkapohja

Academy of Finland, Helsinki, Finland

Remark on the Definition

Malinvaud's paper is a concise general overview of many of the main issues and experiences of incomes policies of the 1970s and 1980s. I especially welcome the views based on the French experience which are less often presented than, say, the British ones.

My first comment is about Malinvaud's interpretation of the notion of incomes policies. He does not give any general definition of the concept. According to the traditional definition, five kinds of policy measures are called "incomes policies". They are guidelines, temporary measures (such as squeezes), statutory norms, indexation schemes and TIPs. I sense that Malinvaud relies on a somewhat broader notion of incomes policy than the traditional one, as he discusses, in addition to the customary aspects, measures such as transfer and tax changes which might rather be classified under fiscal policy. However, this choice may well be an appropriate one, in so far as such actions directly interfere with the formation of wages, prices and therefore incomes in a fairly general way. Note also that TIP has some characteristics of a fiscal measure.

Influencing Wage Bargaining

One of Malinvaud's first points of emphasis is the idea of interfering with the bargaining process in the labor market. He seems to be in agreement with some of the new literature on bargaining and corporatism in that it is not the degree of centralization *per se* but rather the "degree of consensus" about broader issues, such as the macroeconomic circumstances and government policies, that is quite an important element for the success of incomes policies. In fact, it has been the case on various occasions that, at least in economies with centralized bargaining, the government is an active third party in the process, standing ready to introduce tax or transfer policies as part of the deal — the "social contract". Under Malinvaud's broad definition of incomes policies, such actions are included in the concept, although they would not be under the traditional notion.

I might add that one particular avenue for government influence in centralized wage formation processes is the creation of suitable, improved information structures. An example, e.g. in Finland, would be a government body of experts providing consensus statistics on recent macro-economic development (and perhaps forecasts for the future as well) as a background for wage bargaining. We know from the recent theoretical work on dynamic games of incomplete information that the equilibria depend a great deal on the information structure in the game. I am not aware of any formal modeling of this idea so far, but the notion of influence on the game structure might be added to the wide definition of incomes policies.

Some Further Issues

Let me now move on to discuss some points already emphasized by Malinvaud, but from a slightly different angle.

Malinvaud treats the different objectives of incomes policies in turn, but at times he does not make explicit the important distinction between nominal and real magnitudes in wages, prices and incomes. Sometimes, incomes policy measures are justified by the argument that their objective is to influence only nominal magnitudes, when in fact it is real wages and incomes that will also be changed by the policy measures. If this is the case, the policy will typically run into trouble rather easily, as competitive forces will try to correct back the distribution of incomes. This kind of explanation may well be plausible for some of the European experiences in the 1980s, as it is often claimed that Europe is characterized by real-wage stickiness. Explicit attempts to influence real wages are also central in the goal of restoring profitability that is emphasized so much by Malinvaud. Politicians have been very reluctant to state objectives of policy clearly enough, and one can agree with Malinvaud that a clear definition of objectives is important.

The distinction is perhaps not so important when the primary goal is a reduction in income inequalities. In such a case there is an explicit attempt to influence the distribution of incomes in favor of less well-off people, so that the focus is on *relative wages and incomes*. Nevertheless, the success of an incomes policy with redistributive goals probably depends in part on at least small growth of real incomes for all economic agents in the presence of policy restraint. This suggests that the probability of success for policies of wage restraint (aimed at redistribution) is the highest in a period of fairly rapid growth of the economy.

Malinvaud points out that incomes policies may have contractionary or expansionary effects on aggregate demand, depending on the nature of the policy measures. While there can be general agreement about this sugges-tion, we are left wondering about the specific circumstances. Historically, incomes policies have often been introduced as part of a contractionary package, and then wage restraints have added to the depressive elements. However, this need not be the case, as incomes policy measures could perhaps be effective as part of an expansionary policy deal. I interpret the suggestions about TIP voiced in Britain in this light.

Finally, Malinvaud makes no comment about the success or failure of incomes policies as depending on the nature of exogenous shocks that hit an economy at various times. Income policy measures introduce rigidities and restraints which may be less and less appropriate after various kinds of shocks. The policy schemes are typically not flexible enough to work for longer periods of time. It is generally agreed that the market economies were subject to unusually large shocks in the 1970s. Besides the uncertainties about macro relations, e.g. the real wage-employment relation emphasized by Malinvaud, this may provide an additional expla-nation for the currently bad record of incomes policy in the minds of many economists.

Comment on E. Malinvaud, "The Macroeconomic Tradeoffs of Price and Income Policies"

Torsten Persson

Institute for International Economic Studies, Stockholm, Sweden

Malinvaud's stimulating paper covers a range of issues regarding price and income policies. My comment will focus on a narrower set of issues: in keeping with the theme of the conference, I address only policies whose proximate objective is to influence *aggregate* price and wage indices. Furthermore, among ultimate policy objectives, I only consider macroeconomic objectives. This means that I disregard Section III of the paper — about reducing inequalities — altogether. For concreteness, I would like to discuss policies such as direct wage and price controls, or possibly tax-based incomes policies (TIPs), and — again in keeping with the theme of the conference — their potential effectiveness in reducing inflation or unemployment. I begin by addressing the costs of such policies, then their possible benefits.

Costs of Controls

Malinvaud does not emphasize the microeconomic, resource costs tied to price and wage controls, but rather the possible costs in terms of altered macroeconomic outcomes. I think it is important to discuss the microeconomic costs of such policies, however. Indeed, the main point I would like to make in this comment is that the most important tradeoffs are likely to be between certain microeconomic costs and uncertain macroeconomic benefits.

The costs are generally of two kinds. First, managing controls means incurring direct administrative costs: it has not been uncommon in Europe to find whole government bureaucracies largely preoccupied with managing price and wage controls. Second, imposing controls means incurring misallocation costs. To fix ideas, consider an economy with firm-specific, or sector-specific productivity shocks. These shocks are unobservable to the policymaker, at least in the short run. Wage controls at the aggregate level in this economy, would rule out wage increases above a certain level in all firms and sectors, which cut the upper tail of warranted wage dispersion. Imposing wage controls is thus effectively like imposing a prohibitive tax on employment in the high-productivity sectors. Imposing a TIP — with strong disincentives for wage increases above a certain level — is still like a tax, although not a prohibitive tax.

Such costs are certain to appear; their size is an empirical question. At a general level we can only say that the costs are larger, the more effective the controls are intended to be and — to continue the previous example — the larger the need for wage dispersion. The need for wage dispersion, in turn, is larger, the larger the variance of the sectorial shocks and the longer the controls are in place.

Benefits of Controls

Because of the microeconomic costs, price and wage controls are not likely to be used in "normal" situations. Let us therefore concentrate on their possible benefits in "abnormal" situations. To focus the discussion further, I find it useful to consider separately two situations: one where inflation is the main policy problem — which is basically what Malinvaud does in Section IV — and another where unemployment is the main policy problem — which is basically what Malinvaud does in Section V.

Let us first look at an economy with a serious inflation problem: inflation in, at least, double digits. In such an economy the basic distortion is typically in policy itself, with monetary policy accommodating lax fiscal policy, or simply financing large budget deficits via the inflation tax. Without a change in policy incentives — because a new government enters, or because of external pressure for policy change — there is no cure for inflation. Supposing that the right incentives for policy change are there, the fear of high transitional output losses and unemployment may still prevent implementing the necessary stabilization program, a combination of restrictive fiscal and monetary policy. The risk for such transitional costs is particularly high when the economy suffers from "inflation inertia" such that nominal wages and prices continue to rise at a high rate after the stabilization program has been put in place. Inflation inertia may either be backward looking — because wages and maybe some prices are more or less fully indexed — or forward looking — because the government has low credibility in its announcement that the stabilization program will be maintained.

It is conceivable that wage and price controls can help diminish the transitional costs of a serious stabilization program. In theory, such policies are closely directed towards the main distortion causing the output and employment losses, i.e., that nominal wages and prices continue to rise at a pace far above the new and lower monetary growth. According to this argument, controls are not a substitute for, but a complement to, conventional restrictive policies. I think Malinvaud touches on a similar point in his discussion of a broad policy package in Section IV. In practice, stabilization attempts which have used controls as a substitute for policies with a more lasting effect on inflation have failed badly. Among the few examples where controls have indeed been used as a complement to conventional restrictive policies is the successful "heterodox" Israeli stabilization program in 1985–86.

Let us instead look at a problem closer to the recent experience in continential Europe, an economy with a serious unemployment problem: unemployment in, at least, double digits. To identify the basic distortion in this case is, as we know, much harder than in the inflation case. The most popular candidates, both at this conference and elsewhere, focus on distortions in wage and price formation and on adjustment costs, for labor as well as for capital. The candidates have a common feature, however, in that they all suggest a "real", not a "monetary" problem. In that vein, Malinvaud centers his discussion in Section V on affecting the real wage.

Without a clear view of what the distortion is, it is not so easy to come up with a convincing policy analysis. If the distortion has to do with wage and price formation, presumably a policy with long-lasting effects would have to affect the incentives in wage and price setting. It is difficult too see how price and wage controls could do that. Some — such as Jackman and Layard — might argue that TIPs could be part of a policy package that affected incentives in the right direction. Even if this were possible, it seems that the TIPs would have to be effective for a long time, perhaps sufficiently long for the microeconomic costs to become prohibitive. In contrast to the inflation case — where there might be a *short-run* role for price and income policies in correcting a *monetary* problem — it is difficult to see a *long-run* role for such policies in correcting a *real* problem.

Conclusion

I have argued that policymakers who contemplate price and income policies essentially contemplate trading off certain microeconomic costs against uncertain macroeconomic benefits. If inflation inertia is a major problem, there might be large enough benefits to consider temporary price and income policies as complements to conventional restrictive policies in an anti-inflation program. It is difficult to see any conceivable benefits in an anti-unemployment program.

Effects of Productivity, Total Domestic-Product Demand and "Incentive Wages" on Unemployment in a Non-Monetary Customer-Market Model of the Small Open Economy

*Edmund S. Phelps**

Columbia University, New York, NY, USA

Abstract

A small open economy is studied where the labor market exhibits job rationing owing to the elevated wage induced by the "shirking" problem. With the world product market "neo-classical", a (bad) national productivity shock reduces employment and the real wage even in the short run; a "demand" shock is undefined for a country too small to affect price nonnegligibly. With the world a "customer market", employment may rise with the domestic productivity shock before it falls; increased foreign demand raises both employment and the relative world price. But it does not follow that a general increase of demand raises world employment.

I. Introduction

A series of my recent papers work toward the development of a structuralist theory, nonmonetary for the most part yet non-(neo)classical, of long swings in economic activity. A slump — a bulge of unemployment — is shown to result in an *open* economy from positive real-interest shocks and negative "marginal efficiency" shocks in Phelps (1988a); in a *closed* economy from negative shocks to private or public saving in Phelps (1988b); and in *either* economy from a slowdown of productivity in Phelps (1987b). As in the earlier structuralist explorations by Bruno and Sachs (1985), Lal and van Wijnbergen (1985), Fitoussi and Phelps (1986), and

---

*Research for this paper was supported by a grant from the Consiglio Nazionale delle Ricerche to the Department of Economics, Secondà Università (Tor Vergata), Rome, which I visited in June 1988.

Hickman (1987), the mechanisms in these models all operate through a contraction of the derived demand for labor in the face of some sort of real wage stickiness or modified rigidity, which causes increased unemployment.

Here I intend to revisit from a somewhat different viewpoint two findings from my previous work: One is the implication that a slowdown of productivity drives up unemployment. The other is the unorthodox implication that increased foreign demand or domestic demand for the customer good produced by a country will likewise drive up unemployment — insofar as it has the indirect effect of boosting the real interest rate and thus dampening capital-goods output. But these findings were all obtained from one- or two-sector models in which product markets clear and pure competition prevails. If studied in the framework of a more "frictional", yet nonmonetary, model — in particular, one without an auctioneer setting the price level in the product market — would these propositions still find support?

This paper reopens the inquiry with the use of a customer-market treatment of the international product market. An incentive-wage treatment of labor-market equilibrium to generate generalized real-wage rigidity completes the model. The findings are (i) a productivity decline, though ultimately contractionary for employment, causes employment to rise before it falls, and (ii) an increase of foreign demand that is specific to the supplies of our country's firms, not part of a worldwide increase of demand for all firms' output, raises the quantity and the relative world price of domestic output, thus expanding employment and the real wage. But the latter finding does not imply that a global increase of *general* (rather than country-specific) demand will raise employment in all countries since the concomitant rise in the relative world price of every country's outputs is a contradiction in terms. (In fact, an analysis of a closed-economy customer-market model subsequent to this paper shows that increased consumer demand, owing to increased public debt, say, is again contractionary.)

As a member of the middle-age generation I can hear the voices of the older generation saying: "We Keynesian have long known that a productivity decline means that meeting 'effective demand' will (or at any rate may) require increased employment, and we have always understood that increased effective demand will also increase employment." But with regard to productivity shocks, the models of Keynesians and monetarists are *monetary* models possessing some short-term monetary nonneutrality while I dispense with monetary mechanisms in my investigation; similar conclusions would be a coincidence. Further, those monetary models do *not* imply that a negative productivity shock boosts employment. From Colonel Wright and Alvin Hansen to latter-day models, e.g. Nelson (1966) and Phelps (1978), Keynesian analyses have generally held, after weighing opposing effects, that "stagnation" and "oil shocks" have a contractionary impact on the rate of employment.

With regard to the proposition on foreign demand and even domestic demand for the country's product, the Keynesian/monetarist theory likewise does not bring home the bacon. Milton Friedman, in praise of fluctuating exchange rates, argued that a drop of foreign or domestic demand for the home-produced good will set off a depreciation of the currency until employment and the nominal interest rate have recovered to their former levels. The Mundell-Fleming model offers a formalization. To argue contrariwise that employment contacts in the Keynesian model, properly analyzed, one would want to show the expectation of a (partial) recovery of the currency, perhaps based on expectations of rising domestic wealth accumulation, which would operate to prevent the full fall of the currency needed to maintain employment; see Claassen and Krauss (1985).

Section II of this paper introduces the labor market, Section III the product market, and Section IV analyzes the effects of disturbances. Section V reviews the conclusions and makes some needed caveats.

II. "Incentive Wages" and the Labor-Market Equilibrium Locus

Crucial to the relevance of customer-market theory to employment in a country is the premise that domestic and foreign labor are not perfect technical substitutes in the supply of a firm to either overseas or domestic customers. Domestic labor has some advantage over foreign labor, at the same product wage, in supplying the output produced by "domestic" firms, even that sold to foreign customers. For simplicity I treat domestic firms as using only domestic labor, foreign firms as using only foreign labor.

The supply side of the model will be taken up first. Here I use a version of the shirking model of wage policy introduced by Calvo (1977) and Bowles (1979). This model and the earlier turnover model, centering on the quitting problem, are the two pillars of the incentive-wage, or efficiency-wage, theory of nonclearing equilibrium in the labor market. This approach as certain advantages of simplicity over the approach postulating gradual adjustment to some "long-run" ultimate-natural rate.

In this model, the firm uses some employees as monitors to detect the occasional "shirking" — the inattention or lethargy — of the others, dismissing anyone so detected. As long as the unemployment pool is too small to suffice as a deterrent, each firm boosts it wages to heighten its employees' incentive not to shirk (to the point where marginal benefit equals marginal cost). The resulting elevation of the general level of wages causes the unemployment rate to rise until a level is reached at which the representative firm is content not to try again to push its pay to an above-industry level.

The number of firms is taken to be fixed, the events considered here being supposed insufficient to precipitate new entry or exit. The firms are all alike. Let z denote the output, and n the number of employees at such a firm. Then $\tilde{n}$ will denote employment per firm at firms other than the one we are examining, and n^e will denote the firms' expectation of employment per firm elsewhere. With the labor force a constant, the number of persons supplied to the labor market per firm is a constant, n_s. Similarly, v is the firm's real wage, $\tilde{v}$ is the real wage elsewhere, hence approximately the average market wage, and v^e is the expected wage elsewhere or expected market wage. Labor-market equilibrium means $\tilde{v} = v^e$ and $\tilde{n} = n^e$. Since the identically situated firms will behave identically, at least in equilibrium, we also have $\tilde{n} = n$ and $\tilde{v} = v$.

A firm's output is in proportion to the number of employees engaged directly in production, $(1 - m)\, n$, where m is the fraction who are instead engaged in monitoring, multiplied by their average "effectiveness", e, which reflects their inducements not to shirk. Letting A denote the productivity of a unit of labor of standardized effectiveness — an indicator of the technology — the firm's input problem may be seen as choosing v, m, and n, to

$$\text{minimize } vn \text{ subject to } A(1 - m)\, ne = z^0(> 0). \tag{1}$$

Effectiveness is a concave function of m and v; it is increasing in m and in the excess of v over the "opportunity cost" $v^e[(1 - b)(n^e/n_s) + b]$, where b is fixed ratio of the public unemployment benefit to the market wage. This opportunity cost is a rough approximation to the expected value of the income obtainable by an employee if caught shirking and hence dismissed. It is equal to $v^e[1 - (1 - b)\, u^e]$, where u^e is the expected unemployment rate, $1 - (n^e/n_s)$. In this formulation I am following Jackman et al. (1988) and Summers (1989). In equilibrium, therefore, e can be represented by a function $e(m, v - \tilde{v}[(1 - b)(\tilde{n}/n_s) + b])$. Equivalently the firm may be regarded as choosing v and m to achieve the minimum value of unit costs, which in equilibrium is a function of $\tilde{n}$ and $\tilde{v}$:

$$c(\tilde{n}, \tilde{v}; A, b) = \min_{v, m}\left[\frac{v}{A(1 - m)\, e(m, v - \tilde{v}[(1 - b)(\tilde{n}/n_s) + b])}\right]. \tag{2}$$

The existence of this minimum can be taken for granted.

This cost minimum satisfies the first-order conditions

$$ve_2 = e \tag{3}$$

$$(1 - m)\, e_1 = e \tag{4}$$

and the second-order conditions

$$e_{22} < 0 \tag{5a}$$

$$-[2e_1 - (1 - m)\, e_{11}] < 0 \tag{5b}$$

$$e\chi < 0,\ \chi \equiv \left\{ v e_{22} + (v e_{21} - e_1)\, \frac{(1 - m)\, e_{12} - e_2}{2e_1 - (1 - m)\, e_{11}} \right\} e^{-1}. \tag{5c}$$

To see how the cost-minimizing v and thus ultimately $\tilde{v}$ behaves we calculate the total differcntials of equations (3) and (4) and solve for dv as a function of $d\tilde{v}$ and $d\tilde{n}$, obtaining

$$dv = \frac{[(1 - b)\, \tilde{n}/n_s + b](e\chi - e_2)}{e\chi}\, d\tilde{v} + \frac{(1 - b)\, \tilde{v}/n_s(e\chi - e_2)}{e\chi}\, d\tilde{n}. \tag{6}$$

As will become clear, too large a b, meaning a value too close to one, precludes the existence of a labor-market equilibrium at any rate of unemployment. But suppose that b is zero or, if positive, small enough that $b < e\chi /(e\chi - e_2)$ so that the "critical" employment rate $\hat{n}/n_s$ defined by

$$(1 - b)\, \frac{\hat{n}}{n_s} + b = \frac{-e\chi}{-(e\chi - e_2)} \tag{7}$$

is positive. Note that since the r.h.s. of (7) is positive, by (5c), there must exist such b, and since this r.h.s. is less than one, so also is the critical employment rate. Then for all nonnegative $\tilde{n}$ smaller than $\hat{n}$ the coefficient of $d\tilde{v}$ in (6) is, although positive, less than one. Now set $\tilde{n}$ close to zero in equations (3)–(6). Then a firm would find it optimal to offer a positive wage even if $\tilde{v}$ were zero, though in equilibrium the identical behavior of the firms implies $\tilde{v} = v$, so that unless $b = 0$ each firm would find it optimal to offer a higher wage than the former one; this is implied by (3)–(4) as dissected in (6). Since the coefficient of $d\tilde{v}$ in (6) is less than one in the present case it is logically possible that one can find a unique $\tilde{v}$ just large enough that the firm's optimal v is equal to it; only if the coefficient asymptotically approached one as $\tilde{v}$ went to infinity would such a fixed point not be found, and this complication, if it arose, could be excluded by requiring $b = 0$. Of course, labor-market equilibrium here requires $\tilde{n} = n$ as well as $\tilde{v} = v$; but the above analysis is quite consistent with our firm's n being equal to the other firms' $\tilde{n}$. So for $\tilde{n}$ close to zero there is no fundamental obstacle to the existence of a labor-market equilibrium.

As the employment rate, $\tilde{n}/n_s$, is progressively increased, while kept always smaller than the critical rate, the equilibrium market wage rises.

228   E. S. Phelps

With $\tilde{v} = v$ and $d\tilde{v} = dv$, (7) yields

$$\frac{dv}{d\tilde{n}} = \frac{v/n_s(1-b)(e\chi - e_2)/e\chi}{1 - \frac{[(1-b)\tilde{n}/n_s + b](e\chi - e_2)}{e\chi}} > 0. \tag{8}$$

In this "multiplier" formula, the multiplicand (the numerator) is unambiguously positive and the multiplier (the reciprocal of the denominator) is positive for all $\tilde{n} < \hat{n}$.

In contrast, it is clear that for $\tilde{n}/n_s$ above the critical employment rate no labor-market equilibrium exists. In this interval, as before, a positive wage is optimal and that implies that the other firms will have a positive wage too. Yet here one cannot find a $\tilde{v}$ high enough to erase the gap between v and $\tilde{v}$. Hence no equilibrium exists here. If the employment rate could somehow be held at some supra-critical level wages would explode. There is in this interval no economic meaning to the derivative analogous to that in equation (8). The purpose of this analysis of the supra-critical interval has been precisely to avoid the mistake of calculating such a derivative and assuming that it shows the "equilibrium wage" to be decreasing in the employment rate at "high-employment".

Figure 1 illustrates the labor-market equilibrium locus.

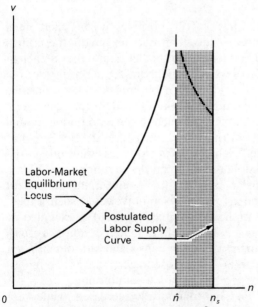

Fig. 1. The labor-market equilibrium locus.

III. The International Customer Market

The objective is a model of a small open economy in which all firms, foreign and domestic, operate in a market subject to informational frictions. In one polar case, all the relevant customers are nationals, and foreign firms (the firms that produce with foreign labor) are successful in competing for some share of that market. This setting is used, without attention to certain complications, in Phelps (1987a). At the other pole, domestic firms export virtually all their final output, nationals comprising a negligible fraction of their stock of customers. The latter setting was convenient in Phelps (1986). The former case poses the analytical complication that the wealth of customers on which their consumer demand depends constitutes a state variable requiring a differential equation. The limitation of the latter case is that it does not shed any light on the effects of changes in domestic demand. But it does permit an analysis of the effects of a change in foreign demand as well as those of a productivity change. I shall take up that case here.

The setting of the firms and their behavior is borrowed as extensively as possible from the partial-equilibrium model in the Phelps-Winter paper (1970). The firms in the economy are many and similar, all in a symmetrical situation so that in the last analysis they will behave identically. They are in atomistic competition — with the numerous overseas firms of the world market and, negligibly, with each other — in the sense that each is too small to have a perceptible effect on the sales of the other firms in the world market.

The firms' respective products, though not identical in every respect, such as location, are essentially perfect substitutes in the long-run sense that price differentials are not indefinitely sustainable: if a firm tried to maintain its price forever above that of the others in the world market (by some nonvanishing differential), that firm would gradually lose its entire "market", or market share, to the latter competitors. Yet, owing to frictions in the transmission of information, a firm that charges less than the "going" price will not instantaneously gain the whole market, and owing to the costs of gathering information about alternative suppliers, a firm that unexpectedly changes more than the going price will not instantaneously or abruptly lose all is market share.

As a result of these frictions, each firm at any moment can be said to have a stock of customers, x, who are consumers regularly buying there and not prepared immediately to buy from any other source. In the case here, x is a stock of apparently homogenous overseas customers, nationals being a negligible share of the world market. At every moment, then, the firm has to set a price, p, for these homogeneous buyers. This price is the firm's relative price in the world market, so the representative firm in the world market always has a price equal to 1; equivalently, p is the firm's real price in terms of the representative overseas firm's supplies.

The dynamics of a firm's market share are represented by the differential equation

$$dx/dt = g(p)x, g'(p) < 0, g''(p) < 0, g(1) = 0, g(p) < \infty \text{ for } p > 0. \tag{9}$$

Again, by choice of units, the average world price, $p^* = 1$, is an implicit constant here, being the numeraire with which to measure a firms' real price and real wage in our small open economy.

At each moment, the firm's output, z, is planned to meet exactly the amount demanded by its current stock of customers at its current price, $D(p; y^*)x$. So, by hypothesis, the product market clears at each firm. Hence one could as well suppose that the firm choses the quantity and auctions it offer to the identical buyers in equal lot sizes. Here y^* can be thought of as real income (in units of the numeraire good) per customer, which is exogenous since virtually all customers are foreign and our country is too small to affect their real incomes; more generally, y^* is a shift parameter, with $D_{y^*}(p; y^*) > 0$, indicating the state of demand, which is essentially foreign demand, for the outputs of the country's firms.

$$z = D(p; y^*)x, D'(p) < 0, 0 < D''(p) < 2D'(p)^2(1/D(p)),$$

$$D(p) = 0 \text{ if } p \geq p^0 > 0. \tag{10}$$

As specified in part I, the firm faces constant costs, given the wage and the unemployment rate on which the propensity to shirk depends, so that its total cost, given by

$$C = v[A(1 - m)e]^{-1}z, \tag{11}$$

is proportional to its own output, z. But aggregate output also enters in implicitly — more precisely, aggregate output adjusted by productivity, z/A. It is an implication of the system comprised by (1), (3), (4) and the equilibrium conditions ($n = \tilde{n}$ and so forth) that, first, economy-wide employment must increase with economy-wide productivity-adjusted output and, second, that what may be called the effective real wage, $v[A(1 - m)e]^{-1}$, which is just unit cost, increases with economy-wide employment. (We noted earlier that the real wage was increasing in the employment rate wherever the equilibrium locus is defined; it is now being added that shirking or monitoring or both increase with employment as well.) Hence the firm's unit cost, c, is increasing in the other firms' productivity-adjusted output, and there may be said to be rising "industry cost" despite constant cost at the individual firm. Total cost may therefore be written

$$C = c(D(\tilde{p}; y^*)\tilde{x}A^{-1}; A^{-1})D(p; y^*)x, c'(\tilde{z}/A, A^{-1}) > 0. \tag{12}$$

The setting in which the individual firm operates is very much like that of the Phelps-Winter firm except that here the effective wage rate moves with aggregate employment as just seen. At each moment the firm's optimal pricing policy must maximize (from that moment forward) the present value of the expected future stream of quasi-rent, or real "cash" flow, resulting from its policy and the informational frictions in the market. Hence the individual firm maximizes

$$\int_0^\infty F(p, x; \tilde{p}, \tilde{x}) \exp(-r^*t) \, dt \text{ s.t. } dx/dt = G(p, x) \text{ and } x(0) = x_0 \quad (13)$$

where $F(p, x) = [p - c(D(\tilde{p}; y^*) \tilde{x} A^{-1}; A^{-1})] D(p; y^*) x,$

$G(p, x) = g(p) x.$

The optimal path of the firm's price has the property that at each moment it maximizes the Hamiltonian,

$$H(p, x) = F(p, x) + qG(p, x). \quad (14)$$

Hence the first-order and second-order conditions are

$$0 = F_p + qG_p \quad (15)$$

$$F_{pp} + (-F_p/G_p) G_{pp} < 0 \quad (16)$$

and q, the shadow price of customers, obeys the relation

$$dq/dt = r^*q - (F_x + qG_x). \quad (17)$$

It should be remarked that all the "prices" in this maximization are being expressed in terms of the supplies of the representative foreign firm, so the real rate of interest here is likewise the world rate, not the national rate; the latter would be higher than the world rate by the amount of the "real inflation", $d\tilde{p}/dt(1/\tilde{p})$, or equivalently, the rate of real exchange-rate depreciation.

IV. General Equilibrium Dynamics and the Effect of Shocks

To describe general equilibrium we use (15) — that is, $q = -F_p/G_p$ — which makes q a function of x and p, in order to calculate the derivative dq/dt in terms of x and p, evaluating it at $x = \tilde{x}$ and $p = \tilde{p}$. The result is

$$\dot{q} = (-1/G_p) \{[F_{pp} + F_{p\tilde{p}} - (F_p/G_p) G_{pp}] \dot{\tilde{p}} + [F_{px} + F_{p\tilde{x}} - (F_p/G_p) G_{px}] \dot{\tilde{x}}\} \quad (18)$$

Using (18) and (15) in (17) then gives

$$\dot{\tilde{p}} = \frac{r^*F_p + (F_xG_p - F_pG_x) - (F_{px} + F_{p\tilde{x}} - (F_p/G_p) G_{px}) G}{F_{pp} + F_{p\tilde{p}} - (F_p/G_p) G_{pp}} \quad (19)$$

232   E. S. Phelps

The character of the contour of points $(\tilde{p}, \tilde{x})$ along which the r.h.s. is equal to zero is quite similar to the corresponding contour obtained in the Phelps–Winter model where increasing cost is internal to the firm, not external. Here the external cost effect of increased x at other firms makes $H_{p\tilde{x}} > 0$ just as the internal cost effect made the analogous $H_{px} > 0$ in the fixed-wage model (which evidently has in mind a small Marshallian industry).

To close the general-equilibrium dynamic system we need only to reuse at the macro (small-country) level the differential equation for the growth of customers previously used to describe the growth or decay of the customer stock at any individual firm in the economy. Hence

$$\dot{x} = g(p)\,\tilde{x}. \tag{20}$$

To study the motion of the economy under conditions of general equilibrium (that is, correct expectations), the standard phase diagram in Figure 2 may be used. The locus of points on which $\dot{p}$ is constant, obtained from (19), is labeled $K(\cdot) = 0$. The lcous of points on which $\dot{x}$ is the horizontal line labeled $G(\cdot) = 0$. This system is saddle-path stable and generates the uniquely-determined price-customer stock relationship shown by the curve labeled $\tilde{p} = P(\tilde{x}; y^*, A^{-1})$. This relationship uses the fact that, starting from an identical situation, the stock of customers of all the firms in the country will remain equal. The diagram shows that, given a

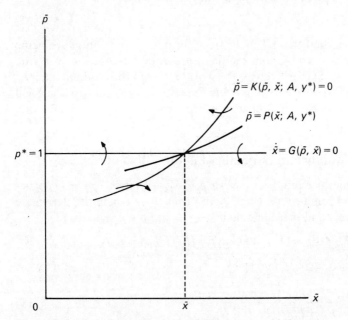

Fig. 2. Macro view of optimal price-level and custom-stock dynamics.

stable environment with respect to foreign demand, national costs, and so forth, the economy gravitates asymptotically toward a unique steady state corresponding to that environment.

Let us now consider the effects of three parameters on the path of the real price, the employment rate, and the real wage. The first is y^*, which serves as a shift parameter measuring the intensity of customers demand. The second will be A^{-1}, an increase of which represents a (positive) cost shock. The third shift parameter of interest is $\hat{n}$, a contraction of which shifts leftward and upward the relevant portion of the wage-employment locus. I will concentrate on the effects of these disturbances over the near term, leaving to the interested reader or discussant the question of long-term effects. The analysis will be confined to small disturbances upon the economy when initially in a state of rest — that is, at the rest point, RP.

An increase of y^* shifts up the P curve, thus causing the real national price level to jump up, if and only it shifts up the $K(p, x) = 0$ curve. Taking the derivative of the ordinate of that curve at the initial x yields

$$(d\tilde{p}/dy^*)|_{K(\cdot)=0} = (r^*F_{py^*} + G_pF_{xy^*})/[-(r^*F_{pp} + F_xG_{pp})]$$

$$= \{r^*F_p[(F_{py^*}/F_p) - (F_{xy^*}/F_x)]\}/\{-r^*(F_{pp} - qG_{pp})\} \qquad (21)$$

upon using $r^*F_p = -G_pF_x$ at the rest point. So the direction in which the curve shifts with an increase of y^* is determined by the effect on the ratio

$$F_p/F_x = [p + (D(p)/D'(p)) - c]xD'(p)/(p-c)D(p) \qquad (22)$$

at $\tilde{p} = 1$, which can be seen to be x times the ratio of $MR - MC$ to $p - MC$, where MR is marginal revenue and MC is marginal cost, multiplied by the price elasticity of demand. (Since $MR - MC$ and the elasticity are negative, the expression is positive.) It is frequently assumed the price elasticity is unaffected by the increase of y^*, the flattening of the demand curve just offsets its outward shift so as to leave marginal revenue unchanged at an unchanged real price. On this assumption, increased y^* increases the critical ratio in (22), and thus increases the price level, if and only if it increases the firms' unit and marginal cost, c. (That is because, as is surely not obvious, the derivative of the ratio with respect to c is unambiguously positive if the elasticity can be taken to be constant.)

As (12) implies, unit cost rises if and only if, given A, there is an increase in the amount of output demanded, $D(p; y^*)$. We just saw that the price level rises if and only if unit cost rises. It follows that there cannot be a net fall (or even a zero change) in the amount demanded as a result of the increase of y^*, with $D_{y^*}(p; y^*) > 0$, for that would imply a fall of cost which would imply a fall of price, and a fall of price would add to the increase in the amount demanded directly caused by the increase of y^*, that would leave the amount demanded up, a contradiction. The reader can see immediately that the same argument rules out a zero net change in the amount demanded, for that would imply no rise of price, which would again lead to a contradiction. So there must be an increase in the amount demanded, hence in the amount of output produced (since the firms clear their respective mini-product markets). The resulting increase of cost induces a rise of the price, but that rise cannot be large enough to prevent a net increase in the amount of output demanded. (Presumably it is unnecessary to note the terminological distinction, preserved in the more careful introductory texts, between an "increase of demand", which refers to a *shift* of the demand curve as represented by an increase of the shift parameter y^*, and an increase of the "amount demanded", which includes movements *along* the curve together with shifts of the curve.) If I am not mistaken, the following algebra goes over the same ground: Write

$$dD/dy^* = D_{y^*} + (d\tilde{p}/dy^*) D\tilde{p} = D_{y^*} + [(d\tilde{p}/dc) c'(D)(dD/dy^*)] D_{\tilde{p}}.$$

Then

$$dD/dy^* = D_{y^*}/\{1 - D_{\tilde{p}}[(d\tilde{p}/dc) c'(D)]\} > 0,$$

$$d\tilde{p}/dy^* = (d\tilde{p}/dc) c'(D) D_{y^*} > 0.$$

So output and the real price of output move up hand in hand. Since employment is thus increased, the movement along the labor-market equilibrium locus must also drive up the real wage. It does not follow, of course, that the product wage is increased. (Recall that only a negligible proportion of our cosmopolitan consumers find themselves customers in their home country so the product wage may fall while their real wage rises.)

We may look beyond the short run. The increase in the real price charged by the firms of our country sets in motion an erosion in their customer stocks. The aggregate stock must go on falling to the point where the real price is no longer elevated above the internationally competitive level of 1. At that point, which is reached only asymptotically, employment will have slid back to its original level, and likewise the real wage. This surprising invariance of steady-state employment and real wage to the demand per customer is a result of the fact that, in the constant cost case adopted here, the supply price of the *individual* firm is independent of the amount demanded by each of present and future customers of his. (The mechanism by which the price was increased in the short run in response to increased demand was simply the rise in unit and marginal cost resulting from the increased tightness of the labor market brought about by the increased output.)

A positive cost shock, more precisely an increase of A^{-1}, seems to be more complicated. Let us begin by again considering the effect of the $K = 0$ curve in Figure 2. The derivative is

$$\left.\frac{\mathrm{d}\tilde{p}}{\mathrm{d}A^{-1}}\right|_{K(\cdot)=0} = \frac{r^*F_{pA^{-1}}+G_pF_{xA^{-1}}}{-(r^*F_{pp}+F_xG_{pp})} = \frac{-[r^*D'(p)+g'(p)D(p)]\,xD(p)\,(c/A^{-1})}{-(r^*F_{pp}+F_xG_{pp})}.$$

It is established, then, that the $K=0$ curve shifts up, pulling up with it the saddle-path schedule which gives the firms' price corresponding to the given stock of customers. It follows that the amount of output demanded falls, so reduced output is implied. But what about employment? There is an employment-contracting effect from the rise in the real price, but this must be set against the employment-expanding effect of the increase in employment needed to produce any given level of output. Clearly, employment will fall on balance if and only if the increase in the price that the firm would require to go on employing the same number as before exceeds the increase in the output "demand price" of its (given) customers that would be displayed if the reduced output producible by an unchanged number of employees were to be auctioned off to them. Since the Phelps–Winter firms operate somewhere on the *inelastic* portion of their demand curves, unlike the textbook monopolist (whose customers are prisoners forever), there appears to be the strong possibility that the short-run effect of the cost increase is actually an *increase* of employment.

Ultimately, as customers drift away as a result of the high price charged by domestic firms, employment must approach a rest-point level that is below the original one. The explanation is simply that, as $\tilde{p}$ approaches p^* again, the real wage must reach a level below its original one; the firm will not absorb the whole increase of unit costs. It follows from the positive slope of the equilibrium locus that the reduced real wage will be accompanied by reduced employment.

The effects of the third and final shock are obvious. An inward shift of the equilibrium locus clearly drives up the real wage and thus induces a rise of the real price level, which entails a fall of sales, output, and employment. Ultimately the effective wage rate must return to "natural" level consistent with $\tilde{p}=p^*=1$. That implies that employment must fall a great deal further in the approach to the rest point.

It is a pleasure to acknowledge that many of the results here have also been obtained in a customer-market model by Kouri (1985). However, Kouri's model strays from the Phelps–Winter price-differential view by invoking the notion of "pricing to market", so it is not to be expected that the model here and Kouri's have identical implications. I recognize the attractions of the pricing-to-market view, of course; it seems realistic, and generates some results beyond the powers of models that resist it. The question is whether that view is not quite misleading for analyzing problems having more than a short-term aspect. The Phelps–Winter model is a formalization of the notion that firms take a long view in their pricing policy, so disturbances believed to be short-term are downplayed

236 E. S. Phelps

in the firm's current price decisions. The pricing-to-market view takes this to an extreme that I find hard to accept.

V. Conclusions and Remarks

A model of the small open economy has been developed in which productivity, country-specific export demand, and the "incentive (or efficiency) wage" are all important determinants of unemployment. Thus the model manages to have a Keynesian flavor, alongside some classical properties, without appealing to any postulated behavior of nominal wages and prices and even the existence of liquidity and paper money.

The model implies that no amount of nominal price and exchange-rate flexibility is sufficient to insulate the economy from fluctuations in its customers' demand. Stability of employment in the face of these demand disturbances would require a *real* wage "flexibility" that is precluded by the incentive-wage model of labor-market equilibrium.

However plausible this result, a large caveat is in order. Suppose *all* countries' customers desired to consume more. It would be an obvious fallacy of composition to assert that all countries' output would go up with such an increase of world demand. That is not a case in which others are offering more of their goods for ours with resulting effects on the relative price.

The model also creates the possibility that a negative productivity shock will actually increase employment, as more workers are required to service the current stock of customers. In any case, subsequent erosion of the customer base entails lower real wages and higher unemployment sooner or later. But there will be no erosion of customers if the shock strikes all countries.

These results all depend on a key result of the labor-market model: that a movement toward lower wages along the equilibrium locus is also a movement toward higher unemployment. The model, though it has its virtues, is still somewhat mechanical, so deeper microfoundations would be welcome.

References

Bowles, S.: A Marxian model of unemployment. Lecture, Columbia U., 1979.
Bruno, M. & Sachs, J. D.: *Economics of Worldwide Stagflation*, Harvard University Press, Cambridge, MA, 1985.
Calvo, G. A.: Quasi-Walrasian models of unemployment. *American Economic Review* 69 (2), 102-7, 1979.
Claassen, E. & Krauss, M.: Budget deficits and the exchange rate. European University Institute WP 86/212, March 1986.

Fitoussi, J.-P. & Phelps, E. S.: Explaining the 1980s slump in Europe. *Brookings Papers on Economic Activity 16* (2), Fall 1986.

Jackman, R., Layard, R. & Nickell, S.: Unemployment. Mimeo, Centre for Labor Economics, London School of Economics, 1988.

Hickman, B.: Real wages, aggregate demand, and unemployment. *European Economic Review 31* (4), December 1987.

Kouri, P. J. K.: Real wage, world demand, and unemployment in a customer-market model of a small open economy. In C.-H. Siven (ed.), *Unemployment in Europe: Analysis and Policy Issues*, Timbro, Stockholm, 1988.

Lal, D. & van Wijnbergen, S.: Government deficits, the real interest rate, and LDC debt. *European Economic Review 29* (4), 157–91, November–December 1985.

Mundell, R. A.: Capital mobility and size. *Canadian Journal of Economics and Political Science 30* (3), August 1964.

Nelson, R. R.: Full-employment policy and economic growth, *American Economic Review 56* (5), 1178–92, December 1966.

Phelps, E. S.: Commodity-supply shock and full-employment monetary policy. *Journal of Money, Credit and Banking 10* (2), May 1978.

Phelps, E. S.: The significance of customer markets for the effects of budgetary policy in open economies. *Annales d'Economie et de Statistique 1* (3), September 1986.

Phelps, E. S.: *Further Development of the Structuralist Approach to Unemployment in the 1980s*. Seconda Universita, Rome, September 1987a.

Phelps, E. S.: A working model of slump and recovery from productivity slowdown. Mimeo, Columbia U., September 1987b.

Phelps, E. S.: A working model of slump and recovery from disturbances to capital-goods demand in an open nonmonetary economy. *American Economic Review 98* (2), May 1988a.

Phelps, E. S.: A working model of slump and recovery in a closed nonmonetary economy. International Monetary Fund, Research Dept., WP 88/82, August 1988b; forthcoming in E. J. Nell & W. Semmler (eds.), *Nicholas Kaldor and Mainstream Economics*, Macmillan, London, 1988b.

Phelps, E. S. & Winter, Jr., S. G.: Optimal price policy under atomistic competition. In E. S. Phelps *et al.*, *Microeconomic Foundations of Employment and Inflation Theory*, Norton, New York, 309–37, 1970.

Summers, L. H.: *Understanding Unemployment*. Harvard University Press, Cambridge, MA, 1989.

Comment on E. S. Phelps, "Effects of Productivity, Total Domestic-Product Demand and 'Incentive Wages' on Unemployment in a Non-Monetary Customer-Market Model of the Small Open Economy"

Michael Hoel

University of Oslo, Norway

Phelps starts by setting up an efficiency wage[1] model for an open economy. He then uses this model to study the effects of (i) increased world demand, (ii) reduced productivity, and (iii) a change in the relationship between wage and efficiency.

Compared with most efficiency wage models, Phelps' model has two original features:

(a) Part of the employment is used to monitor the rest of the workers; this employment share is determined endogenously by profit-maximizing firms.

(b) Phelps uses a "customer-market model". In the short run each firm faces a downward sloping demand curve for the product it produces, as in standard models of monopolistic competition. Over time, however, this demand curve shifts gradually to the right or the left if the price charged by the firm falls short of or exceeds the price of other firms. This latter price is exogenous (set equal to unity) in Phelps' model, since he is concerned with a small open economy in which firms compete with firms in the rest of the world.[2]

It might be true that, in practice, part of a firm's workforce is used to monitor the rest of the workers. However, it is difficult to see that this feature of the model adds any insight to the problems taken up by Phelps.

---

[1] Or "incentive wage", as Phelps prefers to call it.

[2] Rødseth (1985) used a similar assumption for an open economy in a macroeconomic analysis of the relationship between wage setting and trade development.

On the contrary, this feature makes the model much more complex, thus making it more difficult to recognize the driving forces behind the main results. My discussion of Phelps' analysis is therefore based on a simplified version of his model.

A Simplified Model

I follow Phelps' assumptions and notation, except for disregarding labor used for monitoring other workers. Moreover, constant returns to labor are assumed and the labor supply per firm is set equal to one (i.e., $n_S = 1$).

The unit cost of each firm is[3]

$$c(\tilde{v},\ \tilde{n},\ b,\ A) = \frac{1}{Z^0} \min_{v,n}\{vn \text{ s.t. } Ae(v - q\tilde{v})\, n \geq Z^0\} \tag{1}$$
$$\quad\ +\ \ +\ \ +\ \ -$$

where

$$q \equiv \tilde{n} + (1 - \tilde{n})\, b = b + (1 - b)\, \tilde{n} < 1 \text{ for } \tilde{n} < 1 \tag{2}$$

(i.e., q is rising in b and $\tilde{n}$).

In equilibrium the real wage (v) and employment (n) in the firm under consideration are equal to the corresponding economy-wide variables, i.e., $v = \tilde{v}$ and $n = \tilde{n}$. With these equilibrium conditions, the first-order conditions of the optimization problem (1) may be written

$$\frac{ve'((1 - q)\, v)}{e((1 - q)\, v)} = 1. \tag{3}$$

This condition corresponds to Phelps' equation (3), and is often called the "Solow condition" in the literature.

The product price of each firm is a markup (M) over its unit cost, i.e.

$$p = Mc(v, n, b, A). \tag{4}$$

Unlike the simple case of static monopolistic competition, the firms must choose the optimal time path of M taking both short- and long-run considerations into account. The optimal time path follows from maximizing the present value of profits (with an exogenous interest rate). The optimal markup will in general vary over time, but approaches a stationary long-run value asymptotically, provided all exogenous variables are constant.

---

[3] v and n denote the real wage and employment, respectively, in the firm under consideration. The corresponding economy-wide variables are $\tilde{v}$ and $\tilde{n}$. b is the ratio of unemployment benefits to the prevailing real wage $\tilde{v}$, A is an exogenous productivity parameter, and Z^0 is the output requirement. Output per worker is $Ae(v - q\tilde{v})$, where $e' > 0$ and $e'' < 0$.

Finally, supply and demand are equal in equilibrium:

$$Aen = D(p, y^*) x, \qquad (5)$$
$$\quad\;\; - \quad +$$

where Aen is production per firm, x is the number of customers per firm, and $D(p, y^*)$ is demand per customer (y^* is real world demand). As explained above, Phelps assumes that x grows over time if $p < 1$ and declines over time if $p > 1$.

In the short run, x is historically given, and (3)–(5) (with q from (2) inserted) determine the three endogenous variables v, n and p. If $p \neq 1$, x will change over time ($x = g(p) x$ with $g(1) = 0$ and $g' < 0$), until a stationary equilibrium with $p = 1$ is reached. The long-run values of v and n follow from (3) and (4) along with $p = 1$. The long-run value of x then follows from (5).

Properties of the Stationary Solution

In the long run, we may write (4) as

$$c(v, \; n, \; b, \; A) = \frac{1}{M} \qquad (6)$$
$$\;\; + \; + \; + \; -$$

since $p = 1$. As for M, it follows from the present value maximization of the firms that the long-run value of M is larger

- the smaller the short-run demand elasticity $(= - D_p p / D - - D_p / D$ for $p = 1)$
- the less sensitive the number of customers to the product price (i.e., the smaller $- g'$ is)
- the larger the interest rate.

Note in particular that the long-run value of M is independent of world demand, provided D_p / D is independent of y^* (for $p = 1$).[4]

For a given value of M, equation (6) gives a downward sloping curve in the (n, v) diagram, as drawn in Figure 1.

From the "Solow condition" (3) we find

$$\frac{dv}{dq} = \frac{v^2 e'' - v e'}{q e' + (1 - q) e''} . \qquad (7)$$

Since $e' > 0$ and $e'' < 0$, the nominator of (7) is negative. The denominator is also negative provided q is not too close to one. In other words, for q less than some critical value, the Solow condition gives v as a rising

---

[4] More precisely, we find (for $p = 1$) $M = k / (k - 1)$, where $k = - D_p / D - g' / (g + r)$.

foundation of n (since q is rising in n). This curve is drawn in Figure 1. For a given value of b (= unemployment benefits as a share of the real wage), the critical value of q giving $dv/dn > 0$ corresponds to a particular value of $n(<1)$ which Phelps denotes $\hat{n}$.[5]

For $n > \hat{n}$, the Solow condition gives a downward sloping curve in the (v, n) diagram. However, Phelps rules out this part of the curve, since it implies that a dynamic version of the wage-setting process becomes unstable.

The intersection between the two curves gives the long-run values of v and n. We may now proceed to see how this long-run equilibrium is affected by changes in exogenous variables. I consider the first two changes of the three effects mentioned in my introduction.

Increased Consumption Demand in a Closed Economy

Assume for a moment that the economy is closed, and y^* is therefore endogenous. The simplest possible macro framework for determining y^* is

$$y^* = C(y^*) + I(r) \tag{8}$$
$$\quad\;\; + \qquad -$$

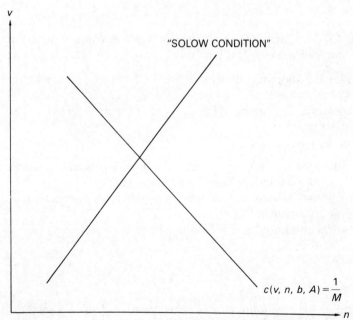

Fig. 1.

_____

[5] Since $q \geq b$, cf. (2), we may find $dv/dn < 0$ for *all* $n > 0$ if b is sufficiently close to 1. I disregard this possibility.

where C is consumption, I is investment, and r is the real interest rate. For any given y^*, r must increase if $C(y^*)$ gets a positive shift, e.g. due to expansionary fiscal policy. But increased r means a higher markup (M), so that the curve $c = 1/M$ in Figure 1 shifts inwards. We thus get Phelps' result that an expansionary fiscal policy will *reduce* output and employment.

This result might seem surprising at first sight. However, it is a direct consequence of this type of model, where output and employment are completely supply determined. In such models, increased demand will typically increase the real interest rate, also in more elaborate frameworks than equation (8). A quite common feature of supply-side models is that an increase in the real interest rate reduces the real wage. It may also — as it does in the present model — reduce output and employment.

Increased Exogenous Real World Demand

In an open economy, y^* is exogenous. Since y^* is *real* world demand, it is equal to real world expenditure (provided there is no rationing). At the world level, an increase in real expenditure corresponds to an increase in real production. Phelps considers a permanent rise in y^*. As we have just seen, such an increase in y^* *cannot* be caused by, e.g. expansionary fiscal policy, if the model applies to the world economy. However, increased y^* can be caused by some supply-side policy at the world level, e.g. a reduction in b.

Since any change in y^* leaves the two curves in Figure 1 unchanged,[6] we immediately see that a change in y^* leaves the long-run values of n and v unchanged. Although world economy supply-side measures which increase world production may have positive spillover effects to our country in the short run, it is thus clear that there are no such spillover effects in the long run.

A Productivity Decline

Consider next an exogenous decline in productivity, i.e., a reduction in A. The parameter A does not affect the Solow condition curve in Figure 1. However, the curve $c = 1/M$ is shifted inwards when A declines. From Figure 1 it is therefore clear that the long-run effect of a productivity decline is to reduce real wages, but that unemployment nevertheless increases.

The above result is somewhat disturbing. According to the model, secular growth in productivity should give ever-declining unemployment.[7] However, such a development is not consistent with history. A natural

---

[6] Provided $D_p(1, y^*)/D(1, y^*)$, and therefore also M, are independent of y^*.
[7] Asymptotically, unemployment will approach $1 - \hat{n}$.

question is therefore whether there is some crucial element of the model which gives us the positive link between productivity and employment.

An Alternative Efficiency Function

The answer to the above question is that the form of the efficiency function $e = e(v - q\tilde{v})$ is crucial to the results. To see this, assume instead that it is the *relative* difference $v/q\tilde{v}$ which matters for efficiency (i.e., $e = e(v/q\tilde{v})$. Along with the optimization problem (1), after inserting $v = \tilde{v}$ and $n = \tilde{n}$ this gives

$$e'\left(\frac{1}{q}\right) = qe\left(\frac{1}{q}\right) \tag{3'}$$

instead of (3). Since (3') determines q, n follows from $q = 1 - n + nb$ for a given value of b. The Solow condition curve in Figure 1 now becomes vertical instead of upward sloping. Changing the e-function from $e(v - q\tilde{v})$ to $e(v/q\tilde{v})$ thus has dramatic consequences for all results. Unemployment is now independent of real world demand and productivity in both the short and long run. Moreover, in a closed economy, an increase in consumer demand (e.g. due to expansionary fiscal policy) has no effect on unemployment, in either the short run or the long run.[8] It is also easily shown that these conclusions remain valid even if we reintroduce monitoring labor in the efficiency function.

It is not obvious which of $e(v - q\tilde{v})$ and $e(v/q\tilde{v})$ is the best description of the true world. However, a property of long-run neutrality of productivity growth seems reasonable, suggesting that $e(v/q\tilde{v})$ is the best choice. In this case Phelps' extension of efficiency wage models to a "customer market" model does not add much new insight into the determination of equilibrium unemployment.

Reference

Rødseth, A.: Dynamics of wage and trade in a fixed-exchange-rate economy. *Scandinavian Journal of Economics* 87(1), 120–36, 1985.

---

[8] In these conclusions, "short run" is defined as before p reaches its long-run value ($p = 1$). However, in a sense, the whole model is of a relatively long-run nature, since the wage-setting process described by the Solow condition is best understood as some equilibrium condition determining wages in the long run. In the short run (up to 1 to 2 years?) it seems reasonable that the real wage may deviate from this equilibrium wage.

Comment on E. S. Phelps, "Effects of Productivity, Total Domestic-Product Demand and 'Incentive Wages' on Unemployment in a Non-Monetary Customer-Market Model of the Small Open Economy"

Matti Pohjola

University of Helsinki and Labour Institute for Economic Research, Helsinki, Finland

I think it is well established nowadays that neither the small open economy model nor the Keynesian export multiplier model can explain the facts very well. The small open economy theory assumes that the economy faces infinitely elastic demand for its products in world markets. There is no effective demand constraint and, consequently, output is determined by supply. The fact is that this story does not fit the apparent dependence of output and employment in small open economies on world demand. Thus it fails to explain cyclical fluctuations in output and employment. Its merits lie in long-run considerations, i.e., in the determination of prices, profitability and economic growth.

The Keynesian multiplier theory captures the short-run dependence on world demand by assuming that the level of exports is determined by world demand while export prices are determined by domestic production costs. Cyclical fluctuations and business cycle transmissions can be accounted for, but the problems now lie in the explanation of long-run events. The model assumes domestic producers to have too much market power in world markets.

Phelps's paper attempts to combine the merits of both the small open economy and the Keynesian models. He studies a customer market model of the small open economy in which firms have some short-run market power owing to informational frictions in the product markets. Firms actively exploit the fact that their customers are imperfectly informed about the prices of competing products. Customers become fully informed in the long run, which makes the model display classical properties.

Keynesian real wage rigidities are introduced via a version of the incentive-efficiency wage model. To elicit greater efficiency from the workers, the firms have to pay higher wages when aggregate employment increases, making outside opportunities more favorable for employees. Domestic demand and the current account play no role in the analysis because the entire output is exported. This is a simplification designed to focus the analysis on the labor market.

The model differs from a previous application of the customer market model by Pentti Kouri in that Kouri assumed export firms to follow passive pricing policies and instead use active marketing strategies to attract customers. Phelps' approach is a more direct application of the pioneering customer market model of Phelps and Winter. Both Kouri's and Phelps's models suggest that it is the combination of labor market rigidities and declines in the demand for exports (and in Phelps's analysis also the decline of productivity) that explains the emergence of large-scale unemployment in small open (European?) economies.

There are a number of points I should like to raise concerning the relevance of the approach in the explanation of European unemployment. First, given the roles that unions play in small European economies, I wonder whether the incentive-efficiency wage model is the most relevant characterization of the labor market. It would be interesting to know the extent to which the results apply if real wage rigidities are modeled using, say, the insider–outsider or the trade-union approach.

Second, given that empirical estimates of real wage rigidity vary from one country to another, we should ask how this theory could explain such a variance; see, for example, OECD (1987). To account for these diffrences in terms of the incentive-efficiency wage model, we should be able to characterize differences among countries in the efficiency factor $e(\cdot)$.

There already exists some work aimed at an explanation of the variation in real wage flexibility using the trade-union theory. Countries differ from each other in terms of the structure of the collective bargaining system, see e.g. Calmfors and Driffill (1988) and Rowthorn (1989), or in terms of industrial relations in a broader sense, cf. Tarantelli (1986). Such differences can explain at least some of the diversity.

Finally, the incentive-efficiency wage model used by Phelps is interesting in the sense that it pays some indirect attention to one aspect of industrial relations, namely the organization and control of work within firms. The variable m measures the proportion of employees — the number of bosses — engaged in monitoring the workforce. It is one of the firm's choice variables. The reason why I find this interesting is the observation, raised for example by Piore (1986), that the ongoing restructuring of industrial production calls for labor market flexibility in a broader sense than intended by mere wage flexibility. Manufacturers are abandoning old Fordist mass production methods in favor of flexible specialization as well as flexible organizations and job demarcation, requiring more flexibility in the deployment of labor. It has been observed that employees are willing to trade off existing job classification systems for increased income and employment security. Some authors, such as Aoki (1988), claim that differences in work organization patterns may explain differences in long-run economic performance better than wage rigidities do. In principle, the framework adopted by Phelps could be used to model the effects of different labor-management systems. In doing this we should explore the explanation of the efficiency factor $e(\cdot)$ more deeply by, for instance, making supervisors' effort levels endogenous and their wages different from those of production workers. We can all agree with Phelps that "deeper microfoundations would be welcome".

References

Aoki, M.: *Information, Incentives and Bargaining in the Japanese Economy.* Cambridge University Press, London, 1988.
Calmfors, L. & Driffill, J.: Bargaining structure, corporatism and macroeconomic performance. *Economic Policy 6*, 14–61, 1988.
OECD: *Structural Adjustment and Economic Performance.* OECD, Paris, 1987.
Piore, M. J.: Perspectives on labour market flexibility. *Industrial Relations 25*, 146–66, 1986.
Rowthorn, B.: Wage dispersion and employment: Theories and evidence. Mimeo, University of Cambridge, 1989.
Tarantelli, E.: The regulation of inflation and unemployment. *Industrial Relations 25*, 1–15, 1986.

Index